# Glamorous Cars

Dear Iain
Happy Birthday!
All my love forever.
Tracy xxx
xxx

{18-3-90}

# Glamor

the apple press

# ous Cars

JOHN McGOVREN

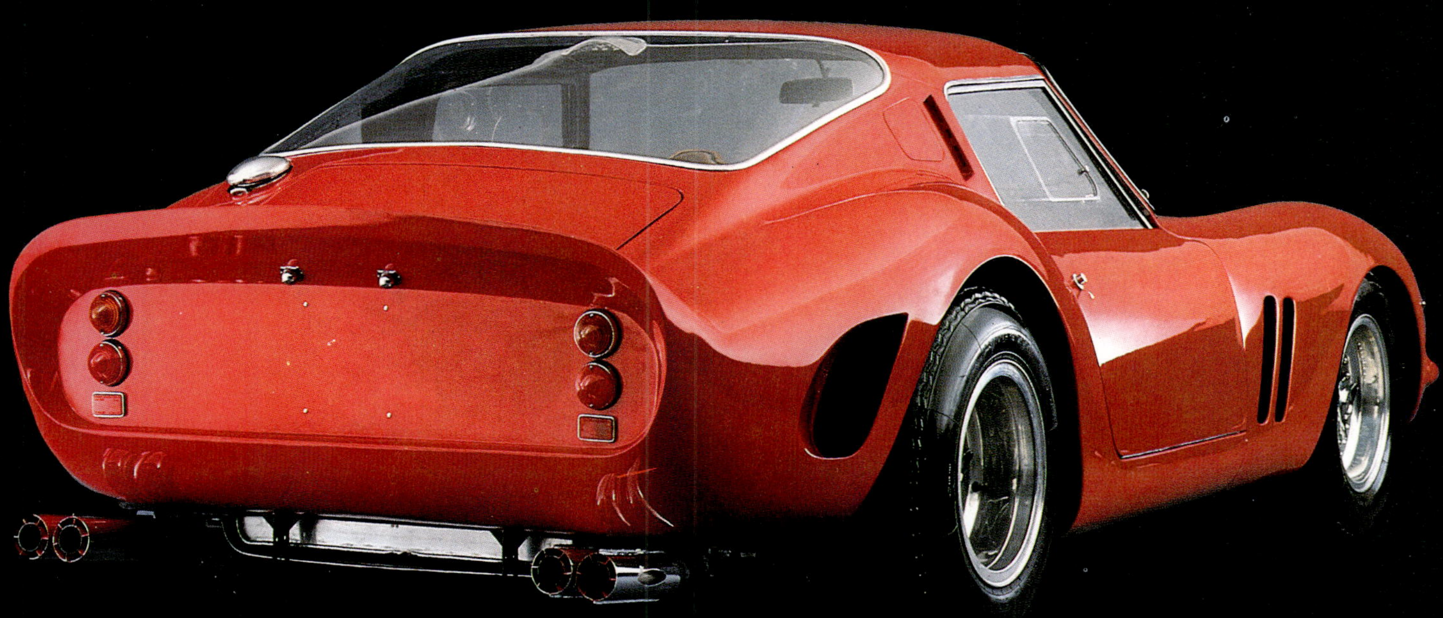

A QUINTET BOOK

First published in Great Britain in 1985 by
The Apple Press
6 Blundell Street
London N7

This paperback edition first published in 1988.



ISBN 1-85076-148-5

This book was designed and produced by
Quintet Publishing Limited
6 Blundell Street, London N7.

Art Director Peter Bridgewater
Editor Nicholas Law
Photographer John McGovren

Typeset in Great Britain by
Context Typesetting Limited, Brighton
Colour Origination in Hong Kong by
Hong Kong Graphic Arts Company Limited, Hong Kong
Printed in Hong Kong by Leefung-Asco
Printers Limited

# Contents

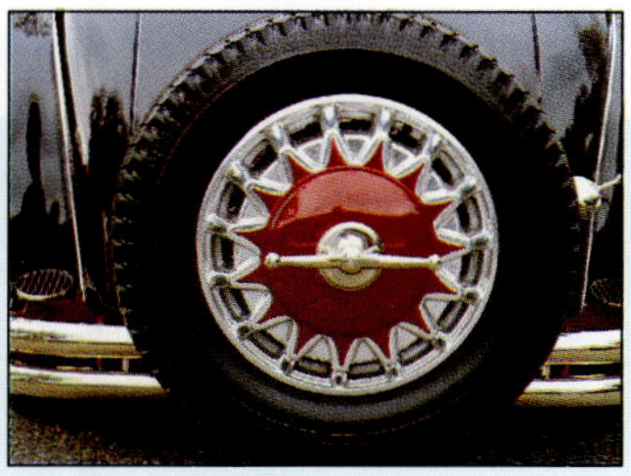

When I was approached to write and illustrate this book I already had a firm idea of what constituted a 'Glamorous Car': an automobile in the grand style, from a prestigious manufacturer, with a pedigree of exotic owners.

I first thought that it wouldn't be a bad idea to really find out the correct definition of the word 'glamorous'. The dictionary defines it as 'magic'. I have taken this definition, in this more modern sense as it is used to describe something or some event as extraordinary; each vehicle in this book meets this criterion.

'Glamour', meaning 'A charm on the eyes, making them see things as fairer than they really are, could also be incorporated in the text, in particular when describing the cars in chapter four. Although these cars have not the pedigree shared by the rest of the vehicles in this book, there is no doubt that they are Glamorous in their own way. In any case the cars in chapter four serve as a counterbalance to the rest of the book.

In gathering the many photographs, and much of the information for this book, I covered thousands of miles by air and by car, in Europe and in the United States of America. I covered a particularly high mileage in November 1984 when I travelled to California to research the three major car collections in that state. In that month I clocked up over 10,000 miles, with only one speeding ticket from the famed Californian Highway Patrol which was collected on the very first day! For the following four and a half weeks I kept a much closer eye on the rear view mirror. The biggest problem in selecting from the very many cars that were available was to sort out the 'glamorous' from the 'very glamorous' and it proved to be a task that was in the end resolved by making a choice based purely on personal preference.

Time, or rather the lack of it, was the next most pressing problem. At that end of the year, even in California, and especially in the northern part of the Golden State, the weather is not uniformly good as it is from March to October. Fog, rain, and a general greyness is the order for most days, but luckily there were two consecutive days of weak sunshine. The situation was slightly better in Los Angeles, 400 miles to the south, but even with the better weather the days were still short, and photography was impossible after 3.30 pm. To have compiled all the photographs and the information on all the Californian cars would have been impossible without the help and co-operation of many individuals: Don Williams and all his staff at the Blackhawk Collection in San Ramon, northern California; Lorelle Levine and Nora Perez at the JB Nethercutt Collection in Sylmar, southern California, and John Burgess, Director of the Briggs Cunningham Auto Museum in Costa Mesa, southern California deserve special thanks for their patience, help, and assistance, without which this book would not exist. In addition, the photography in California could not have been completed without invaluable logistical help and support freely given by the following: Bill Wolf at Mazda Motors Corporation in Los Angeles; Keith, Annette, Ted and Barbara Armstrong and Bill Auda in Modesto, and my very good friend and Rolls-Royce co-driver in the last Cannonball race in 1979, Eddie Harmston, a man who knows how to get things done, whatever the city or continent he finds himself in! Without these people this book would not have been possible.

*John McGovren, Beckenham, Kent. 24th December 1984.*

# CHAPTER ONE

# The very glamorous cars

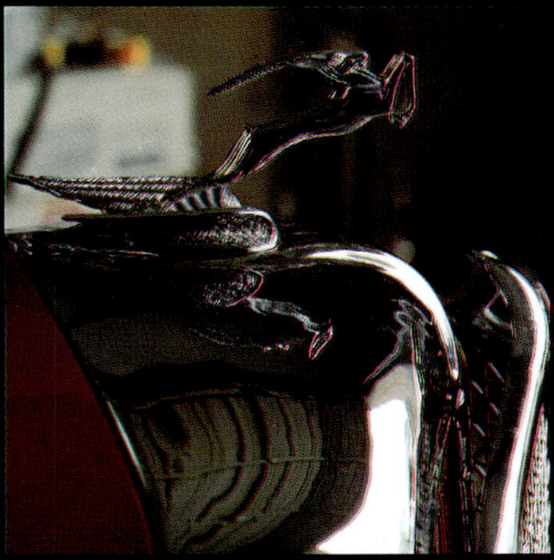

Staking a real claim to be 'The Most Glamorous Car' must be the Rolls-Royce Phantom II that belonged to the Hollywood socialite, the Countess DiFrasso. Determined to outshine her close friend, and deadly social rival, film star Constance Bennett, the Countess commissioned the Paris-based designer and stylist, Dutch Darrin, to produce the most stunning body for her Rolls-Royce, one that would really top anything ever seen in the Hollywood of the mid-1930s.

Darrin, as they say in Las Vegas 'came up trumps!' His coachwork on the Phantom II remains to this day the most beautiful body ever put on a Rolls-Royce. It would not have been unreasonable to have expected the result to be outlandish and vulgar, but Dutch Darrin was too much an artist to fall into that trap and the Countess had too much taste to allow such a thing to happen. The result is simply gorgeous. Their first meeting, in 1936, was at the home of Clark Gable, a mutual friend, and the Countess immediately commissioned from Darrin the re-bodying of her 1933 Rolls-Royce.

It took Darrin two years to complete the work, which was done in his Sunset Strip establishment in Los Angeles. The body is especially notable for the fact that it does not contain a single weld in its aluminium shell. Rudy Stoessel and Paul Erdos carefully gave shape to the detailed Darrin drawings which incorporated several items from the current American automobiles. The car has Buick front and rear bumpers, the door handles and the headlights are from the Packard partsbin, the steering wheel comes from a Lincoln and the rear tail-lights originated from Fords.

After completion, Dutch Darrin was quoted as saying, 'This was the only car I ever designed that came out better in real life than it looked in the rendering.'

There is no record of the Countess DiFrasso's reaction on taking delivery of the Rolls-Royce, but it would appear that she had no cause ever to be upstaged by her friend and rival, Constance Bennett, in regard to their transport!

It is interesting to note that someone, still very involved with the DiFrasso car, once owned it and devoted so much time to it that his wife demanded that he had to choose between it and her. Shortly afterwards they were divorced! That gives just a little idea of the beauty and attraction that the 1933 Rolls-Royce still exerts today.

The 1930 Cadillac V16 is one of the most impressive looking cars ever built. It was designed by the famous Harley Earl who decided to name it the 'Madame X' after a character in a popular play of 1929. Harley J. Earl was an extraordinary character. He began his working life with a Los Angeles Cadillac dealer, Don Lee, who catered to the exotic automotive tastes of the celebrities of the booming Hollywood movie industry. Earl had been recruited into the General Motors Corporation Fisher division (they made all the G.M. bodies) by the acknowledged genius of the American car business, Alfred P. Sloan. Sloan had decided that it was cheaper to restyle the G.M. cars annually with panel

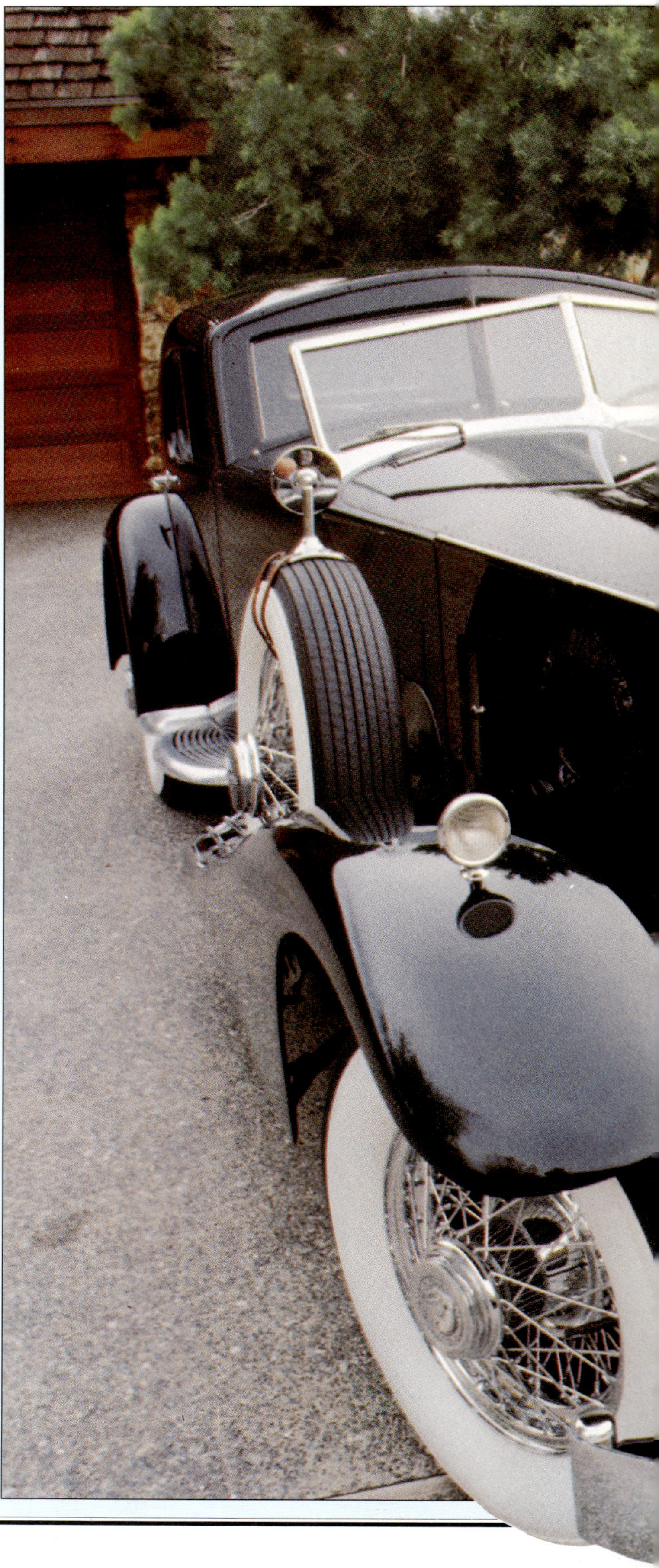

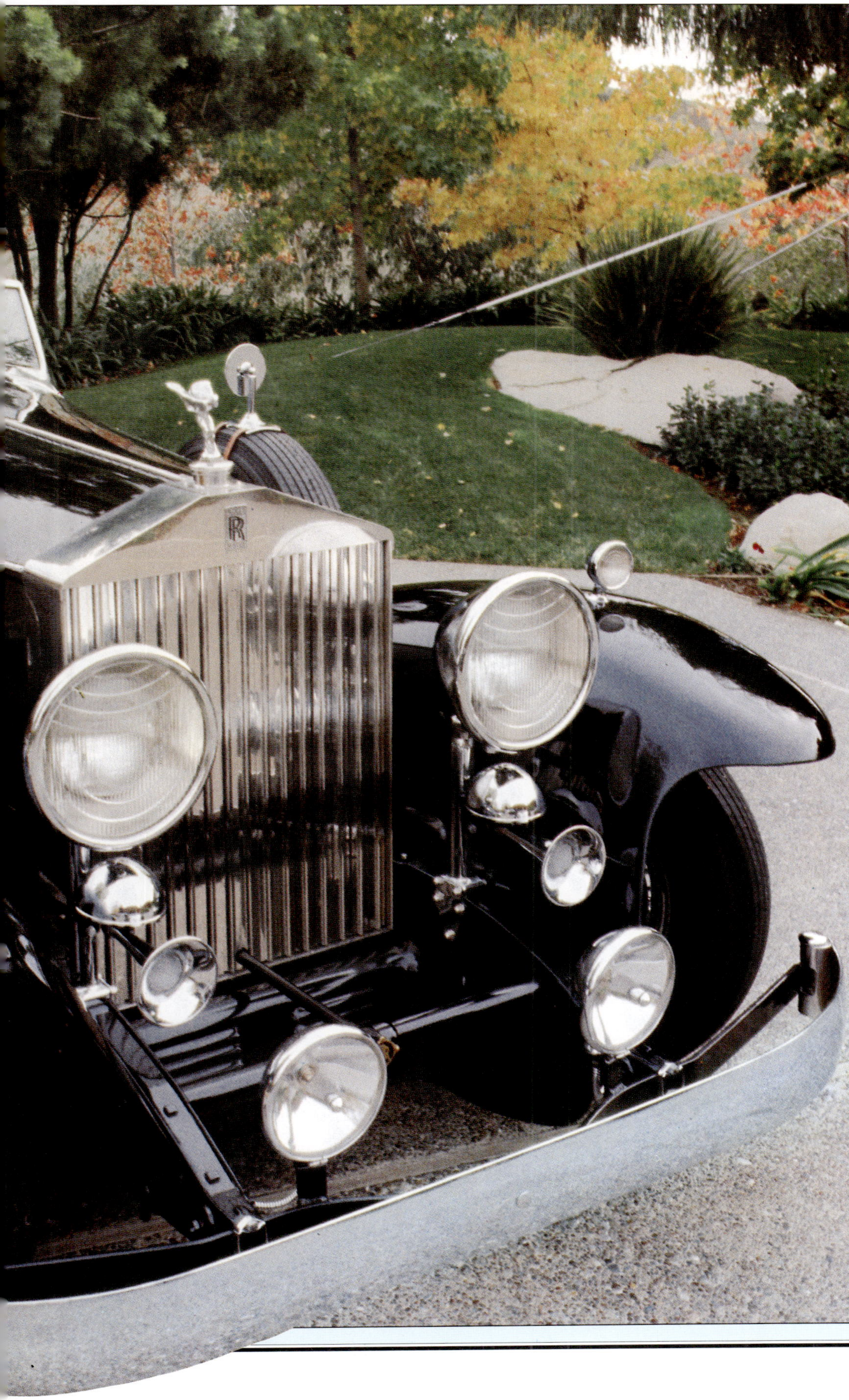

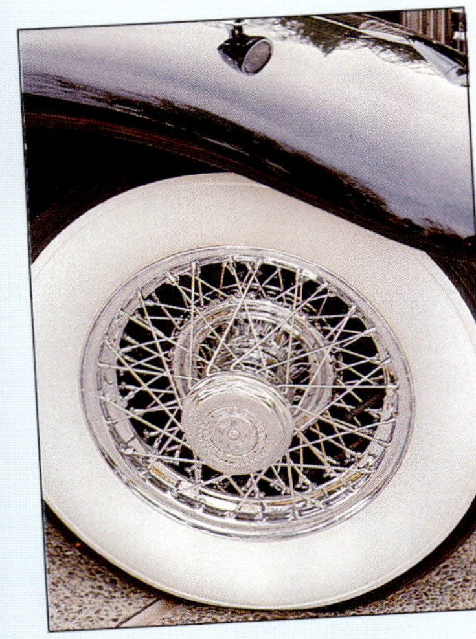

LEFT: The Countess DiFrasso Rolls-Royce is accepted by many experts as the most beautiful body ever to grace a Rolls-Royce chassis. It is perfectly styled and finished as befits the car of a leading Hollywood socialite of the 1930s.

ABOVE: Wire-spoked wheels normally associated with sports cars rather than limousines, nevertheless work perfectly, the delicacy of the wheel design complementing the whole car.

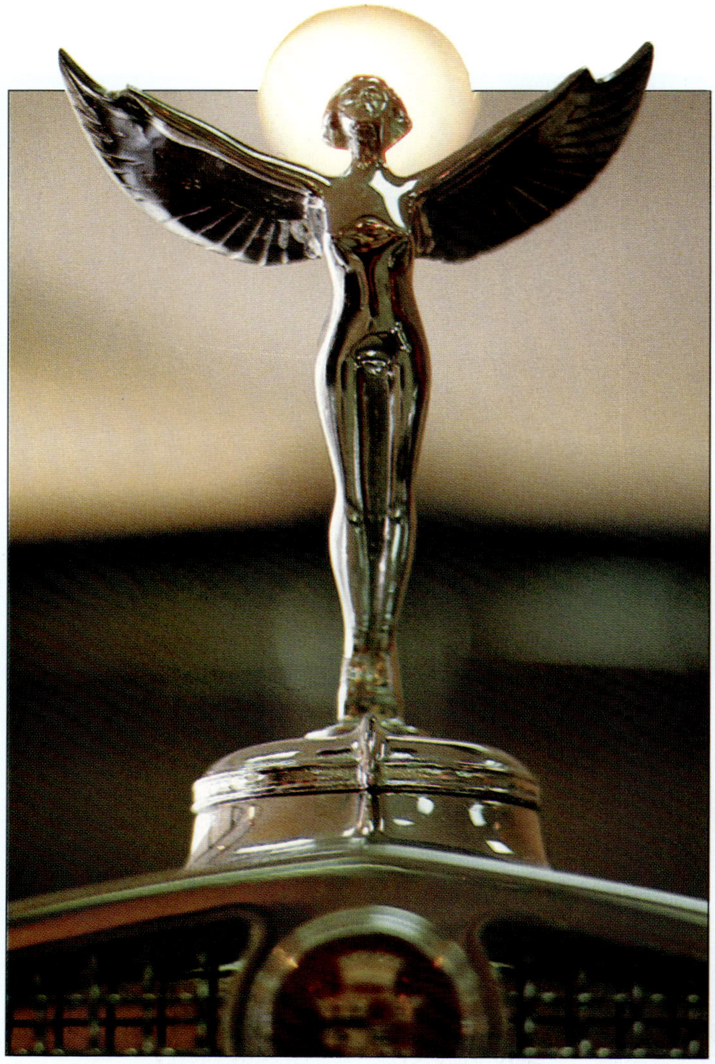

Like Rolls-Royce, Cadillac used a female figure as its radiator mascot. It may not be as elegant as the Flying lady, but its design suits the car well.

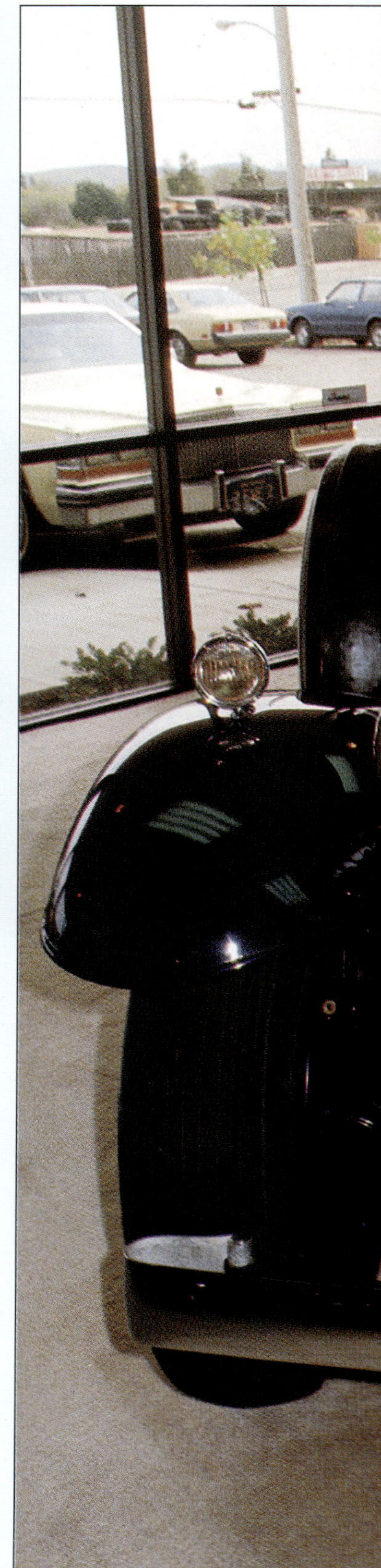

and colour changes, than to undertake very expensive engineering improvements, and Harley J. Earl was just the man to carry out that policy.

Earl soon became the man who introduced 'Hollywood Styling' to Detroit. His own definition of his contribution to the American auto industry is even more revealing; he called it 'dynamic obsolescence'!!

But there was nothing obsolescent or cynical about his work on the 'Madame X' car. It is sober, timeless in its appeal, a stately vehicle in the best possible taste. It is no wonder Harley J. Earl had a long career with G.M., a charlatan could not and would not have lasted for very long in the Corporation with its reputation for high quality.

High quality is what you get from the products of the Daimler-Benz company. The Mercedes-Benz has been voted as the top quality car in North America every year since they were first exported to that continent in any quantity. A car from the Unterturkheim/Singelfingen plants has the highest secondhand value of any mass-produced car made today.

For some people even this fact is not enough to make them

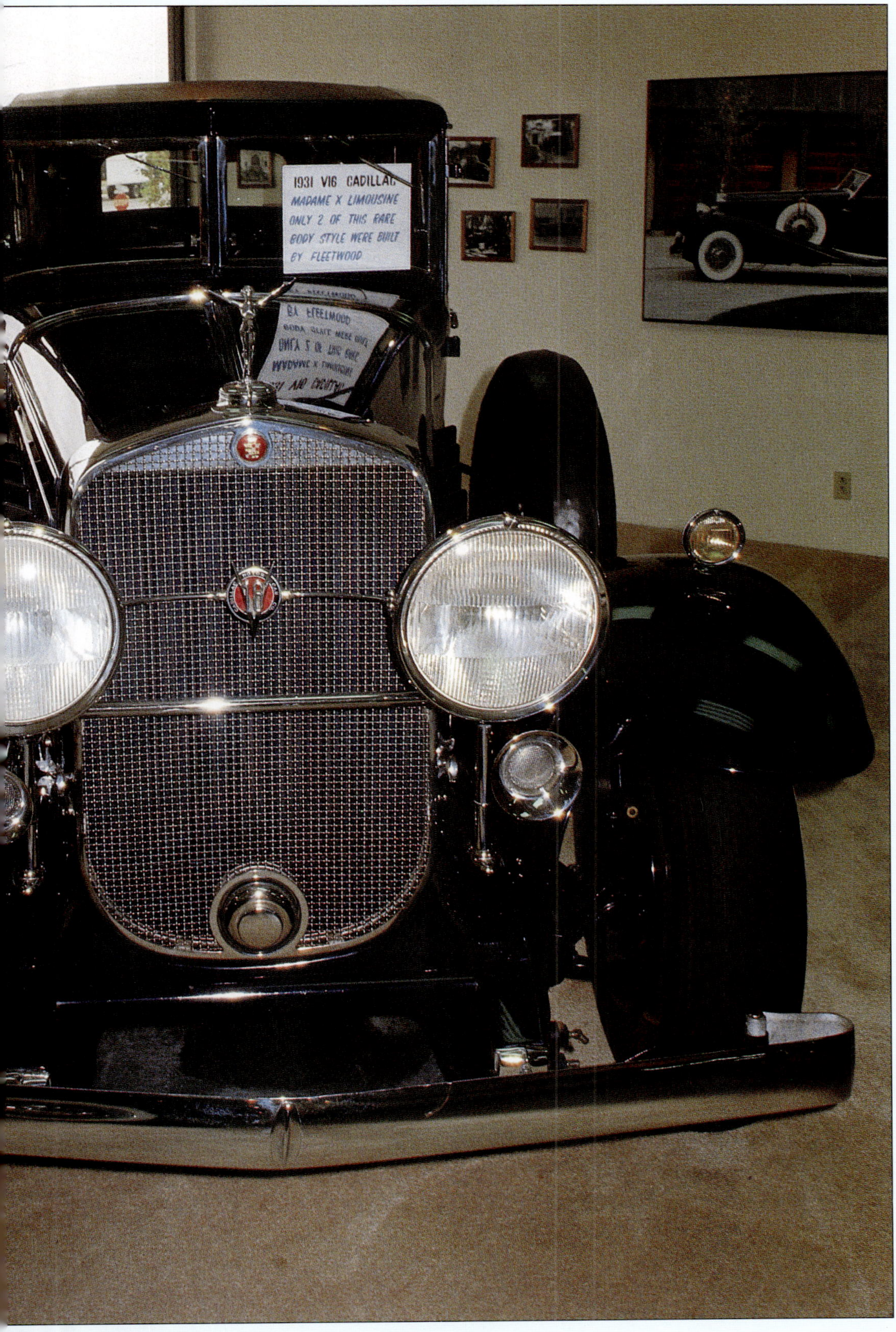


The hand-built Cadillac V-16 town car known as the Madame X, displays all the features necessary to justify the company's slogan 'Standard of the World'.

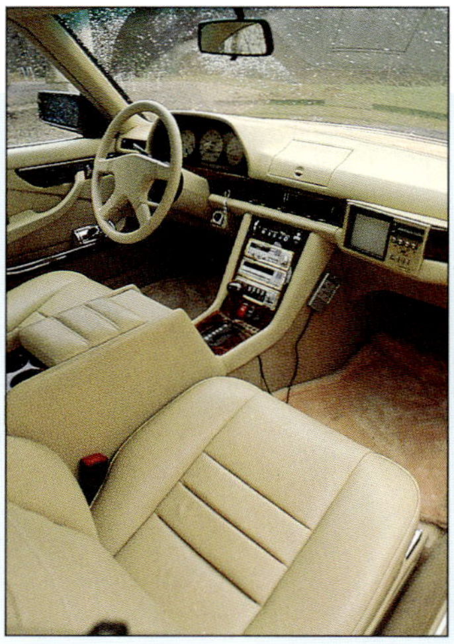

The interior of the original Mercedes is scrapped, and replaced with top quality fittings from the seats, trimmed in the best Connolly leather, to the top quality Wilton carpet.

buy and use a standard Mercedes-Benz. They still insist on having one, but it must be an even better car than that delivered by their Mercedes dealer. One of the few places they can go to for this better Mercedes is Liege in Belgium. In this old industrial city the Duchatelet coachbuilding firm will take your brand-new car, and for a great deal of money turn it into an even better S-class Mercedes-Benz.

The company was formed by Frederic Duchatelet in 1977 with its headquarters located beside the river Meuse close to the city centre. The author met Frederic Duchatelet in March 1984 when preparing this book and the immediate impression was of a man obsessed with attaining perfection in his work. He insists that his workers, some of the very best in Europe, give 101% effort at maintaining and extending the reputation for the very best in craftsmanship that Duchatelet has won. The company can perform every single skill in the production of a finished car, and woe betide any worker who gives less than the best. In respect of his temperament, Frederic Duchatelet is similar to those two other giants of European high quality, high performance motoring, Enzo Ferrari, and Ettore Bugatti. Like them he is a benevolent dictator although sparing with his praise, but with a terrible temper when he finds work done that does not come up to the company's standard of excellence.

During the author's visit the Carat Cullinan, the Duchatelet version of the 500SEL four-door sedan, and the D. Arrow, based on the 500SEC coupe were sampled. Both cars were equipped with just about every accessory that the wealthy owner would want. The re-upholstered seats featured electrical adjustment in every direction and were supremely comfortable and beautifully constructed like every other feature of the car, care of Duchatelet. On the road the car behaved exactly as a standard S-class Mercedes-Benz. The D. Arrow model was taken to nearby Spa-Francorchamps Grand Prix race track, and in the hands of the company's test driver was put through its paces hard. Apart from the Duchatelet bodywork and interior changes this car had a set of BBS alloy wheels and some Goodyear NCT tyres fitted. On the wet race track it stuck to the tarmacas if it were glued, allowing the unmodified engine to deliver all its power in spite of the slippery road surface and the tricky nature of the famous track.

During two very interesting days at Liege, hints were given that the future may well see the development of more power from the magnificent German engines, very probably by using a turbocharging system which is presently undergoing final testing.

The Duchatelet range of Mercedes-Benz cars must represent some of the most desirable vehicles available today. The coupling of the best of German engineering, and the care and attention to detail of the Duchatelet company make for unbeatable value, even though a Duchatelet Mercedes can cost over twice as much as the standard one.

An English company also produces a car that has more than close connections with the mighty giant of Stuttgart.

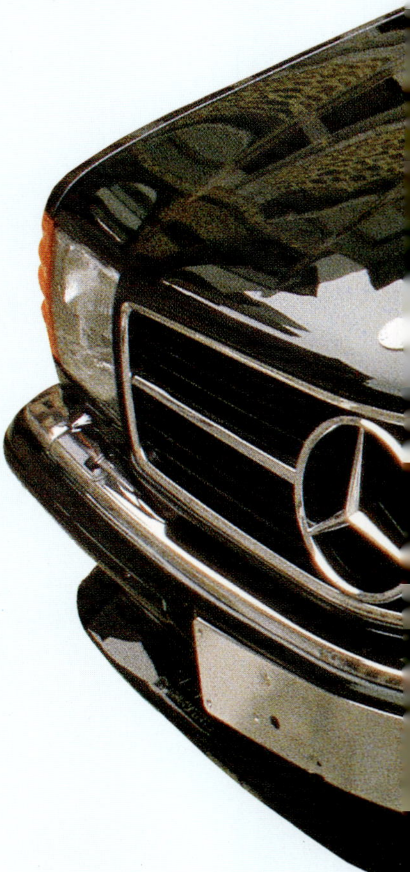

The Duchatelet 500 is one of the very best of today's customized, high-quality cars. Hundreds of hours of work by Belgian craftsmen result in a driving machine that combines the highest quality of finish with a performance to match.

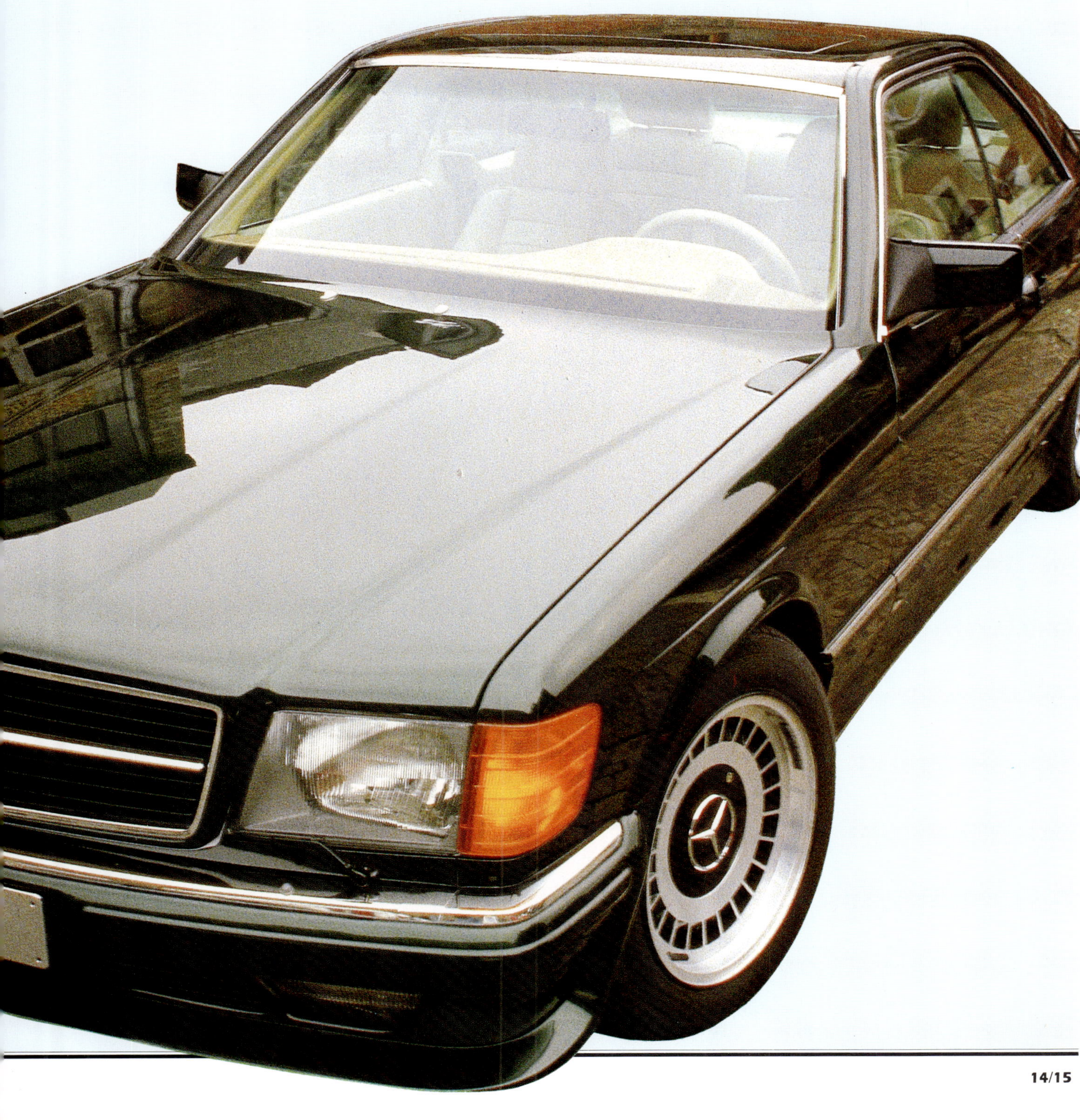

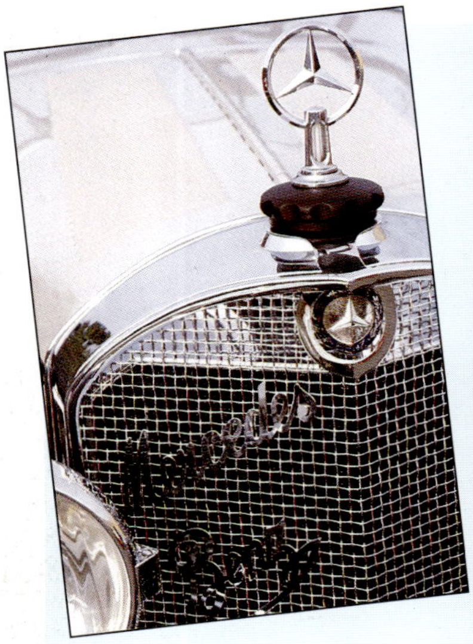

ABOVE: No naked lady or leaping cat mascot—the 1928 Mercedes-Benz SS is graced by the simple, and now familiar, three-pointed star.

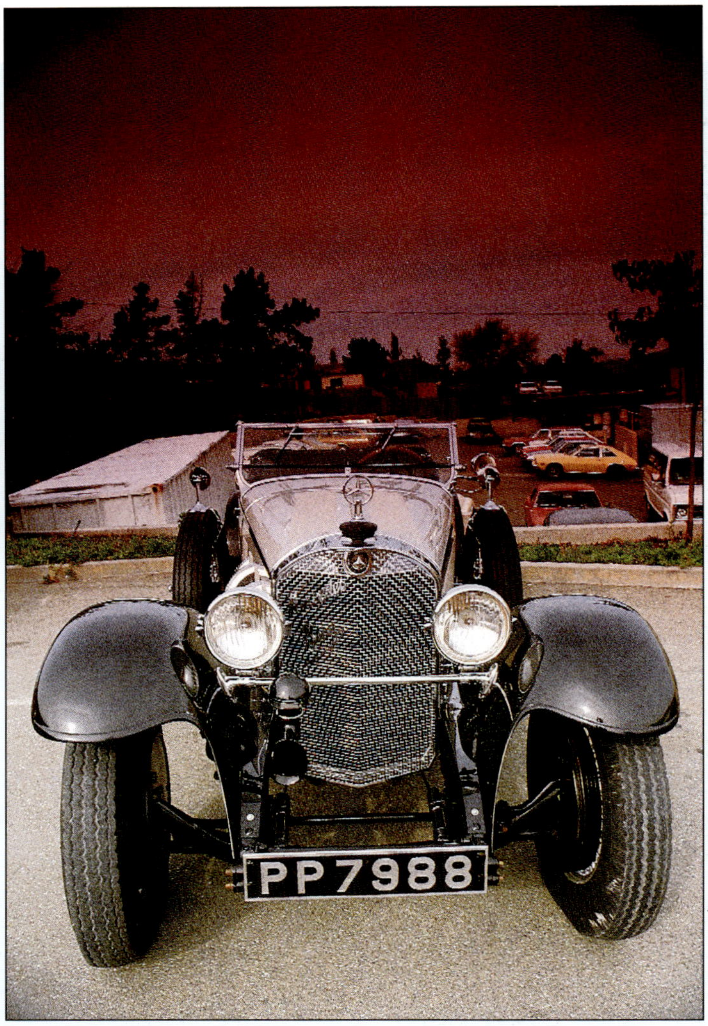


LEFT: Considered to be one of the few great sports cars of all time, the Mercedes-Benz 38/250 SS would compare favourably with more modern cars.

Greenchurch Engineering live deep in the Dorset countryside and led by Paul Weldon they make, to special order, a superb recreation of the 1928 Mercedes-Benz SS/38/259 sportscar. This car came about as a result of a collaboration between Paul and a Japanese company. Their president had always wanted to own a Mercedes-Benz 38/250 sportscar, and commissioned Paul to find him one, restore it and ship it to Japan. Then Paul was asked if it would be possible to manufacture a replica of the Merc. using modern engine/transmission units, but to make the rest of the car as close to the original as possible.

Paul commissioned Len Terry, the ex-Lotus designer to redesign the chassis, keeping the basic layout, but using up-to-date springs, shock absorbers, and location points. The result looked remarkably similar to the 1928 car, but handled and rode so much better. The overall dimensions were the same as the original car and only the engine and transmission were modern—in the case of the car in the photographs, these items came from a 280S model Mercedes-Benz.

The whole car is very well constructed, looks superb and goes even better. It is very easy to drive well and easy to drive very fast as the seating position and all-round view from the high

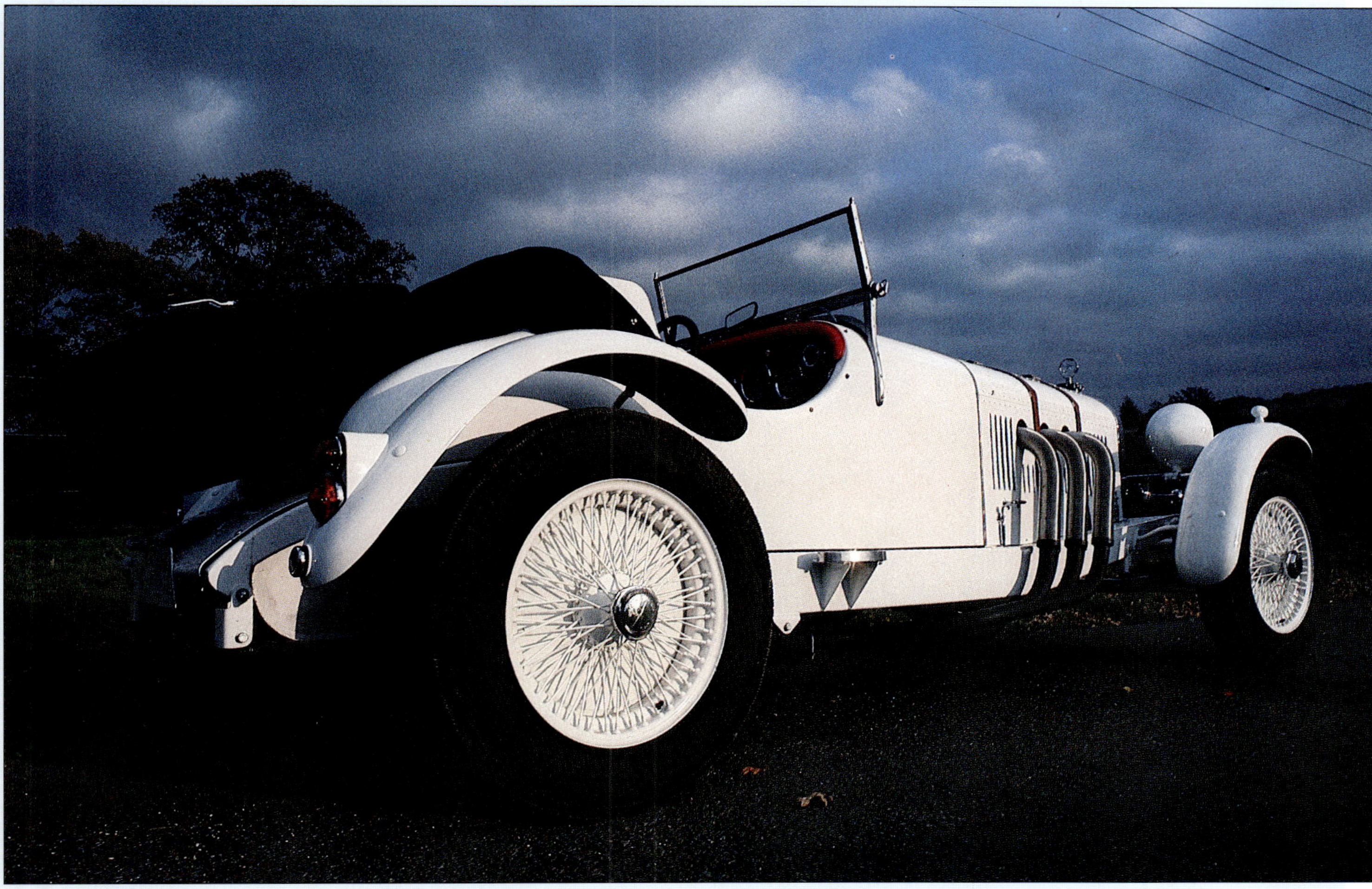

mounted seat allow the car to be positioned on the road to the inch. From the driving compartment the long white bonnet stretches ahead, and the separate front wings enable the fullest advantage to be taken of the road width. The apparently crude suspension works very well with the long wheelbase and gives the car a fine ride with excellent roadholding characteristics. Of course, the Mercedes-Benz engine delivers more than enough power for the lightweight car, and only the lack of aerodynamic efficiency limits the car's top speed to about 118mph.

Paul has named his car the *Gozzy*, and has been paid the highest compliment by Mercedes-Benz who allow him to use a very close facsimile of their famous laurel leaf radiator badge to adorn the Gozzy, which can also be found on the steering wheel centre. Costing over £35,000, the Gozzy is not cheap, but of all the many excellent recreations of famous cars that have been seen in the last five years it must rank with the Favre/Ferrari GTO (which is very much more expensive), and the Red Stallion Cobra as the most usable cars of their type that are available today.

In 1936 Mercedes-Benz converted their excellent sportscar, the 500K into the 540K, and the result was an instant classic. With an engine capacity of 5401cc the supercharged car had a maximum

ABOVE Using modern Mercedes-Benz mechanicals, the British-built Gozzy succeeds in its attempt to recreate the original 1920s Mercedes-Benz.

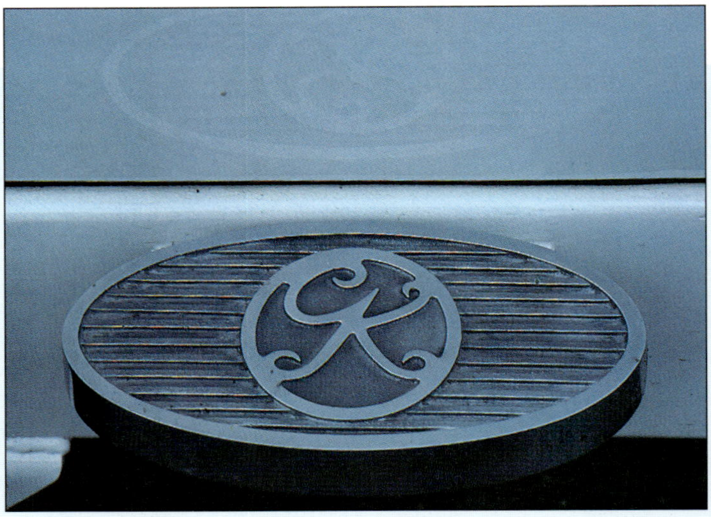

power output of no less than 180bhp, and the car fully justifies the claim to be the ultimate Mercedes-Benz sportscar of the 1930s. Over 700 500Ks and 540Ks were built between 1934 and 1939. In that latter year even the wonderful 540K would have been eclipsed by its planned successor the 580K if war had not brought its production plans to a halt.

As it was the 540K was a very genuine high performance car with a guaranteed top speed of over 110mph. Its supercharger arrangement followed the usual Mercedes-Benz pattern of being engaged by flooring the accelerator pedal, and was only to be used for very short bursts of full power.

Apart from the outstanding performance, the 540K's greatest attraction lay in the stunning bodies that were commissioned for its chassis, which lent itself well for stylish coachwork to be built and fitted easily. Many of the great European coachbuilding houses, as well as Daimler-Benz themselves, constructed elegant and tasteful bodies for the great sportcar.

This combination of power and beauty attracted the attention of the filmstar Barbara Hutton who commissioned one for her new husband, the Georgian Prince Mdivani. The Mdivani 540K is a valued item in the Blackhawk collection at the moment. It is in pristine condition and fully justifies the claim that it is one of the most beautiful sportscars ever built. As it also goes as well as it looks it would appear that this claim is accurate.

The coachwork by Erdmann and Rossi, Berlin is unblemished, the red finish being particularly suited to the body style, and highlighted by the excellent, and discreetly understated chromium plating. It has been said that the Mdivani 540K's lines are rather exaggerated, but in the late 1930s in the social whirl of the Hollywood elite, the car's looks were just perfect. It is one of the most exciting sportscars ever seen. Tucked away in the back of the Blackhawk holding building awaiting cleaning and some slight restoration in 1984, the sheer elegance of the car shone out quite clearly in the gloom.

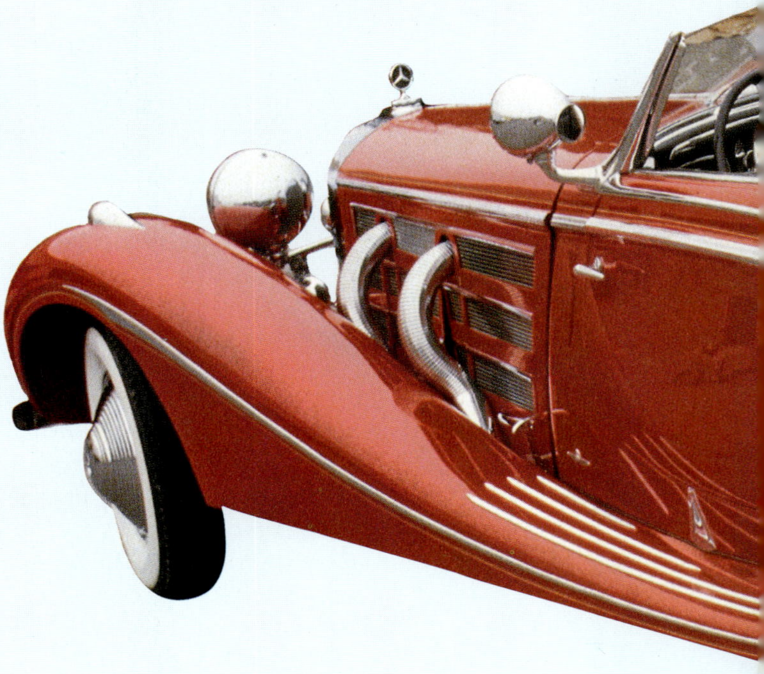

From the time Chrysler was first formed, the company had a fine reputation for good engineering. Enormous stress was placed upon the quality of their engineers' training, and as a compliment their brightest people were constantly being lured away by Ford and General Motors. In the early 1930s it was felt that they should move into the quality car market. As a result of this decision the excellent Imperial model was born. In 1932 only three models of the CL convertible sedan were built, with two being sold in the New York area and one in Los Angeles. The California car fell into a bad state of repair before it was rescued and restored, and now resides in the Nethercutt collection.

One of the New York cars somehow found its way to the West Coast. Nobody knows just when, but it was discovered in a barn in a state that its present owner describes as, 'Unrecognizable as an automobile!' Gerry Jensen was not a classic car expert when he first saw this pile of junk nearly ten years ago, but he was sufficiently alert to feel that it just might be something special and persuaded the farmer to sell him the wreckage. Gerry is not a rich

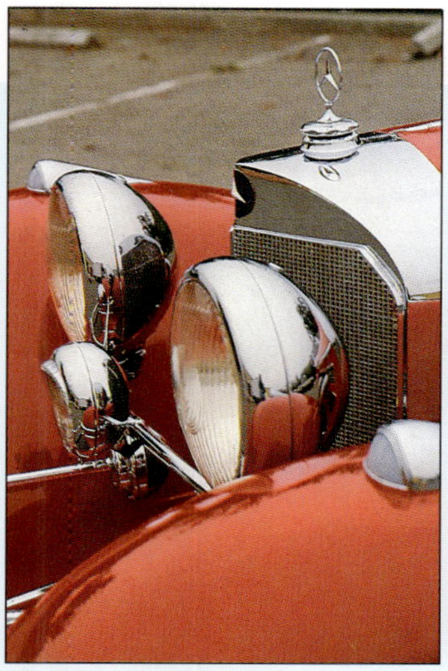

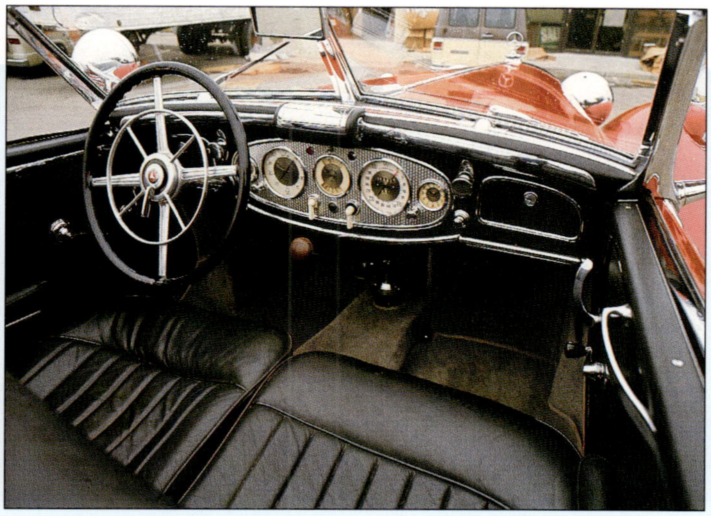

This Mercedes-Benz 540K was specially commissioned from the Berlin coachbuilders Erdmann and Rossi, by Barbara Hutton, the heiress of the Woolworth chainstore fortune.

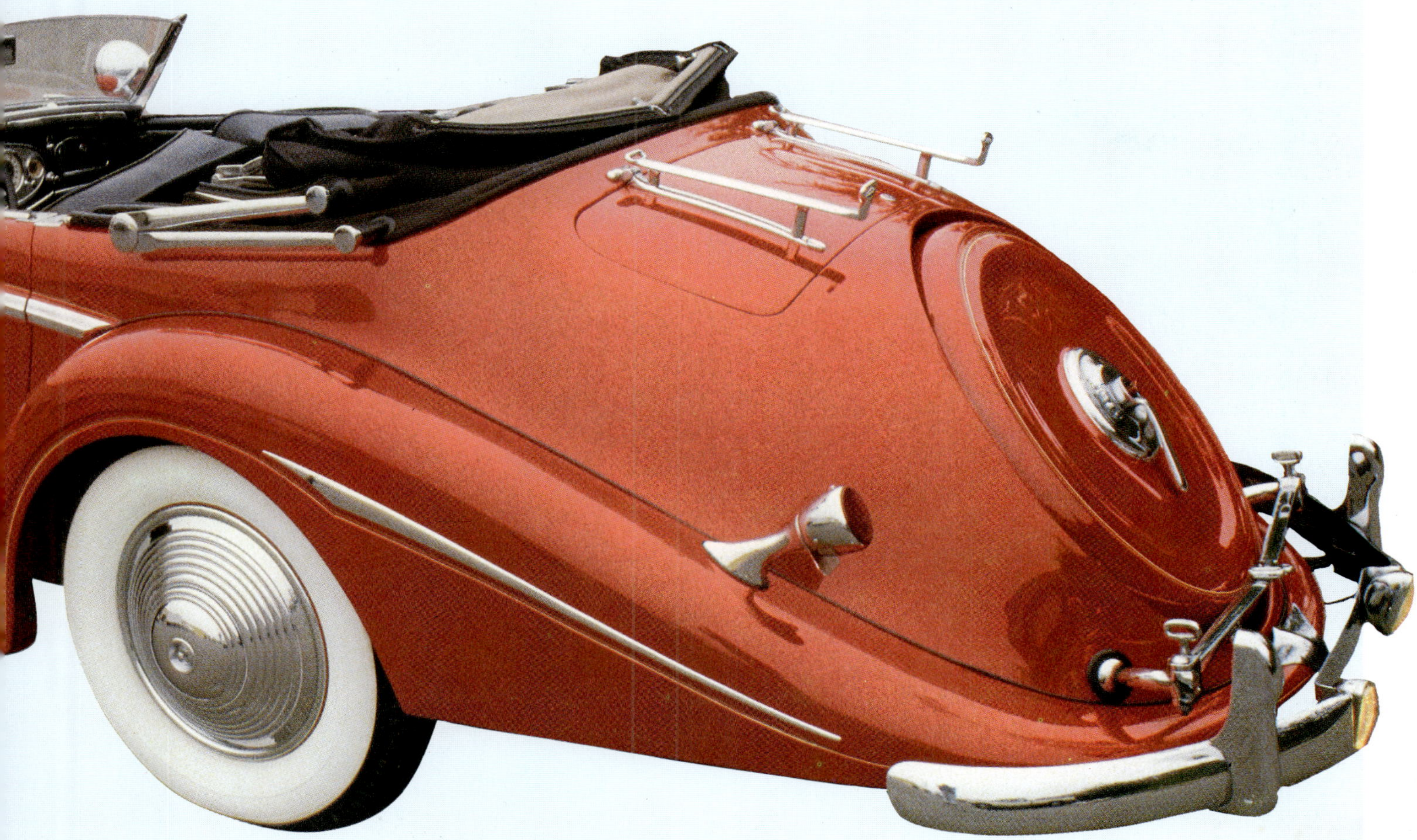

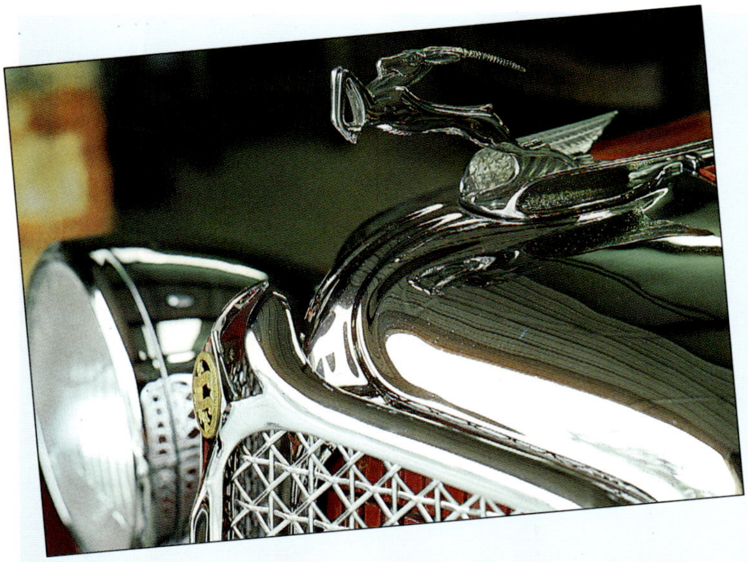

The high build quality of the Imperial is reflected in the mascot and radiator design—the ultimate in good taste and discretion.

man; he works in an auto parts dealership in northern California, lives in a small house with his family, and shares with most Californians a love of the car. Over the next three or four years he saved the necessary money to have the ruins of what he now knew was one of the three 1932 Chrysler CL models restored.

On completion he was persuaded to enter the car into the world's most prestigious concours d'elegance event, at Pebble Beach.

'It was like a fairy story', was Gerry's reaction to that competition, because he not only did well, he won THE award, the Blue Ribbon class of the whole meeting for the Best of Show! For those of a mercenary nature it might be of interest to know that just before the judging started Gerry had been approached by a collector who offered him $200,000 for the car. Three hours later, having just won the top award, the same man increased his offer to $400,000!

At the time of photographing the Chrysler, Gerry had driven the car only 11 miles in three years, out of his garage on to his trailer and off the trailer on to the show stand, with the reverse taking place after the show was finished. In that manner few miles have been totted up, but unlike many other owners of classic cars (for whom this kind of mileage is the norm) Gerry wants to use his car on the road, not as everyday transport, but at the weekend for pleasure driving. Gerry's total expenditure on his lovely Chrysler is relatively low, and he intends exploiting his investment by having some fun with the car in the manner in which it was intended when it was built in Detroit all those years ago.

Italy's entry for the 'Best Car in the World' competition can be claimed by the Isotta-Fraschini concern from Milan. In the 1930s they produced some of the nicest cars for the luxury market, several of which, by virture of their bodywork, turned out to be exceptional cars—for example, the Nethercutt collection model 8A with Castagna coachwork.
This car was in as bad a state as the previous Chrysler Imperial.

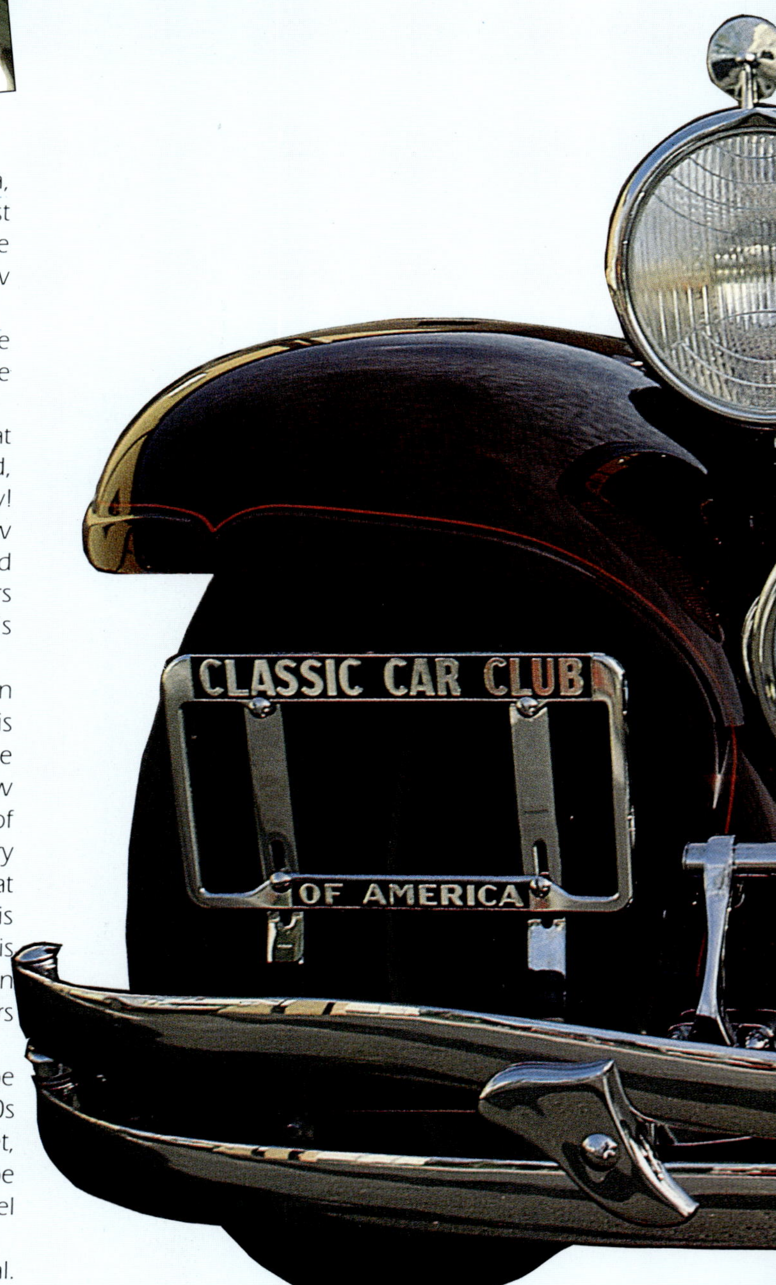

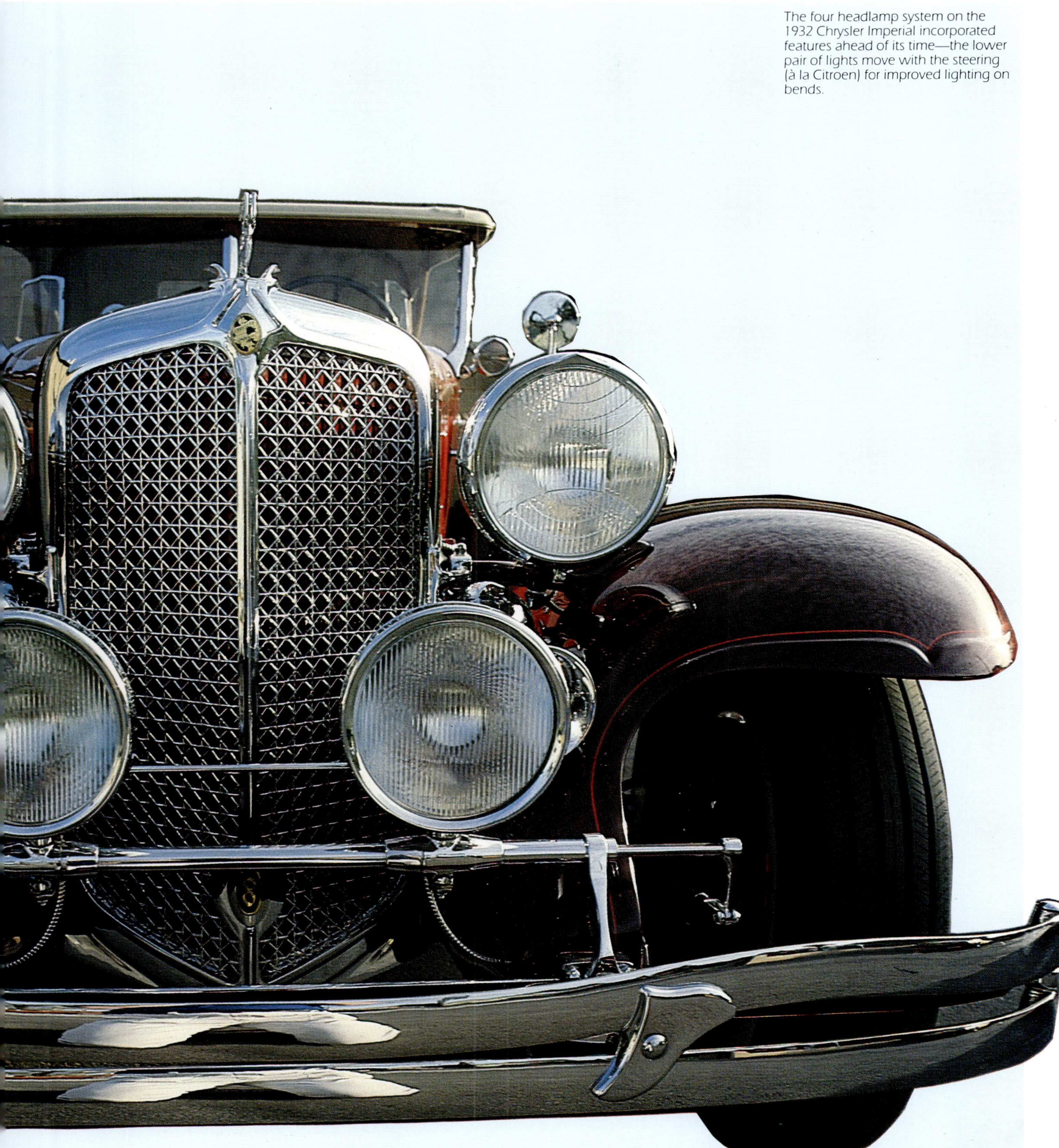

The four headlamp system on the 1932 Chrysler Imperial incorporated features ahead of its time—the lower pair of lights move with the steering (à la Citroen) for improved lighting on bends.

RIGHT: Much more than just a static museum piece, this superb Isotta-Fraschini from the Nethercutt collection, is fully roadworthy.

FAR RIGHT: The radiator mascot of the Isotta-Fraschini is one of the very best examples of Italian decorative design.

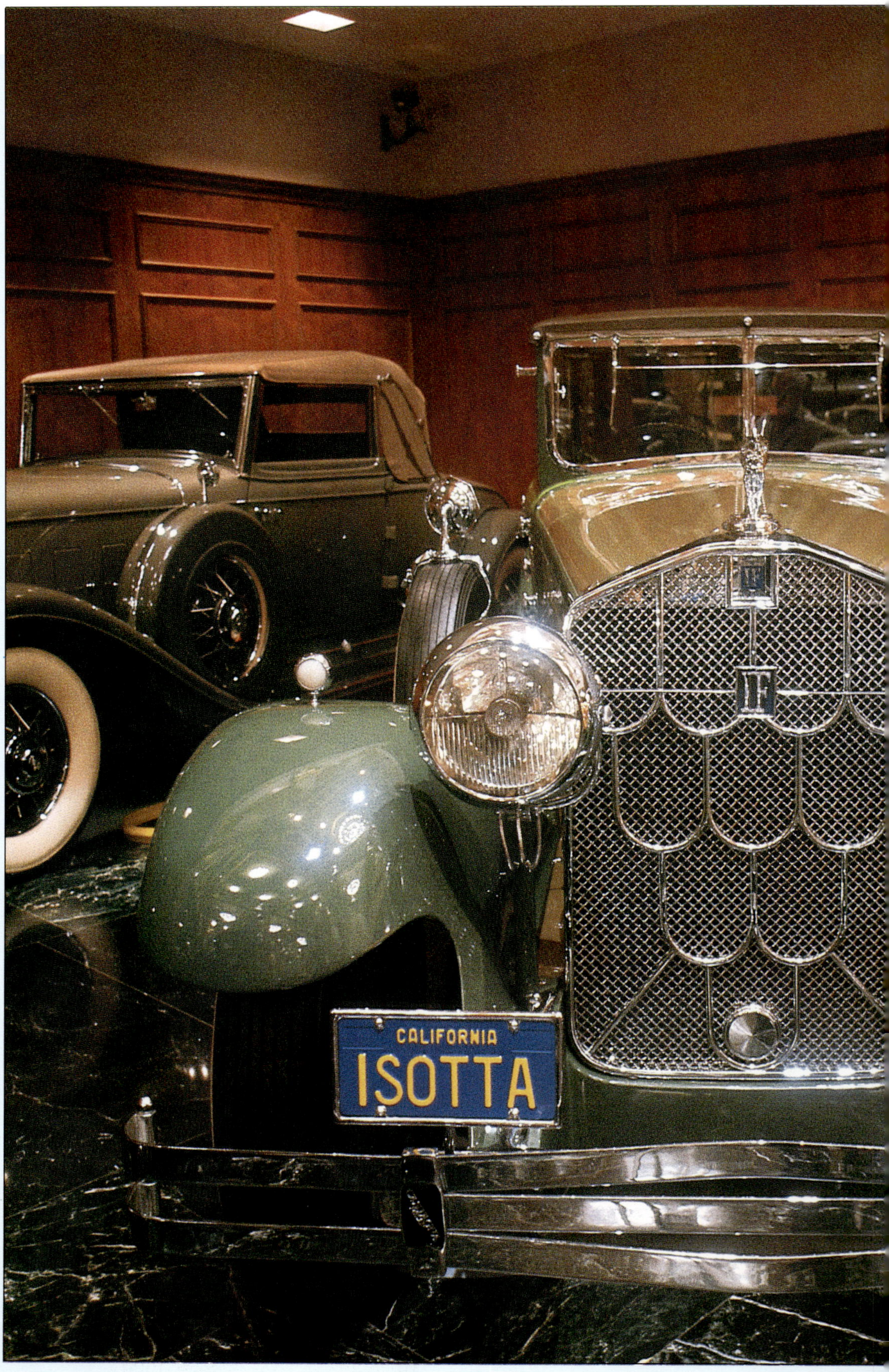

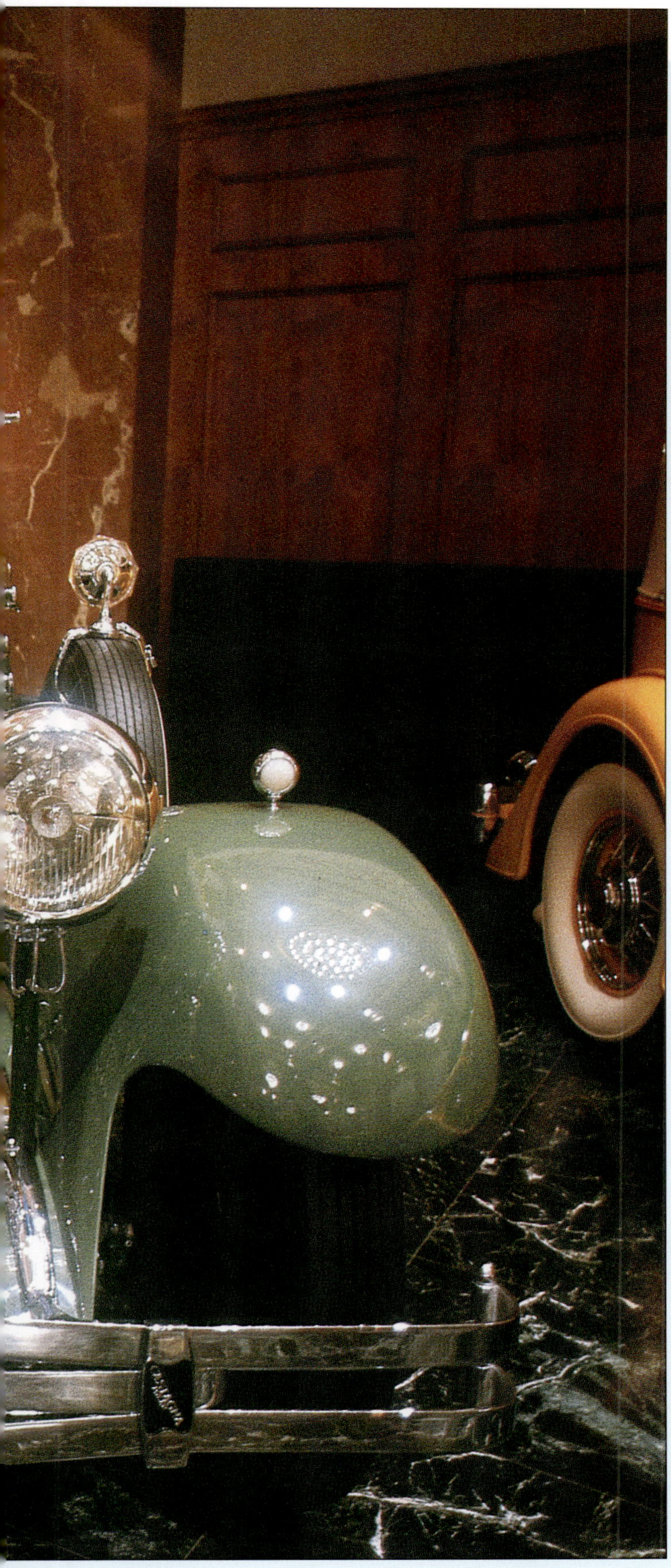

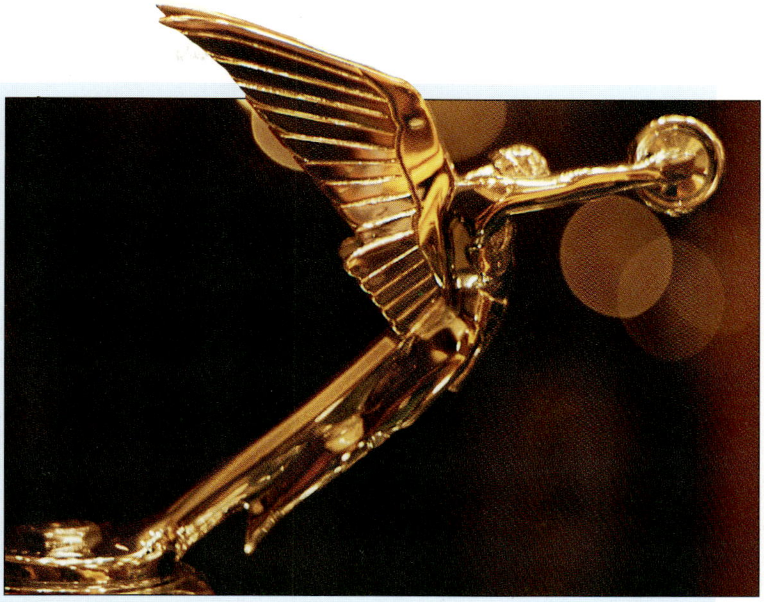

In fact, to listen to the Nethercutt restoration staff it must have been in as bad a state as any car could be, and only just qualified as a rebuild project. Everything on the car, from the mechanicals to the bodywork, trim, paint and plating required attention, but the finished result is magnificent. So good in fact, that the Isotta-Fraschini has taken many prizes in concours events all over the USA and, in particular it has been runner-up twice for the Pebble Beach Best of Show Award.

Emil Delahaye died in 1905, but he left his name to go on a series of very fine French luxury and sporting cars that achieved success both on Europe's race tracks and on the boulevards and fast roads of the Continent. In particular, Delahaye have the distinction of winning the French Grand Prix in 1935 and 1938 in virtually the same car, the first race driven by Phillipe Etancelin, famous for his insistence on wearing his cloth cycling cap, reversed, instead of a racing helmet. The second race was won by the great René Dreyfus in '38. René, now well into his late 70s intends returning to the sport in 1985 when he hopes, health permitting, to drive in the second running of the One Lap of America race. Even that event's 9,000 miles of every kind of difficult driving condition is not enough to put him off.

Of all the Delahayes the most spectacular car must have been the *145MS* model, an example of which is shown here. This particular car is on display in the Los Angeles Museum of Contemporary Art. A remark, 'What a campy car!' was overheard when a spectator saw the Delahaye for the first time. Reference was obviously being made to the driving compartment with its transparent plastic steering wheel and lurid colour scheme, but there is general acceptance that the Delahaye was a fine car from a factory with a long and distinguished history of automobile manufacture. When the Paris factory closed in 1954 another car from the world list of worthy vehicles was lost.

The very name of the Bugatti type 41—the Royale—really says it all. In a letter to a friend in 1913, Ettore Bugatti said that he intended to build a bigger, better, more expensive car than either

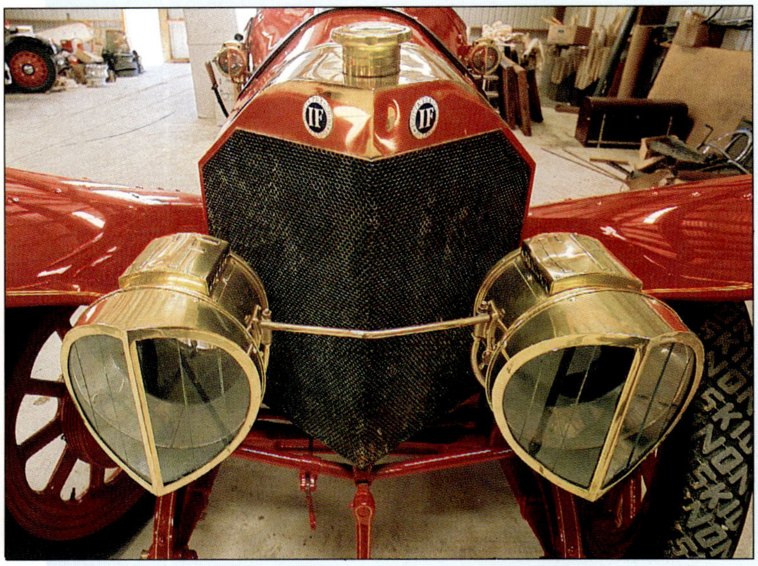

The huge brass headlights sport unique twin lenses.

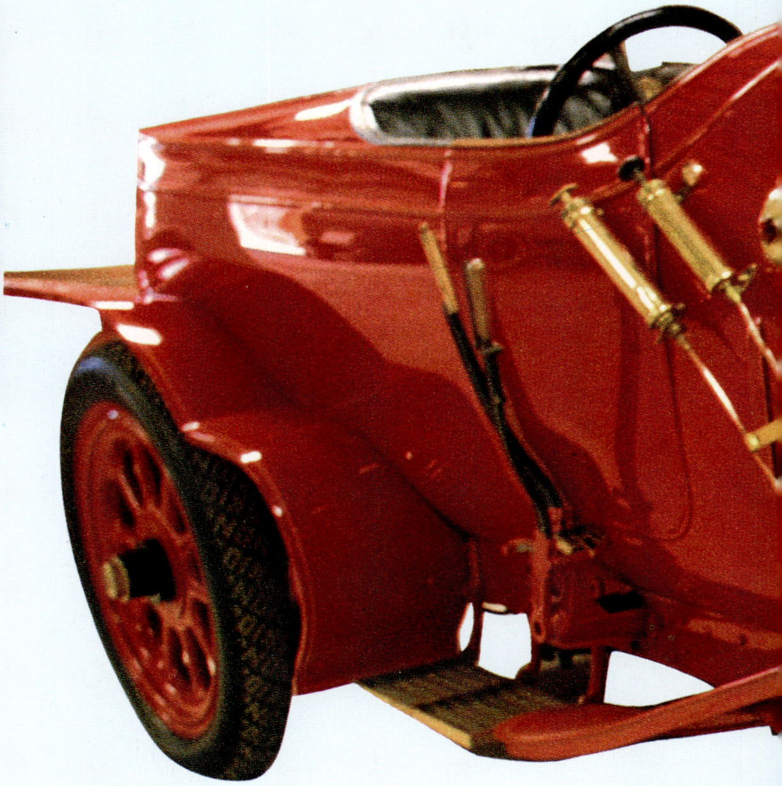

a Rolls-Royce or a Hispano-Suiza. Fourteen years later he had done just that with the type 41. It certainly was bigger; the engine, a straight-8 had a capacity of 12,763cc, the wheelbase was 170 inches and the huge wheels were waist-high. Travelling at 125mph, the vast engine was only turning over at 1680rpm, at which time it was developing over 200bhp.

Only six Royales, plus a prototype, were ever built, as it was hoped that sales could be restricted to the use of the royal families of Europe of the time, or at least heads of state. But, apart from an enquiry from King Carol of Rumania, nobody else seemed interested in the car. Whatever happened to the prototype is not known, but the six customer cars were disposed of as follows; one each to an English, German, and French client of Bugatti's, and the remaining three cars were given to various members of the Bugatti family.

One of the ex-Harrah Collection cars (Bill Harrah had owned 2!) on display in the L.A. Museum of Contemporary Art, and some details from the car were photographed in the Cunningham Museum. At the Cunningham Museum, John Burgess pointed out that the type 41 had the most perfectly arranged steering system ever put on a large car. He said that it made no compromises in catering to the driver who wanted to be isolated from road shocks. It is even more direct and free from deficiencies than a modern Grand Prix car, yet could be easily used by a woman driver, as was the Cunningham car which had been owned by Ettore's daughter, L'Ebé. He went on to say that at all the speeds the car was capable of, the steering remained light, with full feel and very responsive, a remarkable achievement for such a gigantic machine.

In 1927 a type 41 cost $25,000, and a body would require another $10,000 to be spent. The Cunningham Royale was hidden from the Germans in 1940 by being bricked up between two walls for the duration of the War, and in 1950 Briggs

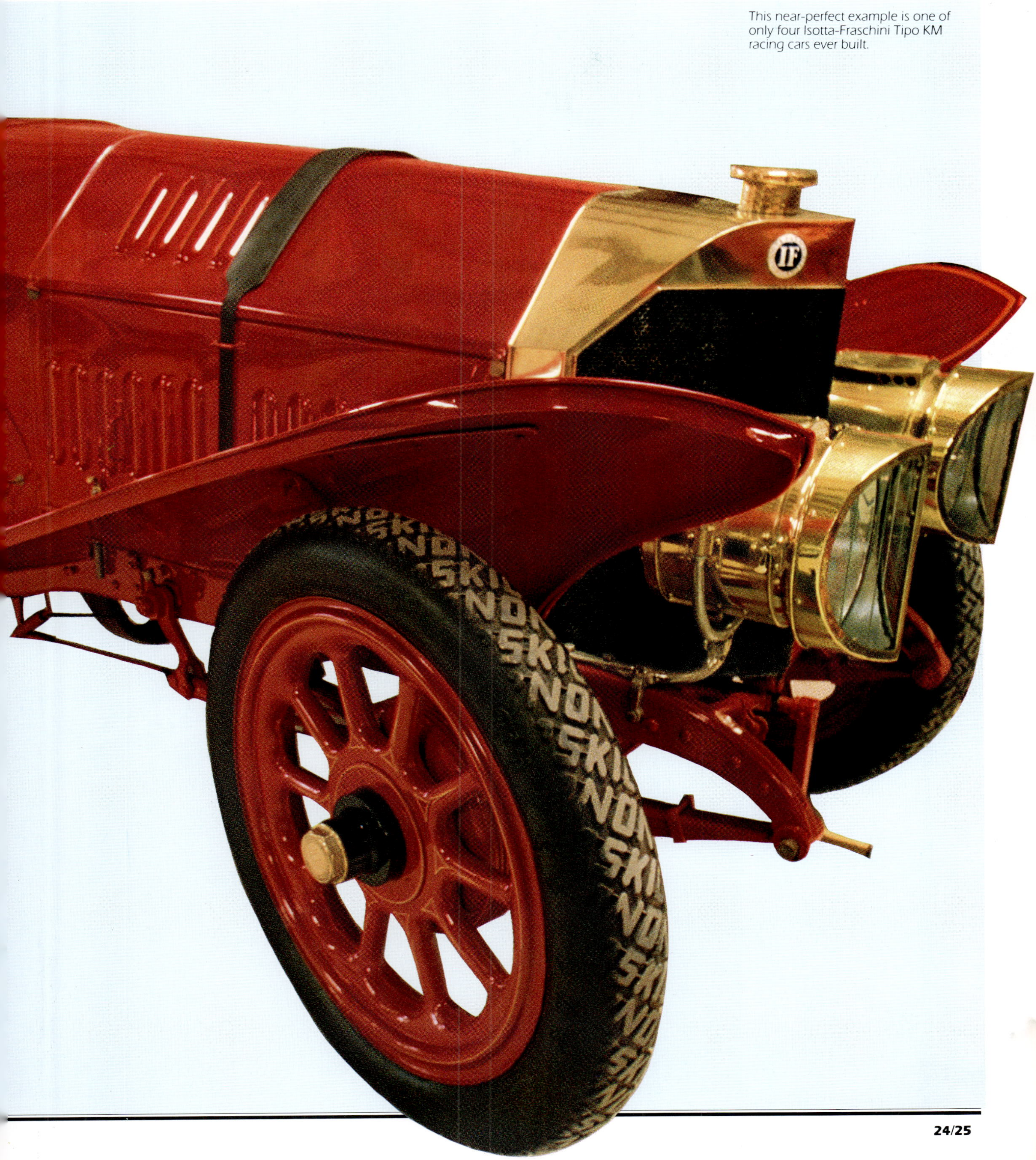


This near-perfect example is one of only four Isotta-Fraschini Tipo KM racing cars ever built.

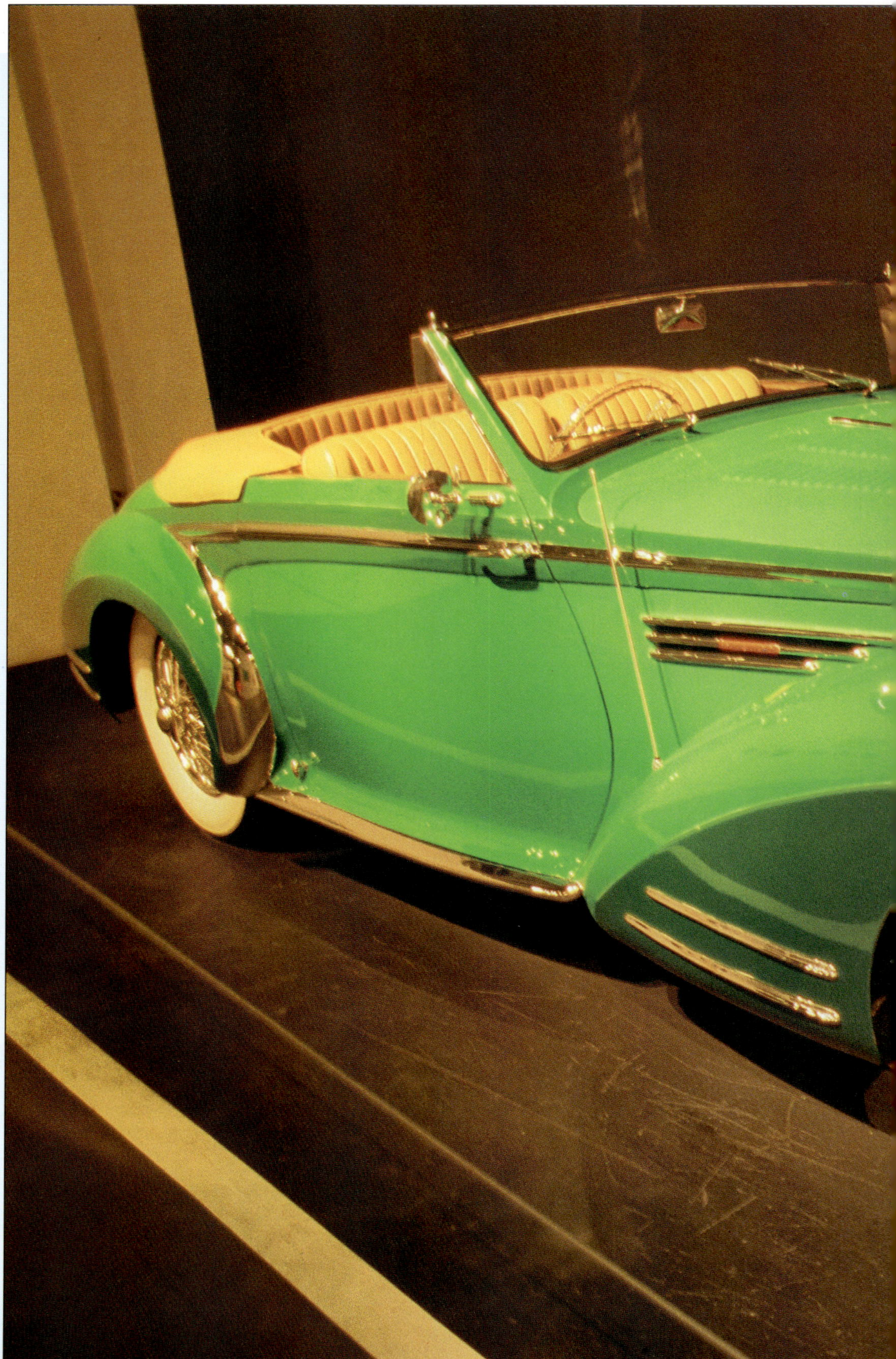

An example of extravagant French automotive design? This Delahaye 145 sports the most exotic body styling available on the car.

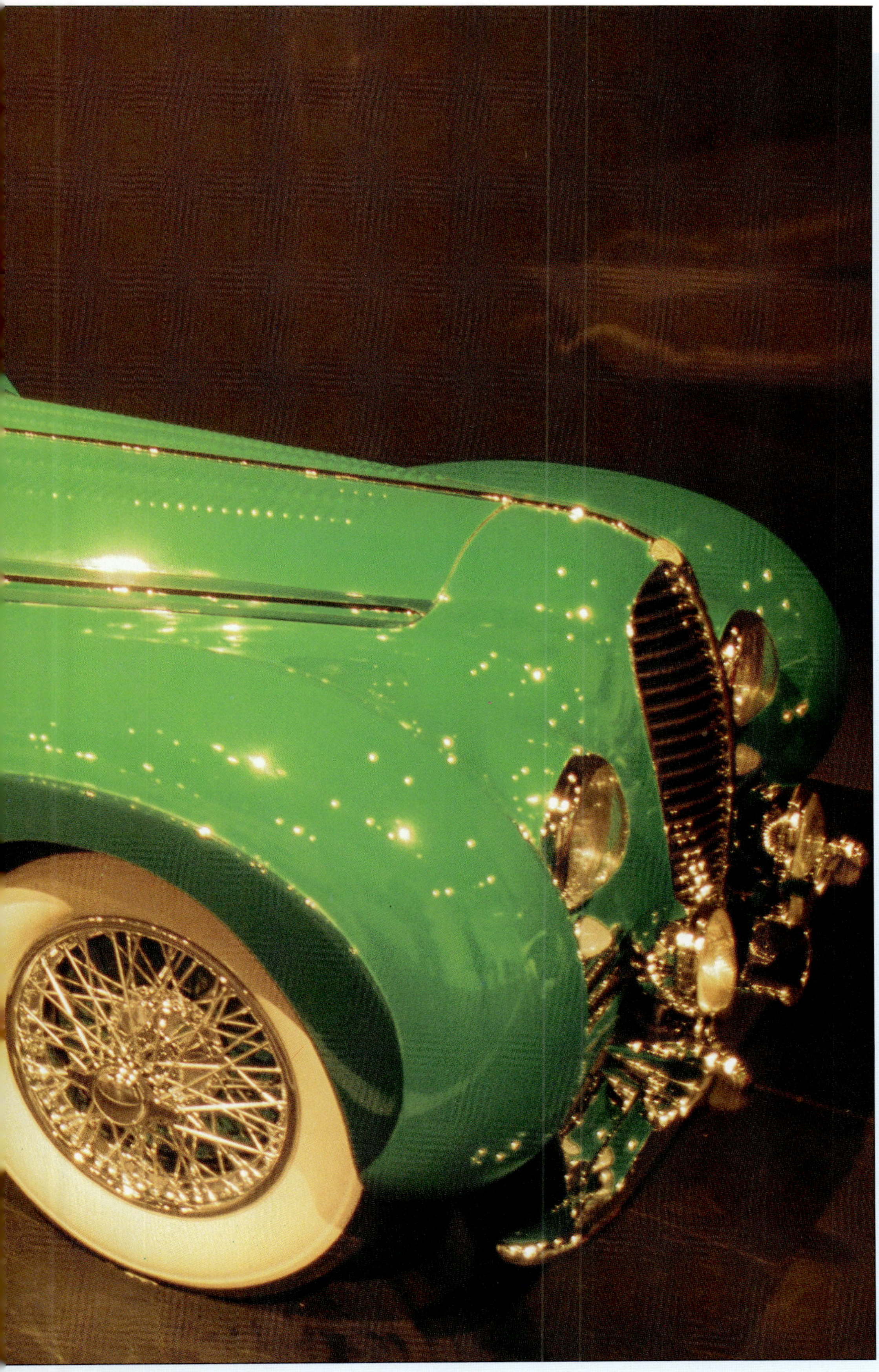

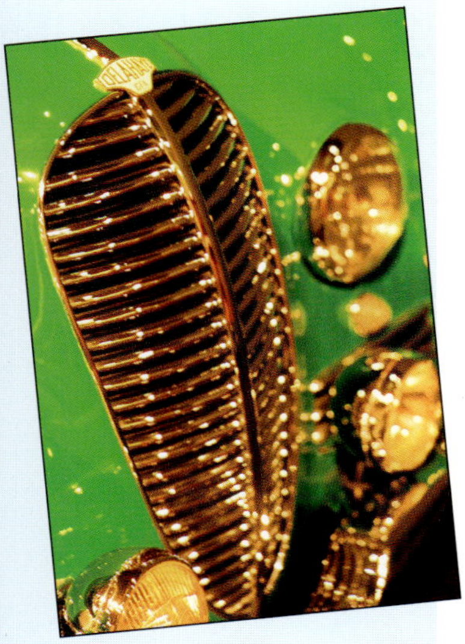

The lattice-work radiator grille design is said to have been influenced by the face guard of an Olympic fencer.

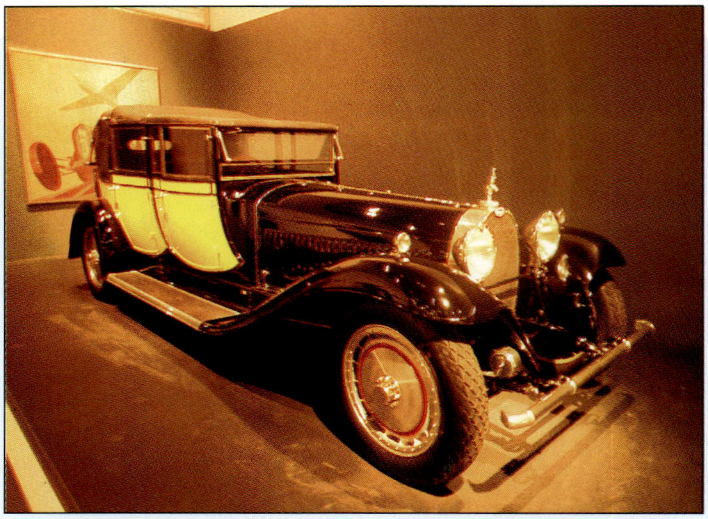

The massive Bugatti Royale Type 41 was not a sales success. It failed to find favour with royalty and heads of state for whom it was intended, and of the six offered for sale, the Bugatti family ended up with four.

Cunningham bought it from L'Ebé. It is no wonder that Ettore chose an elephant for the radiator mascot for this very large, splendid automobile.

The Napier car company had a short but hectic history of only 24 years, ending in 1924. The name is always linked to the name of S. F. Edge, the company's managing director. Edge firmly believed that racing, and more importantly, the publicity gained from that activity, sold cars. The Napier company had already a very fine reputation for precision engineering long before they became involved with the automobile, and this tradition carried over into their cars.

In 1902 Napier won the prestigious Gordon Bennett Trophy, and also gave Napier green to future British racing teams as the official British racing colour. At the then new Brooklands Racing Track in 1907 S. F. Edge averaged 65.9mph in a Napier 60hp model, a track record which stood for 18 years. In fact, THE record for the Brooklands Track is held by a Napier-Railton at 143.44mph, set by John Cobb in late 1939. As the Track was never opened for motor-racing after 1939, this remains its ultimate speed record. After Napier stopped making cars in 1925 they put all their efforts into aero-engines, and were world renowned for their work in this field. But in 1931 they were nearly tempted back into the car market in a tie-up with W. O. Bentley of Bentley Motors fame. The Bentley company had gone into liquidation earlier that year, and W.O., as he was known to everybody, had been approached by Napier to design an expensive, high performance sportscar for them, to be known as the Napier-Bentley. Napier would bid for the assets of the old Bentley company, pay off all that company's debts, and then go into production of the new car. There was even a new aero-engine contract for W.O. to be involved with in the new deal, so all was looking rosy for both companies when the Bentley receiver came to apply to the court for approval of the Napier contract in late 1931. Terms had been agreed, everything seemed to be tied up, and the court was simply expected to go through the motions of the hearing to finalize the deal. At this point a representative of Rolls-Royce stood up in court and offered

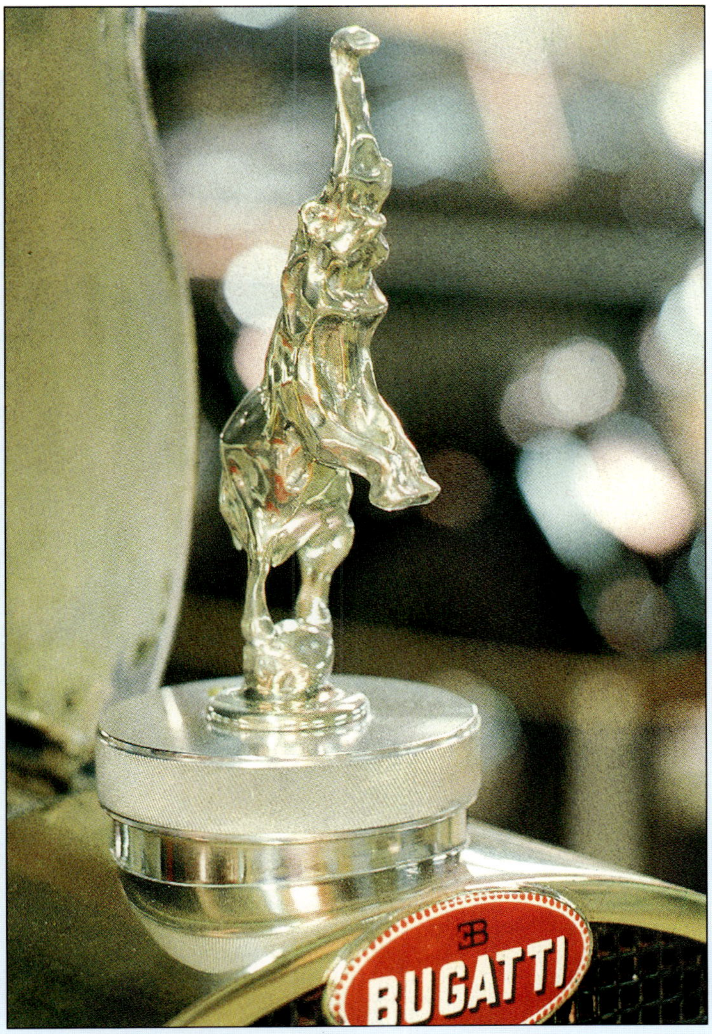


Ettore Bugatti chose the elephant mascot for the Royale because he felt it typified the size and engineering of the car.

slightly more than Napier for the assets and goodwill of the Bentley company. Napier upped their offer and were again topped by the R–R agent! Finally Napier gave up in disgust, not expecting or wanting to be involved in a public auction for the defunct Bentley company. The new Napier car never came to anything, W.O. finally joined Rolls-Royce to work on the 'Rolls-Bentley', and Napier as a car-maker was lost in the whole sordid mess. They went on with their aero-engine work and prospered, but for the car enthusiast it is still sad to drive through Acton in west London, past the D. Napier & Sons factory, and think what might have come out of the collaboration between Bentley and Napier.

The Auburn 852 Speedster with the boat-tail bodywork could be described as the epitome of the Hollywood special, the sort of car that the filmstars of the 1930s would be photographed in against a background of palm trees and white painted, Spanish style houses, under a bright Californian sun.

Unsurprisingly, that is where many 852s did finish up, being owned by film stars.

The 852 Speedster was a very large two seater roadster with sweeping lines and good proportions, which gave the car a very

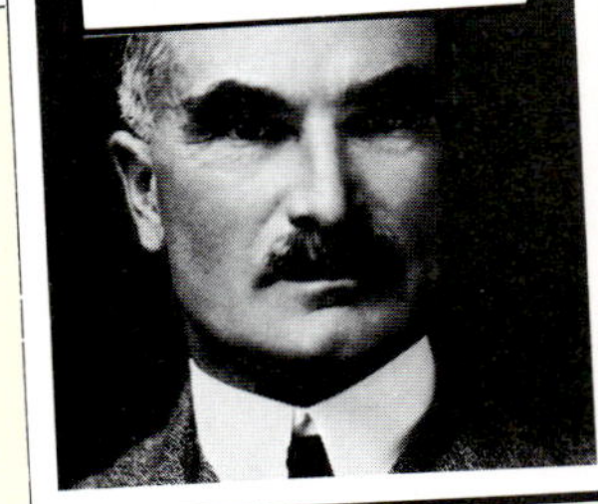

## SELWYN FRANCIS EDGE

Selwyn Francis Edge (1868-1940), was born in Sydney, Australia and came to England where he achieved success as a racing cyclist. He joined the Napier company and proceeded to race and promote the British luxury car at every opportunity. His brashness and peculiar brand of Australian enthusiasm rather shocked the staid British auto industry but he was nevertheless an able promoter of Napier's products.

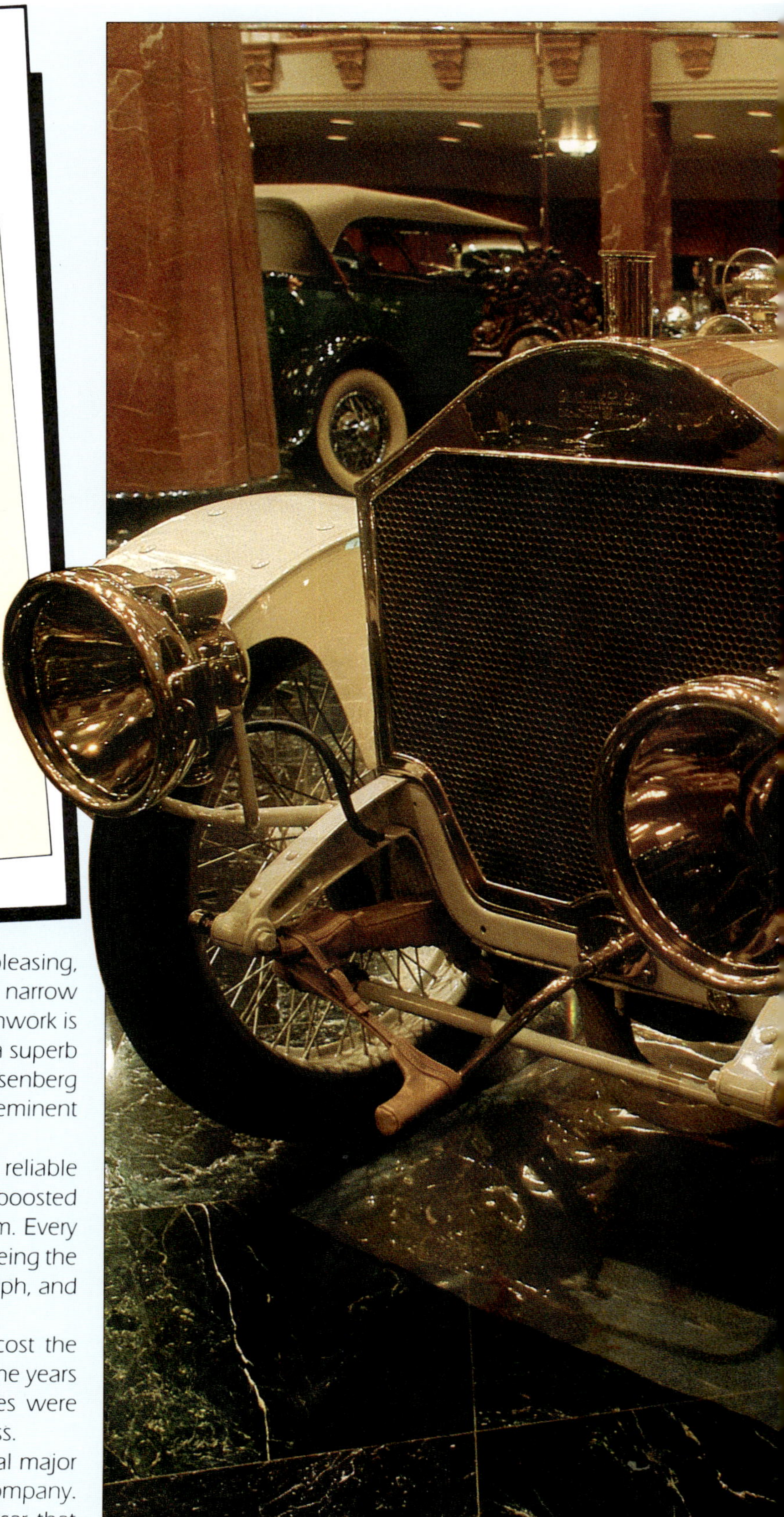

muscular, virile appearance. In profile it is particularly pleasing, but from the front some consider that it has a rather too narrow look, emphasized by the high build of the car. The coachwork is the result of a collaboration between Gordon Buehrig, a superb stylist and August Duesenberg, chief engineer of the Duesenberg company, a collaboration of the happiest kind of two eminent practitioners of their respective art forms.

August Duesenberg produced an efficient and reliable supercharger for the straight-8 Lycoming engine which boosted the power from 115hp at 3500rpm to 150hp at 4000rpm. Every 852 carried a plate mounted on the dash panel guaranteeing the top speed, which was always on the high side of 100mph, and the car sold for a very modest $2245 when new.

About 200 model 852s were built and every one cost the Duesenberg company hundreds of dollars, because in the years of the Depression the days of such exotic automobiles were numbered, so each and every 852 had to be sold at a loss.

The loss of money on the 852 was one of the several major factors in the demise of the Auburn-Cord-Duesenberg company. In the harsh climate of the American depression, any car that

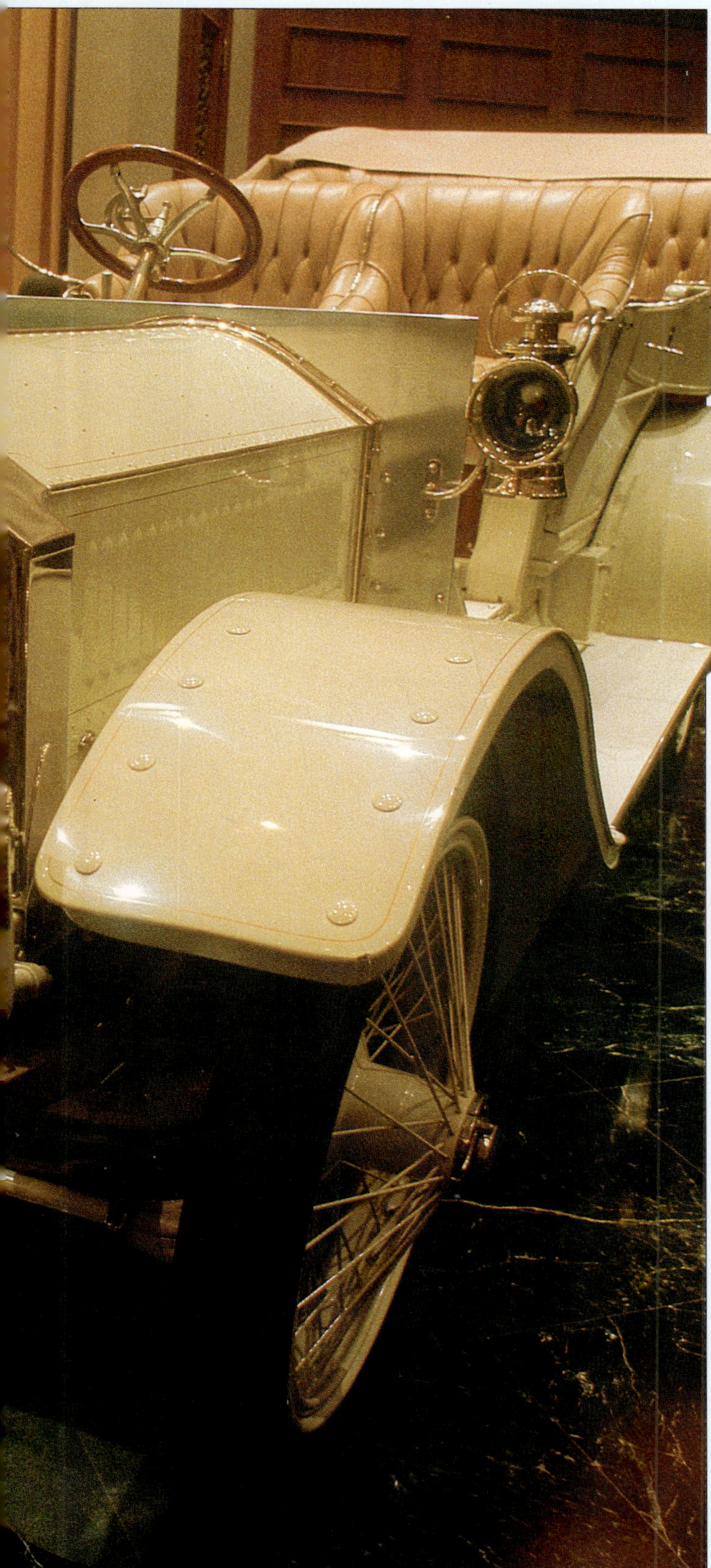

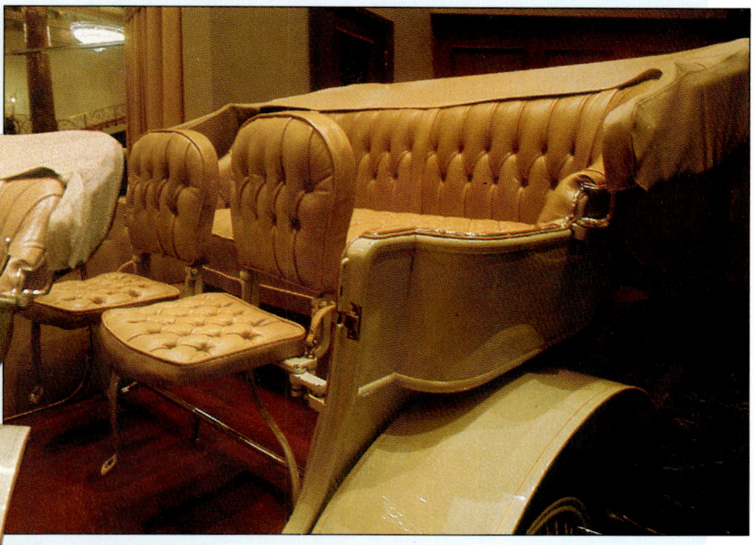

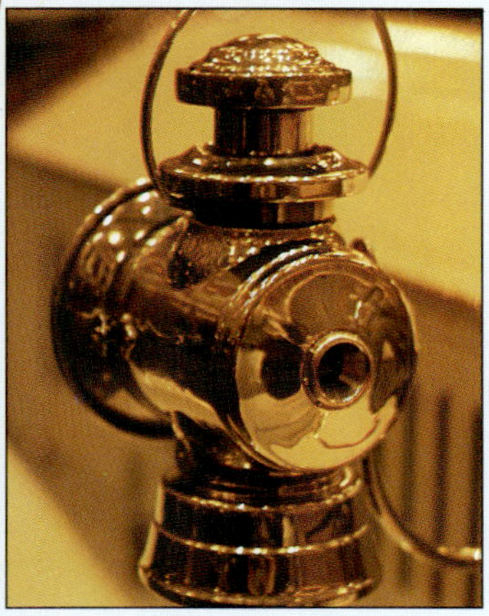

FAR LEFT: The Napier touring car is typical of the type of high quality vehicle favoured by the rich before WW1.

ABOVE: The interior of the Napier exudes class—all the seats are trimmed in the finest quality British leather.

LEFT: The brass acetylene lamps, although complementing the car's styling, did little to light the way ahead.

required as much hand work as the Auburn body, with 22 sections needing hand fitting and finishing, was doomed from the start.

The combination of the superb Buehrig body styling, and Duesenberg mechanical design and excecution has resulted in a car that from its very beginning was destined to be one of the most striking looking cars of all time. Not only is the 852 Auburn from the Blackhawk Collection a 'looker', it is also still a fast car and able to dash to 100mph when the opportunity presents itself.

Considered by many experts to represent the ultimate in classic cars', the Hispano-Suiza J12 did not burst upon the public conscience out of the blue. It came into being as the fullest expression of the genius of Marc Birkigt, the Swiss-born chief engineer of the Hispano company.

Between 1904 and the demise of the Hispano-Suiza company in 1938, Marc Birkigt penned the design of every engine that the company built for their cars, and made a very considerable contribution to the war effort against Germany in the 1914-1918 conflict by designing the V8 water-cooled engine that powered so many of the fighter and bomber aircraft in the allies' air fleets.

The choice of the rich, the film star and the sportsman, this 1930s Auburn 852 sportscar combined sweeping lines with a 100mph plus performance.

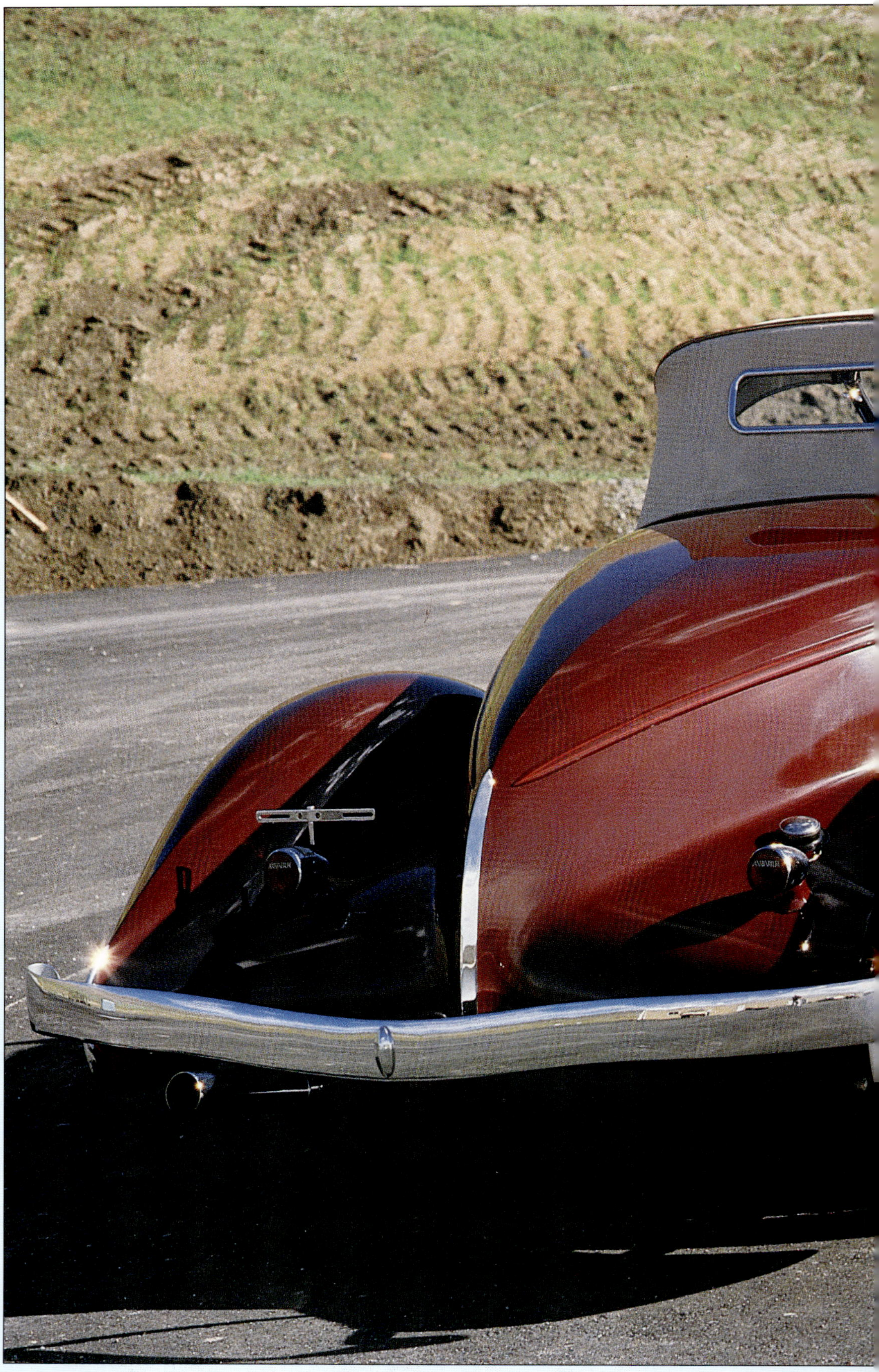

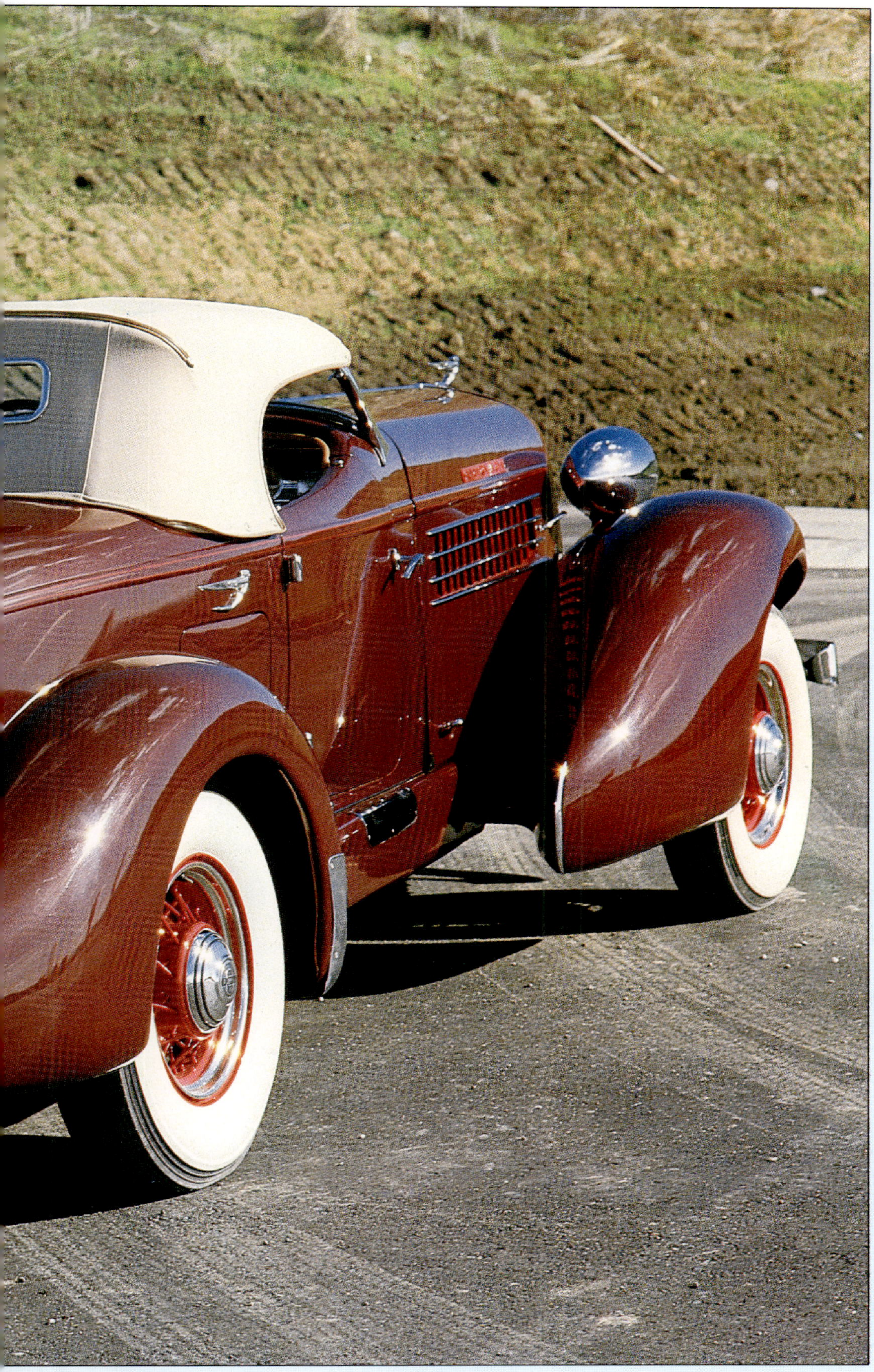

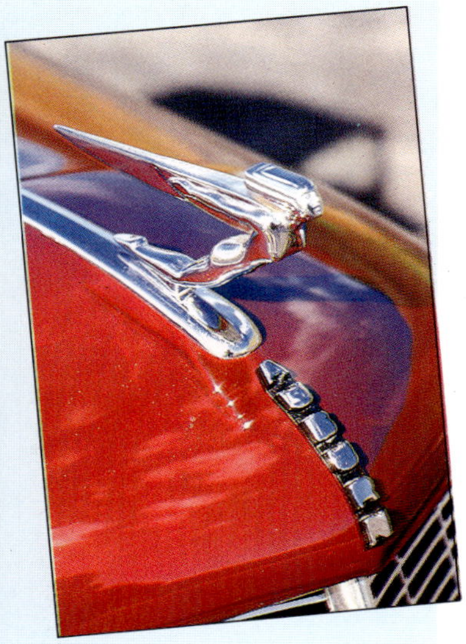

Despite its flamboyant styling, the Auburn's mascot was a distinctly plain affair.

A high-performance car, with power braking to match, the Hispano-Suiza rivalled and often beat the Rolls-Royces and Cadillacs of the day.

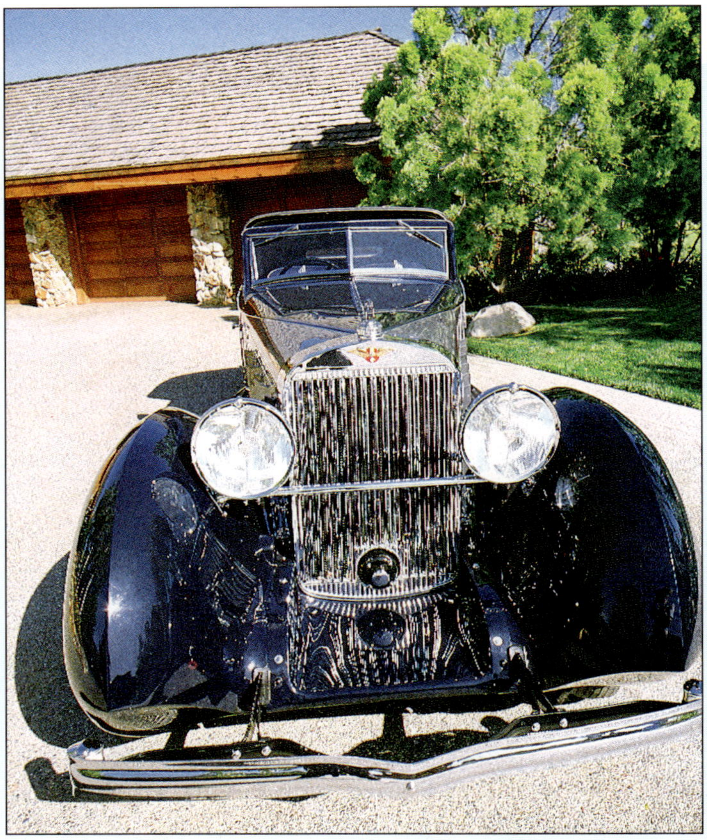

By 1918, 49,893 models of his aero-engine had been built by 21 different engineering firms in America, France, and Great Britain. Marc Birkigt received his technical education in Barcelona, where he was living with his grandmother, qualifying with the highest honours in Mechanical Engineering. Between 1904 and 1920 he is credited with designing no fewer than 35 different vehicles! He stayed with the Hispano-Suiza company for 34 years, in one of the most productive partnerships in automotive history.

He was brutally honest about his abilities, as he viewed them, and in one of his rare speeches he said, 'I am only an engine designer', which must be one of the great understatements of all time. One has only to consider his work on power assisted braking, which was fitted to all his cars from the early 1920s. Braking performance was the Achilles' Heel of many automobiles of the period, some cars being equipped only with rear wheel brakes, most of the rest having only mechanically operated means of stopping. The Hispano-Suiza patented friction motor powered braking system was so good that even those arch-conservatives in the Rolls-Royce company negotiated to use the system, built under licence, in their own cars, as did many other European car makers.

Birkigt was a perfectionist in every sense and his car reflected his care and appreciation of just how cars should be made with no concessions, half measures or compromises at any stage in their construction. He repeated his aero-engine success 21 years later with his 20mm automatic cannon design, just to display that

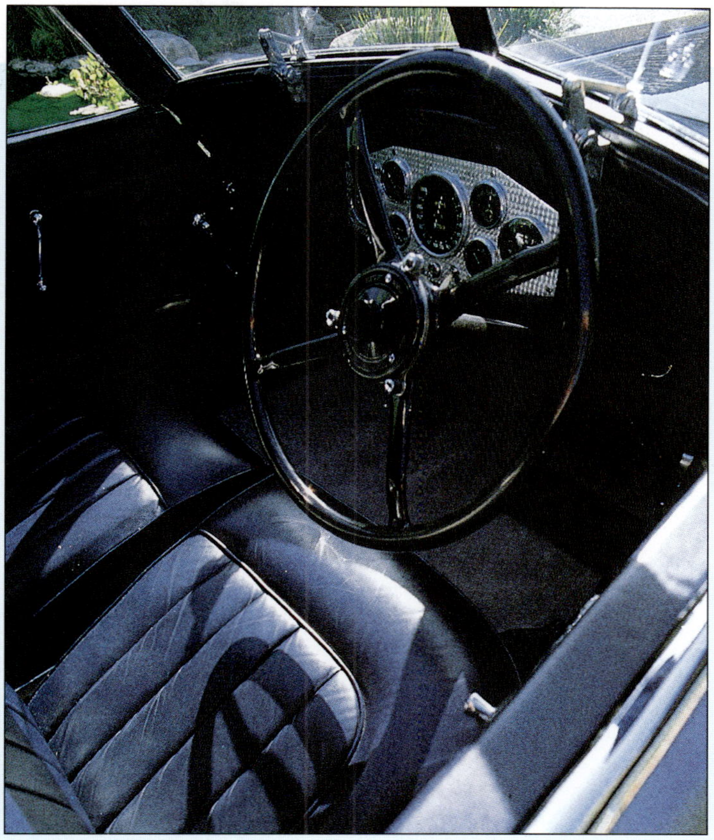

Simple but elegant—the subtlety of the car's styling extends even to the cockpit of the Hispano-Suiza J12.

34 years of designing cars had not blunted his ordinance-trained abilities—the cannon was used in aircraft in World War II.

The J12 was, at one and the same time, a town carriage par excellence, a high performance machine capable of covering hundreds of miles a day across continents in great comfort and a superbly good looking vehicle. Figures can give only some idea of the J12's ability when it was tested at the famous Brooklands track—it lapped at over 95mph in 1933. 0-60mph in 12 seconds, over 108mph top speed and an amazing braking performance of 30mph-0mph in 26 feet were all amazing for a two ton vehicle then and are still very respectable now. The car's fuel consumption, at an average of 11mpg, was more than good bearing in mind the weight and performance. Suspension could be adjusted by using the driving compartment located shock absorber control to compensate for varying loads and speeds.

Between 1931 and the closure of the factory at Bois Colombes in 1938, 120 J12s were constructed at a chassis price of £2750. Any of the many high-class coachbuilders would equip the chassis with the customer's choice of body for £750-£900 in those days. The quality of the J12 can be appreciated by the knowledge that over a quarter of the 120 J12s built are still in use. During its lifetime the J12 faced stiff competition from the Rolls-Royce Phantoms II & III, the Cadillac V16, and the Packard V12, all marvellous cars, and it matched them in all respects, even bettering them in the engine department by an appreciable margin. With the J12 Hispano-Suiza, Marc Birkigt has earned a place in the hearts of lovers of great cars the world over.

CHAPTER TWO

# The Duesenberg

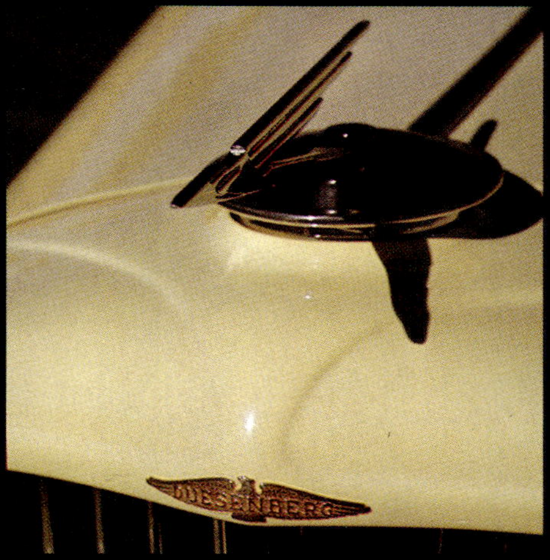

OVERLEAF: The sales appeal of the Duesenberg was based as much on its performance, as on its styling. The basic simplicity of this JN radiator emblem bears this out.

RIGHT: The choice of Hollywood filmstars—the supercharged Duesenberg SJ speedster became the most famous American sportscar of the 1920s and '30s.

CENTRE: The huge flexible, exhaust outlet pipes of the Duesenberg leave absolutely no room for doubt that the engine is supercharged.

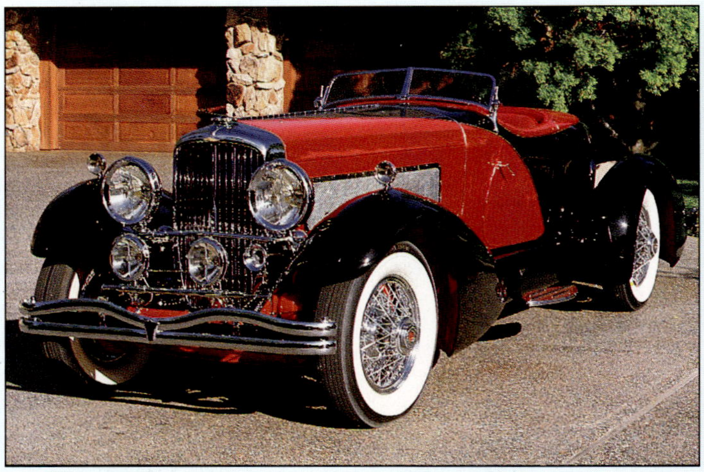

The Duesenberg holds a special place in American automotive history, even though production stopped nearly 50 years ago. The Duesenberg is one of the most collectable of all cars in the USA and no real car enthusiast can fail to be impressed at seeing one of the Indianapolis-built cars for the first time—its massive construction in all respects promises both high performance and great durability. It also reminds the modern day motorist of the features that his counterpart looked for in the 1920s and 1930s: glamour, style, power and more than a hint of the fabled days of the Hollywood of the pre-World War Two period. Many of the great stars of that time owned and used Duesenbergs; Gary Cooper, Clark Gable, Carol Lombard and Tyrone Power to mention just a few.

Fred and August Duesenberg were automotive engineers in the true American pattern of the early part of this century, trained by a combination of theory and very practical experience, interested only in producing the best possible product that carried their name. They were more engineers than businessmen, a combination that did not, sadly, stand them in good stead during the years of the Depression.

In one respect they, in their small way, anticipated a trend of automobile production still current today. They were assemblers rather than makers; a modern-day parallel would be to compare them to the Lotus Car company of 15 or 20 years ago. The Duesenberg brothers subcontracted out their engine and transmission work to specialists such as the Lycoming engine company who made all their production motors. Bodies were handled by many of the excellent American coachbuilders like Murphy, Le Baron, La Grand, Darrin, Fleetwood and Rollston. In the factory the various components were brought together and assembled into the finished vehicle. Engines were checked by Fred Duesenberg, adjusted where necessary, then road-tested for hundreds of miles before going to the customer. An interesting fact emerged when researching this book: John Burgess, the director of the marvellous Briggs Cunningham Auto Museum in Costa Mesa, California, told the author that the

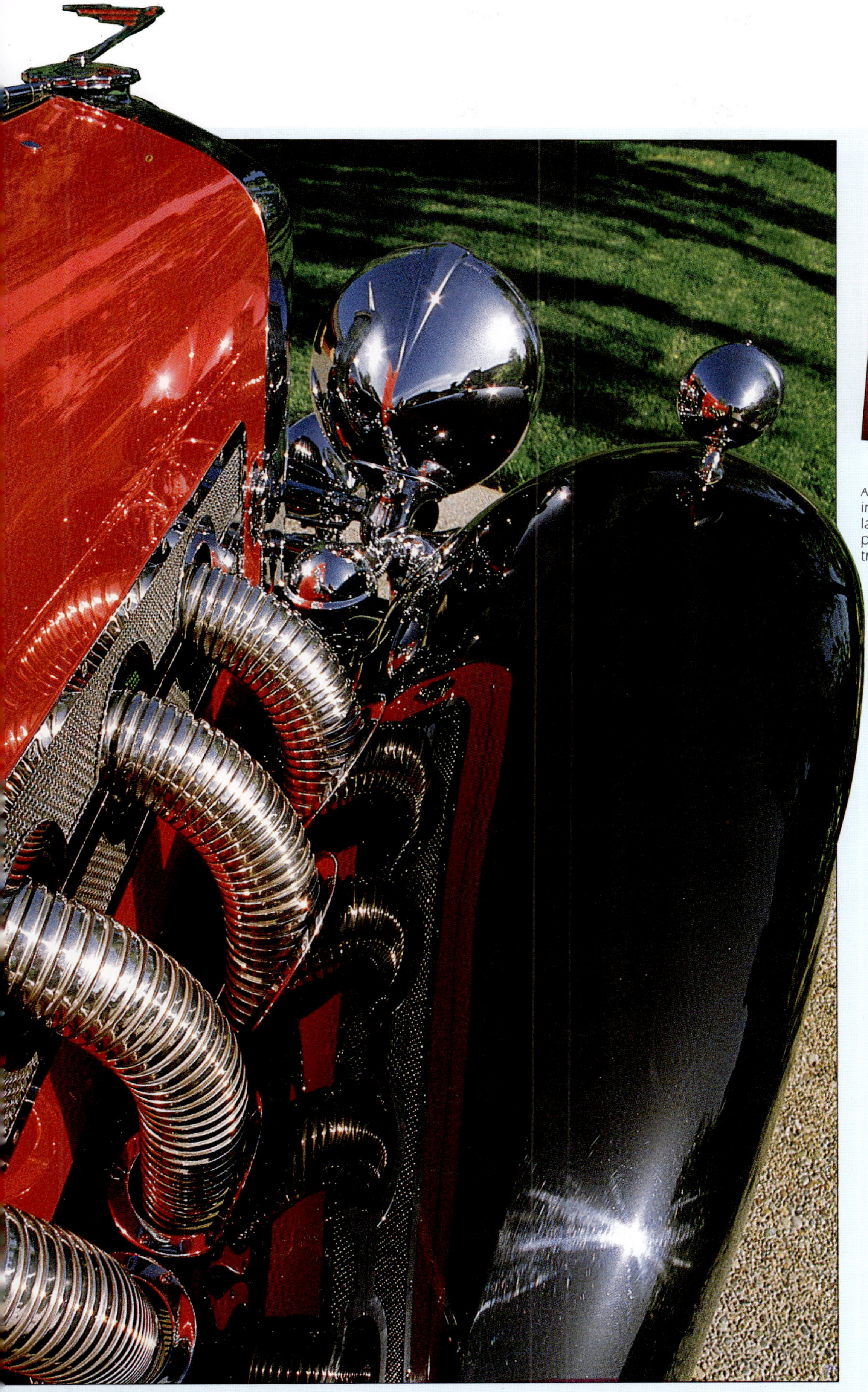

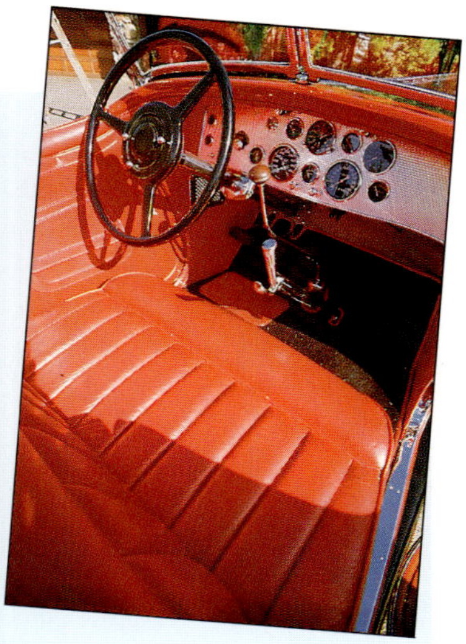

ABOVE: Comprehensive instrumentation, and a simple cockpit layout gave the Duesenberg SJ the purposeful air of a high-speed travelling machine.

Duesenbergs would give the Lycoming factory a brief of what kind of engine they wanted, and leave it to Lycomings to build, produce and deliver the finished engines to the Duesenberg plant. This meant that the engines did not always conform to design tolerances, hence the post-production work by Fred Duesenberg. In this he was not always successful—so many of the Lycoming-built engines were down on power when delivered to the customer, many of whom never knew or experienced this fact. Recently the Cunningham restoration shop undertook to 'blueprint' an unsupercharged engine out of a J-model car; this is the lower powered version of the basic two model Duesenberg range, the SJ carrying the blown engine with much more horsepower. After very carefully reworking the engine to bring it up to the original design tolerances it was found to be capable of outperforming the SJ model by an appreciable margin!

The Duesenberg engine is a massive affair, looking more suitable for service in a large ocean-going yacht than a mere automobile. Luckily, there is an exhibition engine, available for photography, mounted on a stand in the J. B. Nethercutt Collection and a very good idea of the size and proportions of this huge straight-8 powerplant can be gained by looking at it with the knowledge that the engine alone weighed over 1200lbs. The 420 cubic inch engine was equipped with double overhead camshafts which operated four valves per cylinder and produced a claimed 265bhp. The SJ blown model with its twin carburettors and special supercharger was supposed to develop 397bhp at 5000rpm. Both of these engines were fitted with three-speed gearboxes, but their torque ensured that in most circumstances the second and top gears alone were quite adequate for normal driving conditions.

All Duesenberg cars carry quite beautifully designed bodies, most carefully constructed and finished. The very best of some of the most famous Duesenbergs are illustrated in the accompanying photographs in this chapter.

1932 saw two great Duesenberg cars appear on the automotive world scene, the 'Twenty Grand' Chicago World Fair car, and the model that has been known as either 'The French Speedster' or simply 'The Figoni'. A J model, it was given a boat-tail body by the Paris-based company Figoni, a body of great beauty and style which carried all the glamour and excitement of the marque Duesenberg. In the hands of its early owners the car won many honours in concours d'elegance competitions in Monte Carlo and Cannes. It was raced and rallied, although it did not enjoy great success in these events. However, the rallies were not as they are today, being more like reliability runs, but even so the Duesenberg must have been out of its element, far too valuable to throw around for the sake of a silver cup or two. At one time it was owned by a Peruvian playboy, Antonio Chopitea. Looking at the 'French Speedster' today, it is so very easy to imagine it being driven, fast, from the Negresco Hotel in Nice along the coast road to Monte Carlo on a warm summer's

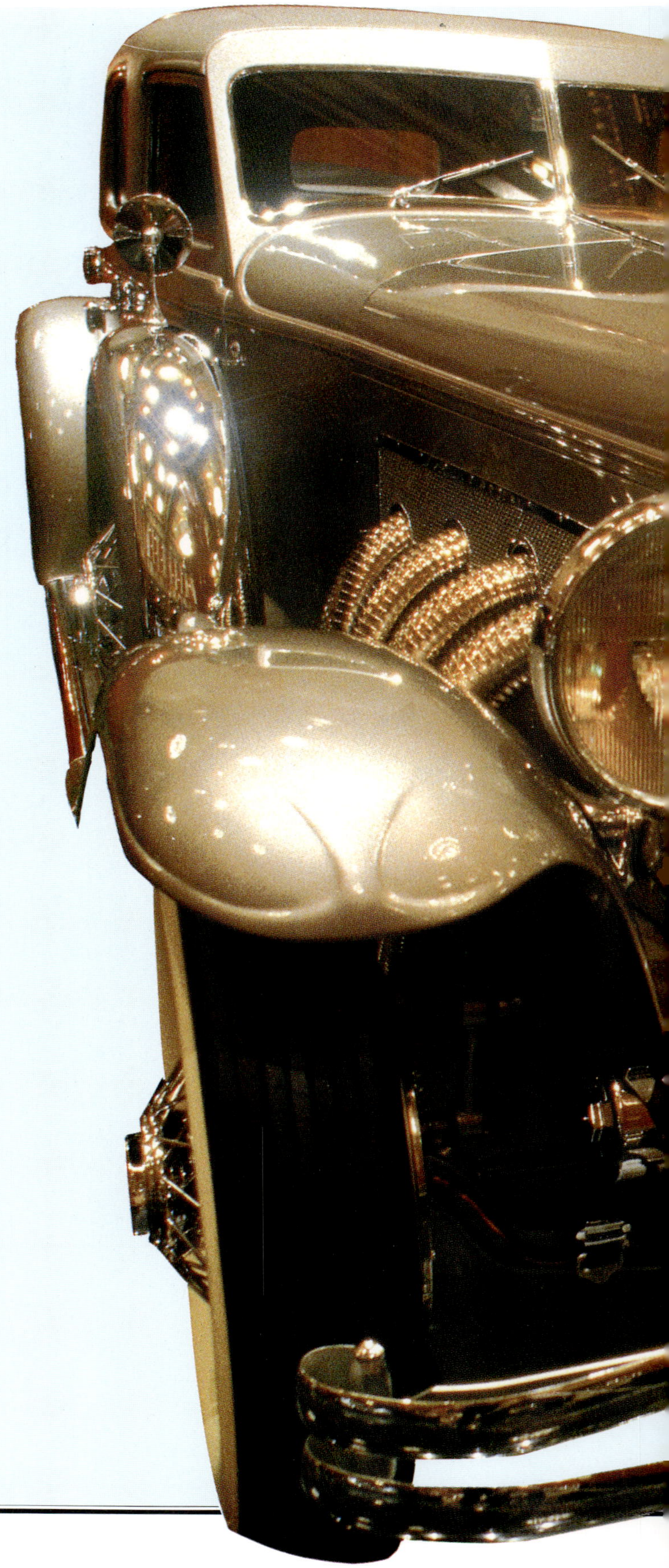

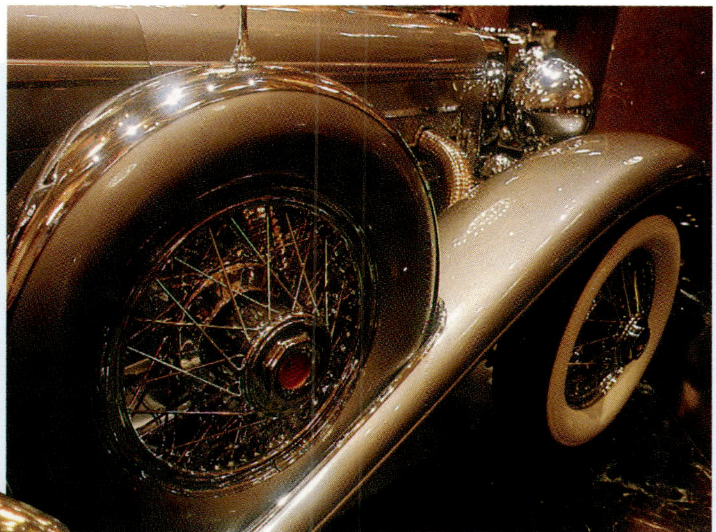

Built to grace the Chicago World Fair of 1933, the Duesenberg 'Twenty Grand' is unique. Superb workmanship and materials combine to make the 'Twenty Grand' a fabulous car.

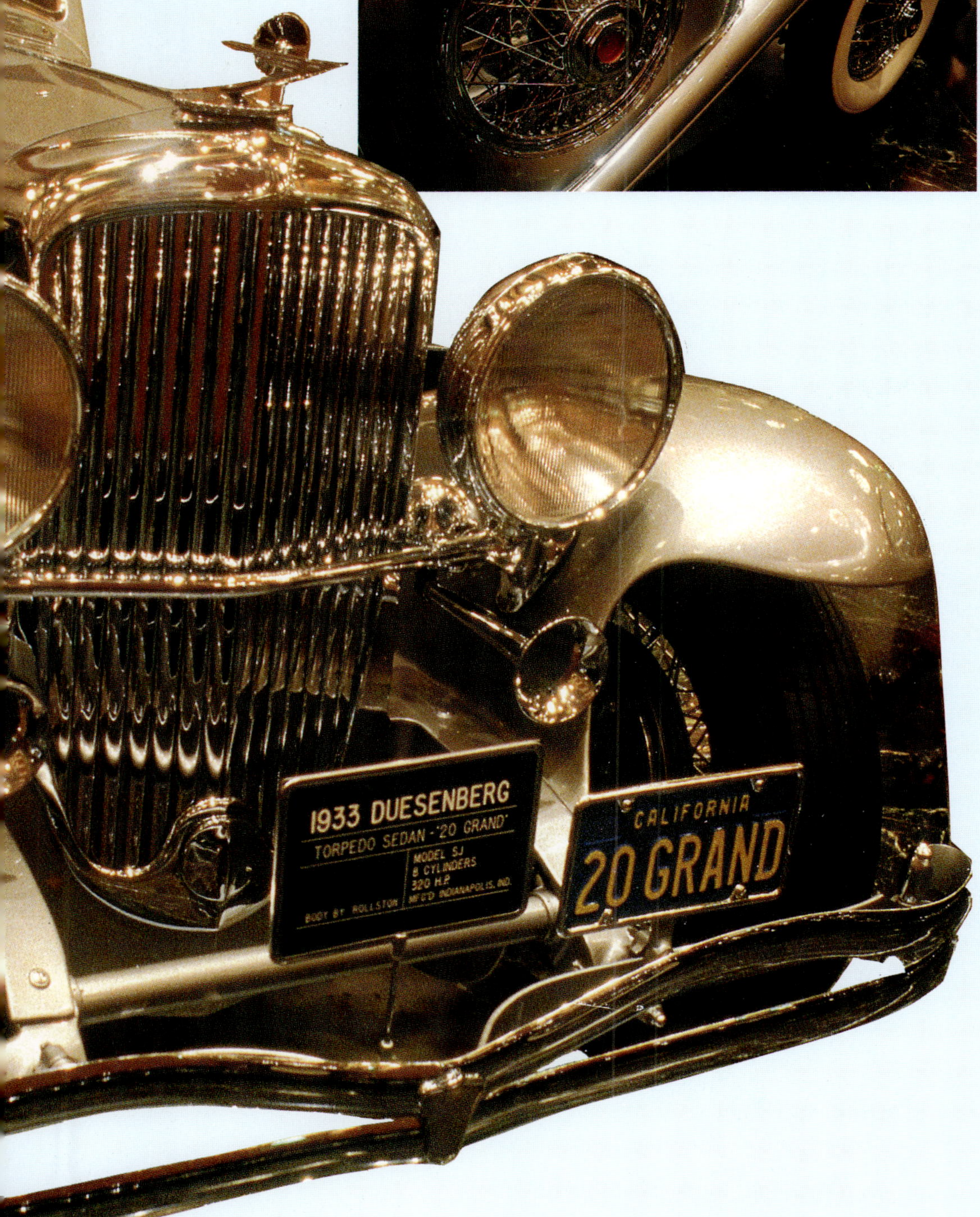

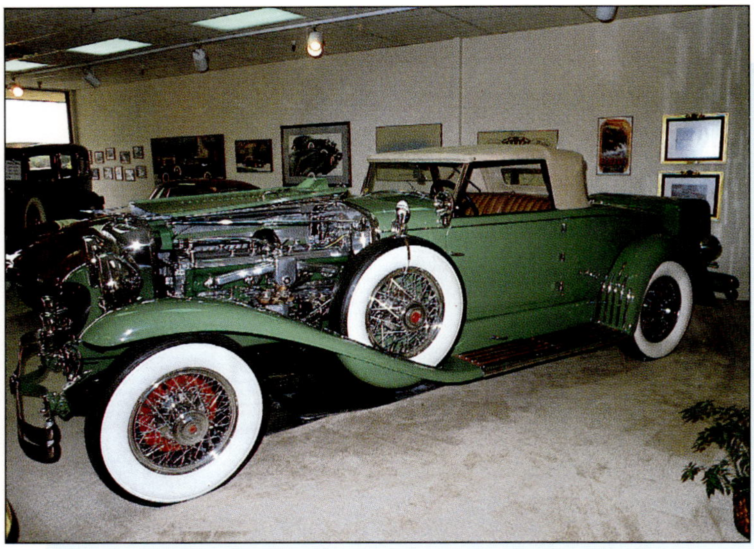

The Murphy coachbuilding firm from California designed and made 125 bodies for Duesenberg cars—most striking of all is this 1929 model J.

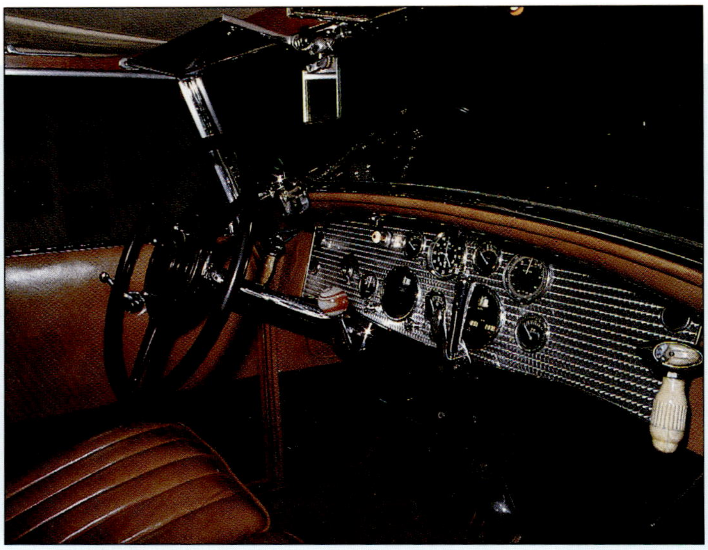

Attention to detail has resulted in a superb finish—the interior of the Murphy-bodied Duesenberg J after restoration.

evening for dinner, followed by a night's gambling at the tables of the famous casino. Today this car is a treasured exhibit in the marvellous Blackhawk Collection in northern California where it shares garage space with other rare and beautiful automobiles.

To the north of the city of Los Angeles at the top end of the San Fernando valley lies the sprawling town of Sylmar. It is typical of many of the small townships around L.A., the houses arranged in square blocks of single-storeyed timber-framed structures. At first it would appear that Sylmar has nothing to commend it to the visitor, but for those in the know it has within its boundaries one of the greatest, and certainly THE best displayed collections of desirable automobiles in the world. The Merle Norman Cosmetic Company is fortunate in having as its President Jack Nethercutt, who together with his wife Mary, have assembled inside a purpose-built building a unique collection of functional art. Furniture, musical instruments and automobiles are gathered together in the Tower of Beauty right next door to the main cosmetic factory and administration block. The second floor, known as the Grand Salon, is the setting for a display of cars that we once described as an 'automotive Aladdin's cave'. The room is nearly as big as three tennis courts, with the ceiling over 50 feet high. Bavarian crystal chandeliers illuminate the vast room, assisted by other supplementary lights and a giant mirror covering half of the back wall from floor to ceiling. The floor is marble, as are the pillars that support the painted ceiling. At one end there is a splendid curved stairway with a grand piano sitting on a level halfway up. The whole setting exudes style and good taste and is the most perfect place to display the 24 cars that occupy the floorspace.

The collection's most recent acquisition, or rather, re-acquisition is the SJN Duesenberg that sits on the green marble floor in front of the mirror; it was previously owned by Jack Nethercutt between 1956 and 1961. Jack had bought the SJN in 1956 for $5000, (the transaction taking place on 6 October at exactly 2.13pm!) Bill Harrah had purchased it from the Nethercutt Collection five years later for the same amount of money. This

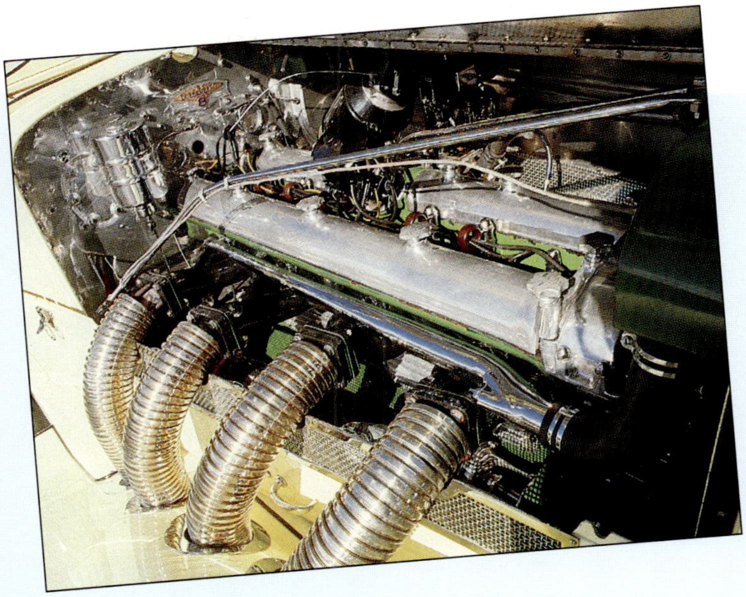

Equal care and attention have been lavished on the engine and engine compartment of this Duesenberg JN, once owned by Clark Gable.

year it returned to the Tower of Beauty for a rather larger sum of money, exactly $800,000, an inflation factor of 1600%!! It goes without saying that the SJN Duesenberg is in as new condition, its Rollston-built body with black paintwork flawless, and the interior featuring butter-coloured leather upholstery looks as though it has never been sat in. If ever an automobile looked to be worth its price tag this one most certainly does.

While all Duesenbergs were extraordinary, one of the most glamorous was a J model 1929, Murphy-bodied example. This car is displayed in the current showroom of the Blackhawk Collection in San Ramon, California. (In 1985 the Blackhawk Museum building will be finished, and a selection of cars from the Collection will be exhibited in it.)

The J cost $13,000 in 1929, a very large sum of money to spend on an automobile, when a model A Ford cost less than $600. The car featured the straight-8, DOHC, 4 valves per cylinder engine, which delivered a claimed 265bhp at 4200rpm. Mercury vibration dampers, consisting of 2 cartridges containing 16 ounces of mercury were mounted on the webs of the crankshaft. As mercury finds its own level quicker than any other element, dampers effectively suppressed any periodic vibration that the crankshaft might suffer while the engine was running.

The carburettor was manufactured by Schedler and it drew fuel from a 26-gallon fuel tank. When tuned by Fred Duesenberg a J model would reach 89mph in second gear, with 116mph available in top. Not only could the J cover the ground fast, but it could stop, its hydraulic drum brakes 375 mm (15 in) in diameter and 75 mm (3 in) wide saw to that, and the handbrake drum on the propshaft of 200-mm (8-in) diameter and 75-mm (3-in) width.

Walter M. Murphy of Pasadena, California built 125 bodies for Duesenberg cars, and this distinction gained them the reputation of being 'Young, new coachbuilders', as E. L. Cord, who by the mid-1930s had gained control of the Duesenberg company, described them.

In all, 481 Duesenberg J and SJ cars were built in Indianapolis. 175 different body styles were listed in the company records (the

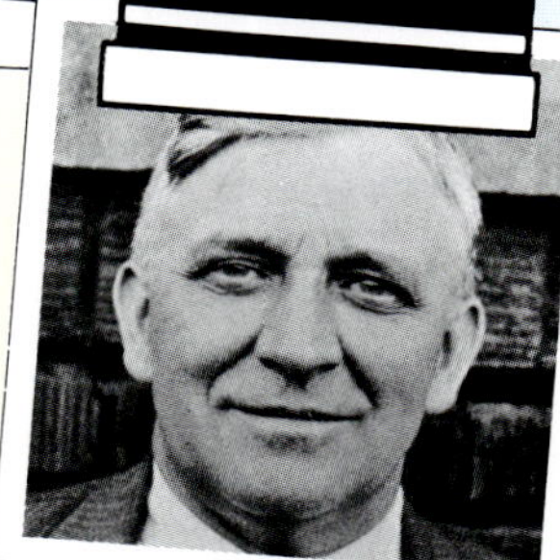

**DUESENBERG**

Frederick and August Duesenberg came to car production late in their working lives in 1930. They had already established themselves in 1913 designing and building aero-engines and formed the Duesenberg Motor company — Frederick had pencilled his first car as early as 1904. It was not until the extraordinary E. L. Cord took over their company in 1927 that they had the money, and the support, to realize and build the marvellous luxury J and SJ models. E. L. Cord had enough good sense to leave them out to get on with the job making one of the all-time great cars. One has only to examine any Duesenberg to appreciate a product of superb engineering.

Fred and Augie were racing enthusiasts too. Their various Indianapolis 500 cars are, of course, essentially competition machines. Although they combined all the latest racing technology they were nevertheless so well made as to be displayed as works of art.

Fred died, tragically, in a car crash in 1937, and the car world lost a great car man.

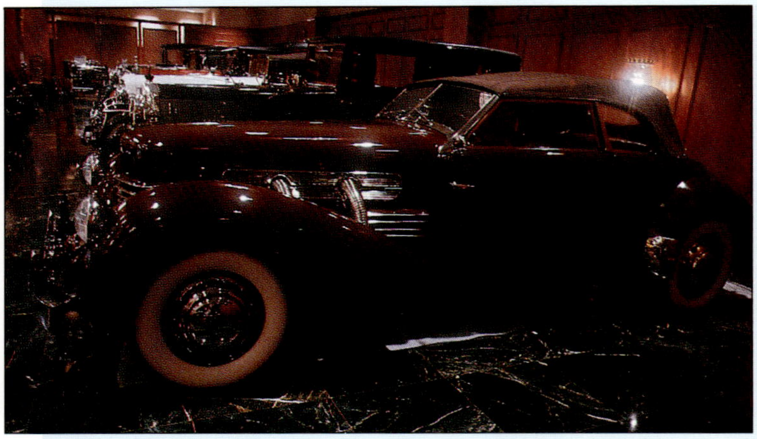

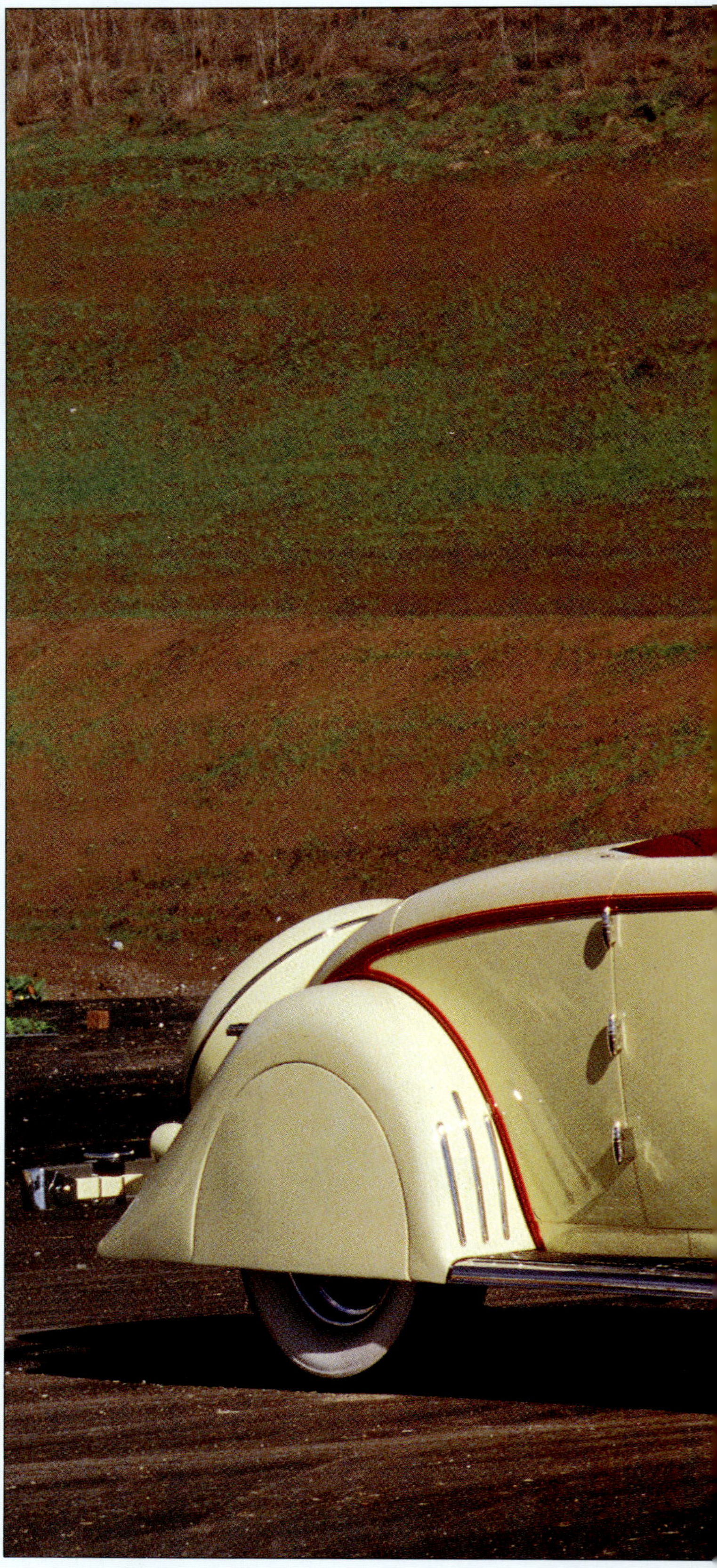

N suffix was attached to both SJ and J cars to denote the fact that they were built during the last two years of production up to 1937.

Possibly the most famous and glamorous Duesenberg JN model car was once owned by Clark Cable. He commissioned the Rollston coachbuilders to build a body of elegant proportions and balance, although it now looks rather extravagant for a mere two-seater, in its day it was exactly the RIGHT car for the most famous filmstar to be seen driving. After his marriage to Carol Lombard, Gable gave her the car as a wedding present, and she used it extensively until her tragic death in an air crash in 1942. After this, the Duesenberg was stored never to be driven again by Clark Gable. It is in quite splendid condition in the Blackhawk Collection waiting to go into their new museum in 1985.

One of the most extravagant Duesenbergs must be the 1932 Chicago World's Fair 'Twenty Grand' model. Attracting as it did the attention of the rest of the world, the 1932 World's Fair provided a splendid platform for displaying the quality of the Duesenberg company. At that time the Twenty Grand must have ranked as one of the world's most, if not the most, expensive vehicles: $20,000 was an enormous sum of money to spend on a car at that time. The Twenty Grand is massive, beautifully built and finished, and could only have come from a confident American manufacturer such as the Duesenberg company in those days. Today the car resides in the Nethercutt Collection.

Of all the many excellent American luxury cars made up to the 1940s the Duesenberg is the most widely known to the general public. It was massively built, it usually carried spectacular looking bodies painted in equally spectacular colours, and the engines promised vast amounts of real horsepower. Their appeal for today's spectators must lie in their direct association with the glamorous personalities and times of the dizzy Twenties and Thirties—a motoring era that will never be repeated.

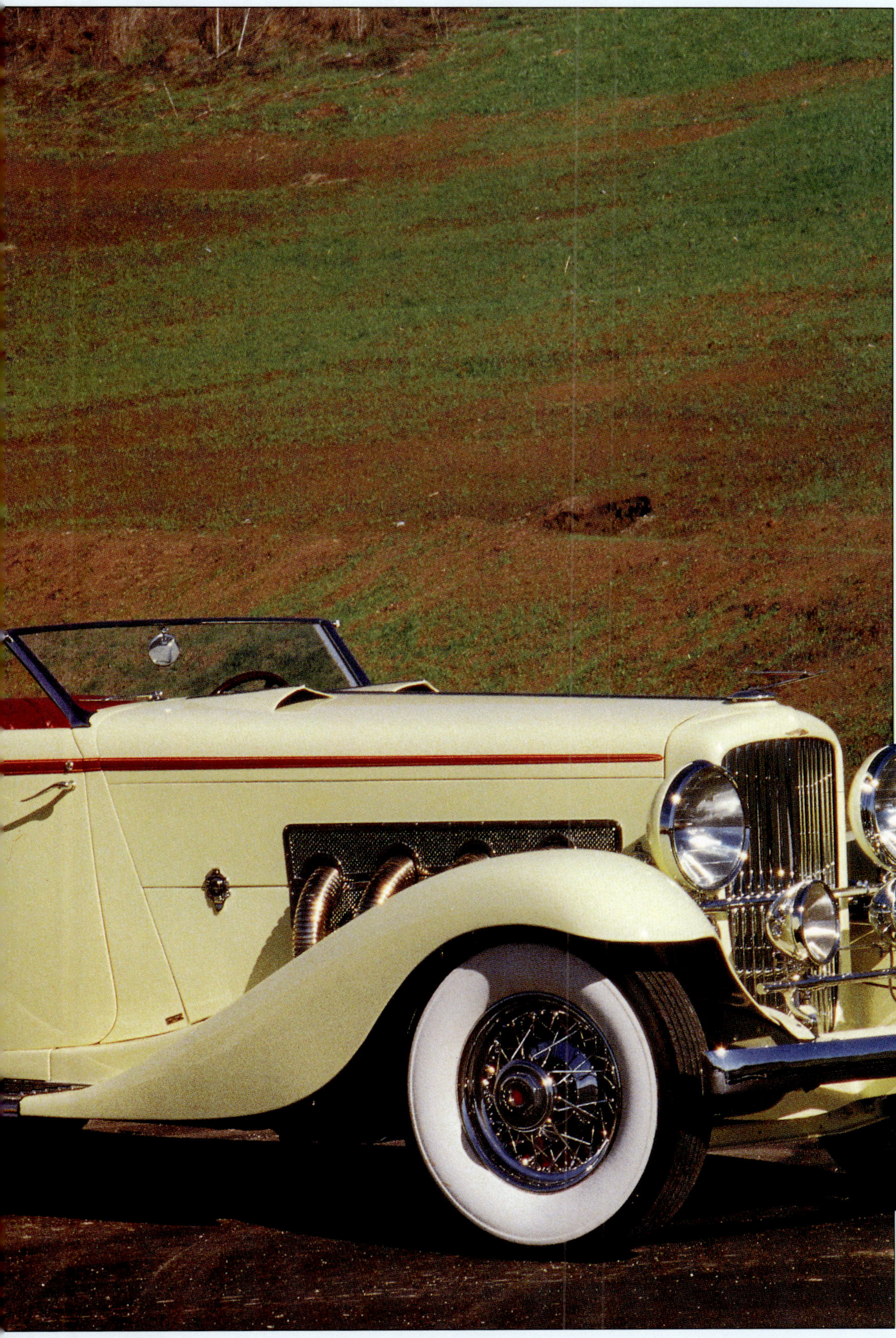

FAR LEFT: the Cord was the car responsible for the collapse of E. L. Cord's business combine. It came too late, and failed to live up to the buyer's expectations. Its failure contributed to the demise of Duesenberg and Auburn.

LEFT: Formerly owned by the filmstar Clark Gable, this Duesenberg JN has been lavishly restored.

CHAPTER THREE

# Sporting Coupés

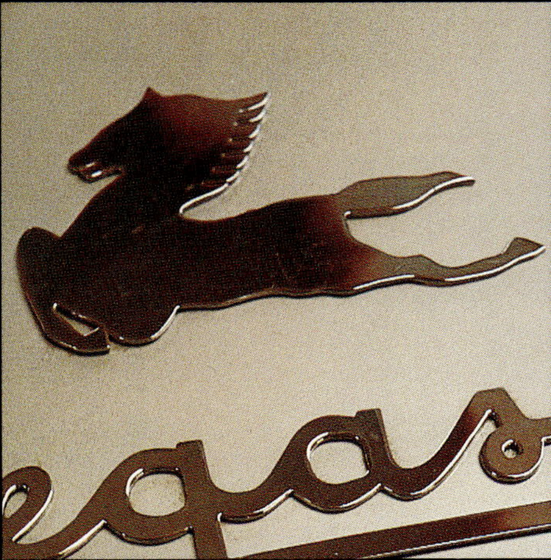

OVERLEAF: Mythological overtones in the mascot hint at the grace and power of the Spanish-built Pegaso sports car. This bounding horse badge adorns a Z102-B model, a world record holder in its day.

BELOW: A formidable car in standard form, the Mazda RX-7 becomes a truly exhilarating sportscar in its turbocharged form. The additional aerodynamic aids have both practical and cosmetic value.

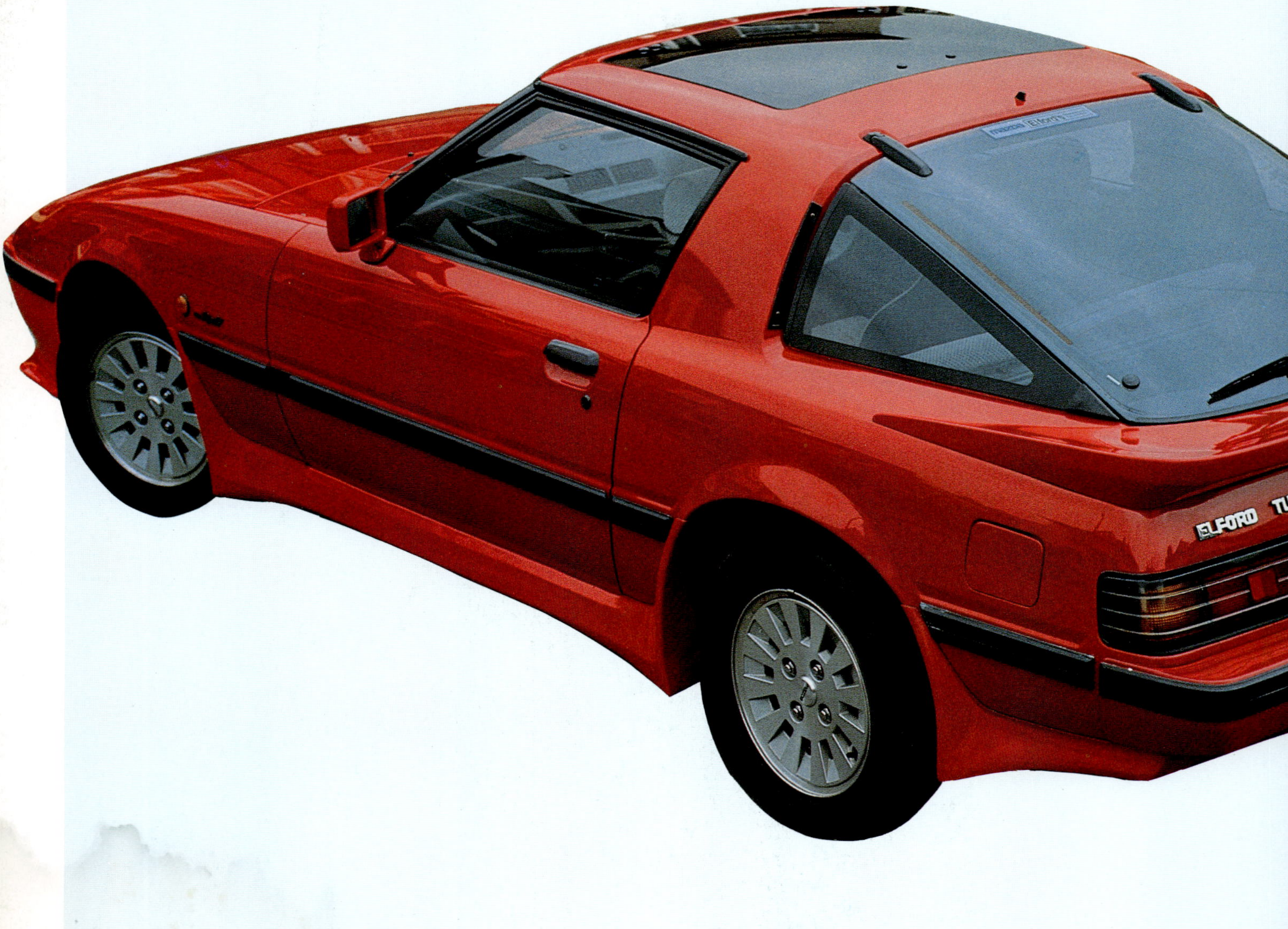

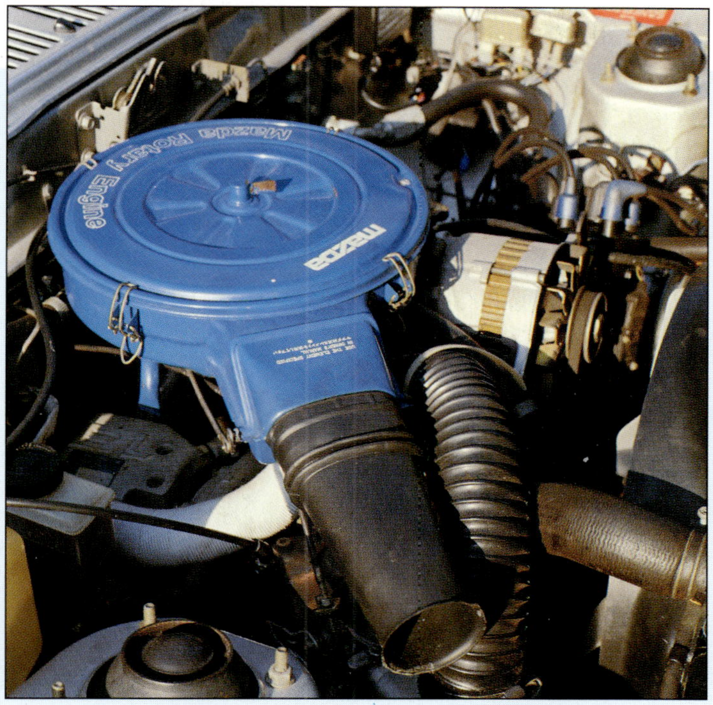


No longer the black sheep of the motor industry, the rotary engine in this RX-7 is fitted with an Elford Engineering turbo conversion.

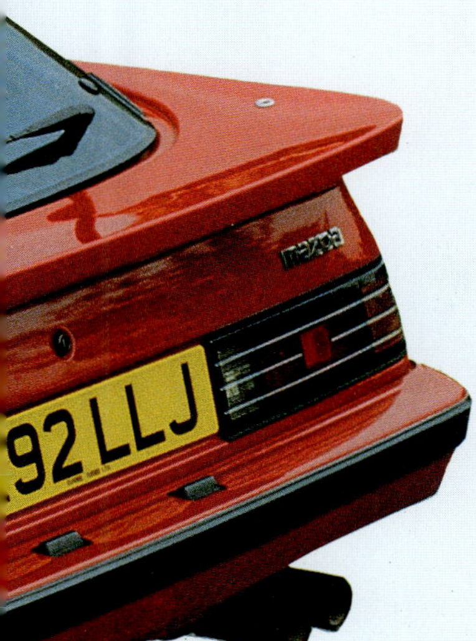


When the Japanese company Toyo Kogyo (Mazda to the man on the street), introduced the RX-7 model in 1978 they, maybe unwittingly, produced an instant classic in the sporting coupé market.

The RX-7 had a beautiful shape, was very well made, trimmed and finished, and had a rotary Wankel engine. The rotary engine had five years earlier very nearly brought the company to its knees. To be strictly accurate, the rotary engine came along at a time of worldwide gasoline shortage and rotaries are inherently quite thirsty, although solutions to this problem are now being found. These two factors, the fuel crisis, and the natural thirst of the new Mazda engine, drove customers out of Mazda showrooms across the world, and left the company with thousands of unsold cars stocked in fields and storage areas in their Western export markets.

But Mazda was not allowed to die, they effected a rescue act that very nearly duplicated the BMW resurrection some years before. Not only did they come back from the dead, but they persevered with the rotary engine and made it considerably more economical while retaining the smoothness and power that characterizes this type of power unit. They designed the hugely successful RX-7 body around the rotary engine, and within two years had a smash-hit seller on their hands. The story of the financial and technical difficulties Mazda faced and defeated would fill a book. In short they succeeded by 'keeping the faith'; they knew that they were right in staying with the Wankel engine, and with very hard work, technical brilliance, and the leadership of one of today's great automobile engineers, Kenichi Yamamoto they won through.

A two-seater coupé of good aerodynamic shape, fine driving habits, and a very smooth, powerful engine was exactly what the

Perfect styling and proportions contrive to give an appearance of speed, even when parked.

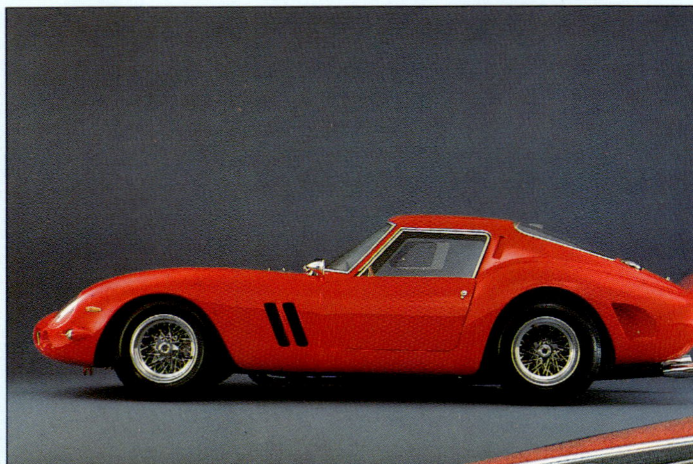

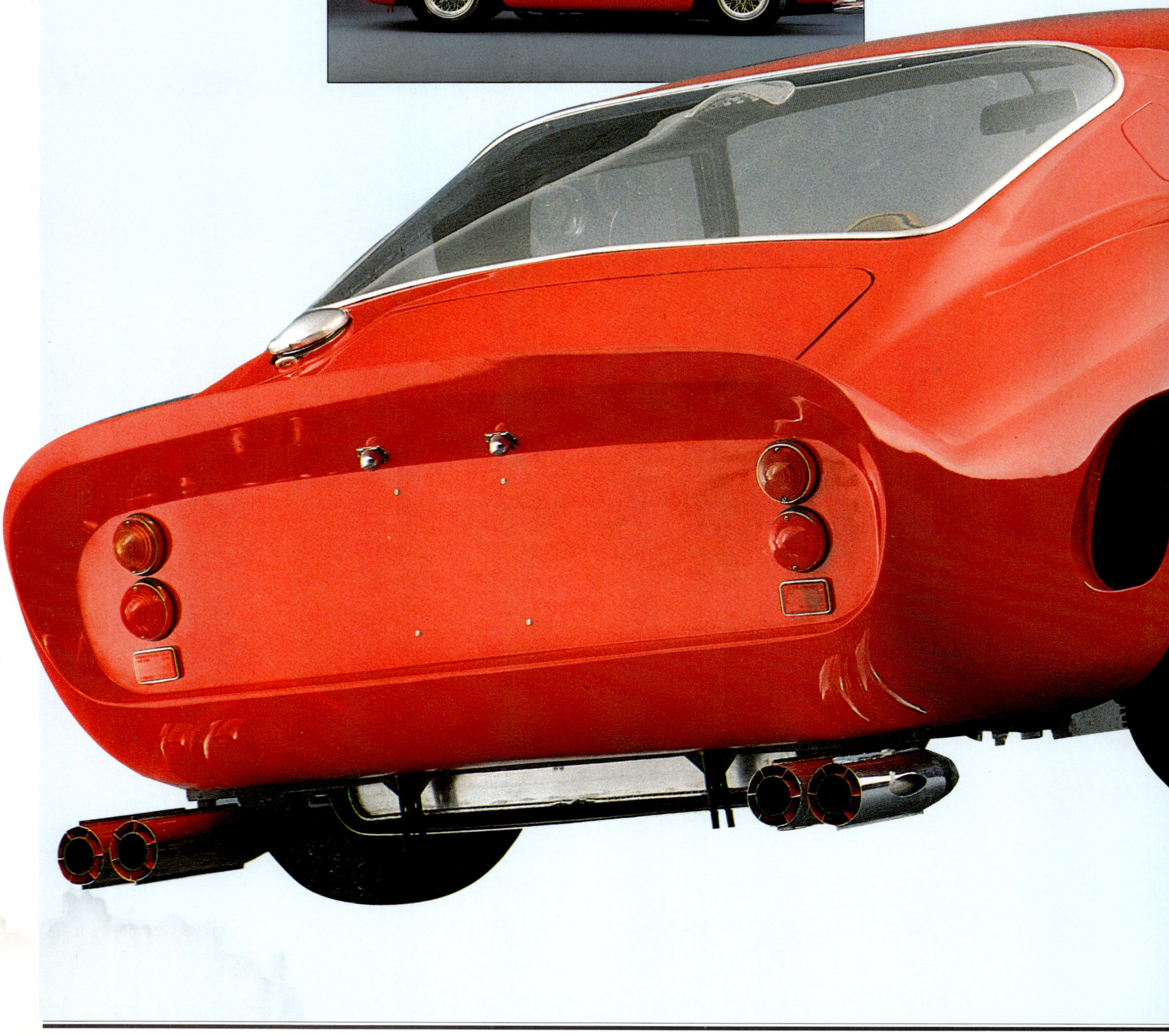

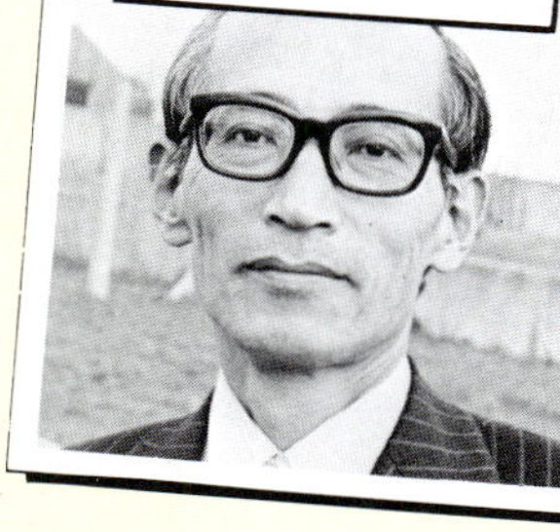

**KENICHI YAMAMOTO**

When in 1961 the Toyo Kogyo car manufacturing company took out their licence to carry out research and development on the Wankel rotary engine it brought to light the talents of a young, virtually unknown, engineer Kenichi Yamamoto. He had previously completed his education at Tokyo University and first worked on the T.K. assembly line making their three-wheeled truck. Yamamoto rose rapidly through the company ranks and was a natural choice to head the small team on the Wankel project. He was to take on, with the chairman of T.K., Tsuneji Matsuda, the seemingly impossible task of making this new type of engine work, not only work in laboratory conditions, but installed in a car, to be sold to the general public, the hardest test for any mechanical device! The success of the rotary engine after 24 years' work, as a very durable, reliable automotive power unit, has contributed largely to the popularity of the Mazda RX-7.

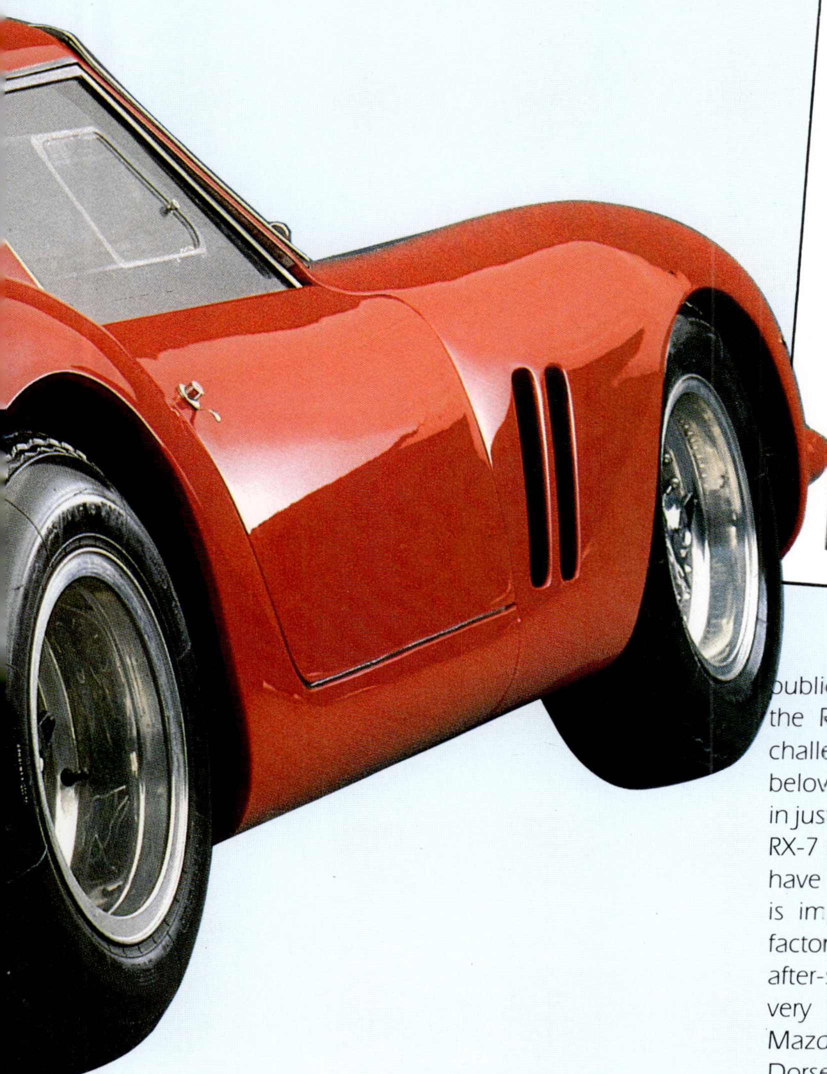

public wanted. In Great Britain the Mazda importers decided that the RX-7 was so special that it would be sold as a direct challenger to the Porsche 924 model and the RX-7 was priced just below the Porsche. As it was able to match the Stuttgart machine in just about every possible way, and soundly beat it on price, the RX-7 became a desirable automobile to own. Specialist builders have modified the engine and bodywork of the car and the RX-7 is impressive all round—the only reservation being that the factory cars lack power when compared with several of the good after-sales turbocharged versions that are available. One of the very finest turbocharger installations comes from the British Mazda dealer, Elfords Ltd., of Tuckton, near Bournemouth in Dorset. Under the guidance of their technical director, Ted Marchant, the Elford turbo installation is so good that Mazda retain the guarantee warranty on the converted car, an almost unheard of arrangement. The Elford turbocharged RX-7 is very reliable and almost totally untemperamental. The car revels in the extra power, performing even better than the standard version, and the fuel consumption difference is so small as to be of no consequence.

Recreating one of the greatest sports cars ever built, the Favre GTO duplicates the 1963 Ferrari original in every detail except that the engine is even more powerful.

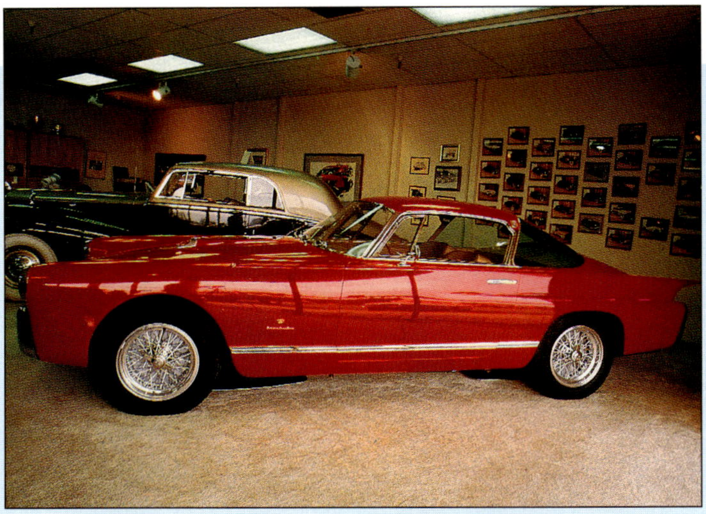

A Ferrari with a custom-built body, this Super America model features bodywork by Italian coachbuilders Boano.

The RX-7 has progressively been improved by the factory—each new model has been significantly better than the one before, but after nearly seven years the time has come for an all-new Mazda coupé. Nobody knows exactly what it will be like but it is one of the most eagerly awaited new cars for some years. Private rally drivers have experimented with turbocharged four-wheel drive RX-7s, so it seems likely that the next version will make use of some of this experience. Whatever happens to the RX-7, it will always remain one of the only genuine classic Japanese automobiles, a magic car.

Another magic, or glamour, car but from the recent past must be the Ferrari GTO model. It combined good looks with outstanding performance and only 39 examples of the original Ferrari GTO were ever built.

A young Frenchman, William Favre two years ago took the decision to recreate the Ferrari GTO, not to make a replica, but to re-make the 1963 GTO in the finest detail, using Ferrari chassis, engine, transmission, steering, and braking components taken from very similar Ferrari models and reclothing the finished mechanicals with a brand-new body, identical to the original, made by ex-Ferrari craftsmen in a factory near Turin.

William is a Geneva-based lawyer, and because of his training in the law, he did not go into this project with his eyes closed; he planned minutely before starting up. He invested a huge amount of his own money and already has his factory working on producing 27 new Favre/Ferrari GTOs. The cars look like perfectly restored genuine GTOs, just as they must have over twenty years ago when they came out of the Ferrari body shop. The Favre GTO will not be cheap, but at $130,000 it will be much cheaper than buying one of the original 39 GTOs and then having to pay the bills to bring it up to as-new condition. William has gone to great lengths to ensure that in all the important respects his car is exactly like the original. He discovered that the one item that really was in short supply was the four-speed gearbox. Everything else, V12 engines, chassis, brakes and steering components were available, albeit at a price, but the gearboxes were like hen's teeth, very, very scarce. So he took the expensive

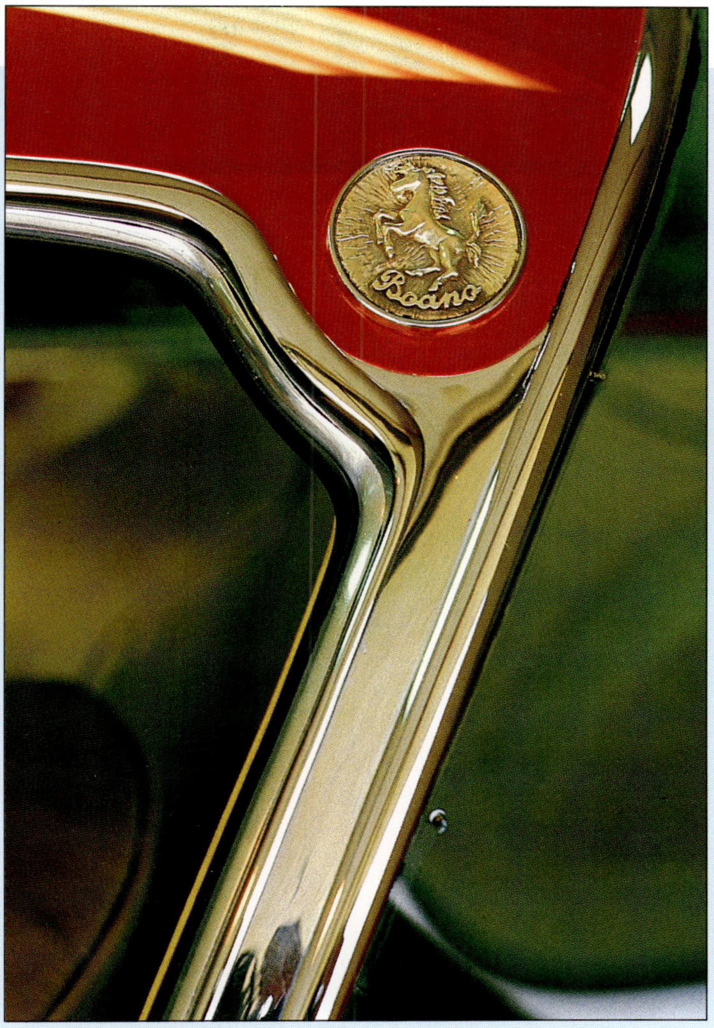

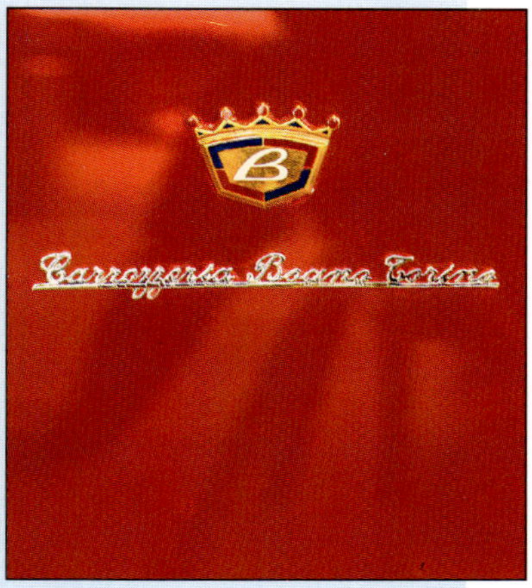


The distinctive Boano badging on the rear quarter panel and wings.

but very necessary step, of remaking them in his new factory exactly as the originals.

The original Ferrari GTO came out of the factory in Maranello with 290bhp from its V12 3 litre engine. The Favre GTO 3 litre engine is blueprinted i.e. it is built to exact blue-print specifications of the original engine design using the latest engine assembly technology, and as a result delivers 325bhp!

The owners of each of the 27 Favre/Ferrari GTOs will get a car that has glamour in the true sense of the word.

The Blackhawk Collection contains two rather special Ferraris, both are 410 SuperAmerica models, one a coupé, and the other a convertible. Designed by the Pininfarina company and built by the coachbuilding concern of Piero Boano they are two of the most beautiful Ferraris ever built.

In 1956, the coupé model first saw the light of day and was the hit of the Brussels Auto Show in that year. It differed from the previous 410SA Ferrari in several respects: the front leaf spring was replaced by coil springs and the V12 single overhead camshaft engine had a compression ratio of 8.5:1; breathing through 3 twin-choke Weber 42DCF carburettors the 88mm × 68mm, 4963cc (310 cu in.) powerplant produced an easy 320hp at 6000rpm. With an all-up weight of 3080lbs the coupé had performance well in keeping with its attractive lines and proportions. A top speed of over 160mph made sure that the car went as well as it looked. With its 25-gallon fuel tank the 410SA coupé could also cover 450 miles between stops to refuel.

The Shah of Iran bought the actual Brussels Show car, and many personalities in the worlds of showbusiness, banking, property development, socialites, and simply lovers of the big-engined Ferraris bought similar models.

The cabriolet version went into production the following year, 1957, and with the 410SA coupé, continued to be turned out in small quantities at Boano's until the end of 1958.

The car in the Blackhawk Collection is simply superb in its appearance—the engine compartment looks almost too good, more like a piece of perfectly finished metal sculpture than simply motive power for an automobile. The alloy engine parts are stove enamelled grey, the valve covers are the familiar Ferrari crackle black, and the six-a-side exhaust manifolds are chromium plated. The whole compartment for this magnificent engine is spotless, every nut and bolt is plated, and look as though they have never seen or felt a spanner in their life.

Likewise the interior, which has been so carefully maintained that the evidence of light usage only increases one's regard for the car and its previous owner. The exterior of the Ferrari is a combination of tasteful, ageless lines, and a hint of the future in the elegant, rear fin arrangement that was taken to such excess in many American cars of that period. On the Boano Ferrari, Pininfarina has managed to combine these fins with the rest of the car most successfully, from their beginnings at the point in front of the door openings, across the door gradually, then swelling into the full fin shape past the bottom edge of the rear screen and becoming the complete fin at the back of the body shape. To some people it looks too American, even flashy, but to see it in the metal is to observe just how well the theme has been handled by designer and builder. The 410SA has a most distinguished appearance. Add the perfect Ferrari red paint finish, and the excellent chromium plating and it fully justifies its inclusion in any list of glamorous cars.

In 1950 the Spanish Empresa Nacional de Autocamiones, builders of some of Europe's best heavy commercial vehicles, decided to venture into the field of high quality, high priced, sportscar production. They engaged the services of Wilfredo Ricart, a designer with many years of experience at Alfa Romeo, gained while working on their Grand Prix and sportscar competition programmes.

Wilfredo Ricart drew up a design for a car that, on paper, had all the elements for performance and striking good looks and was equal to any car that had gone before. When it was introduced to the World in 1954 it had the necessary qualities to put it on an equal footing with the very few other contenders for the title of 'Best Sportscar', cars such as the Mercedes-Benz 300SL, the Jaguar XK120, and the Ferrari 250 Europa.

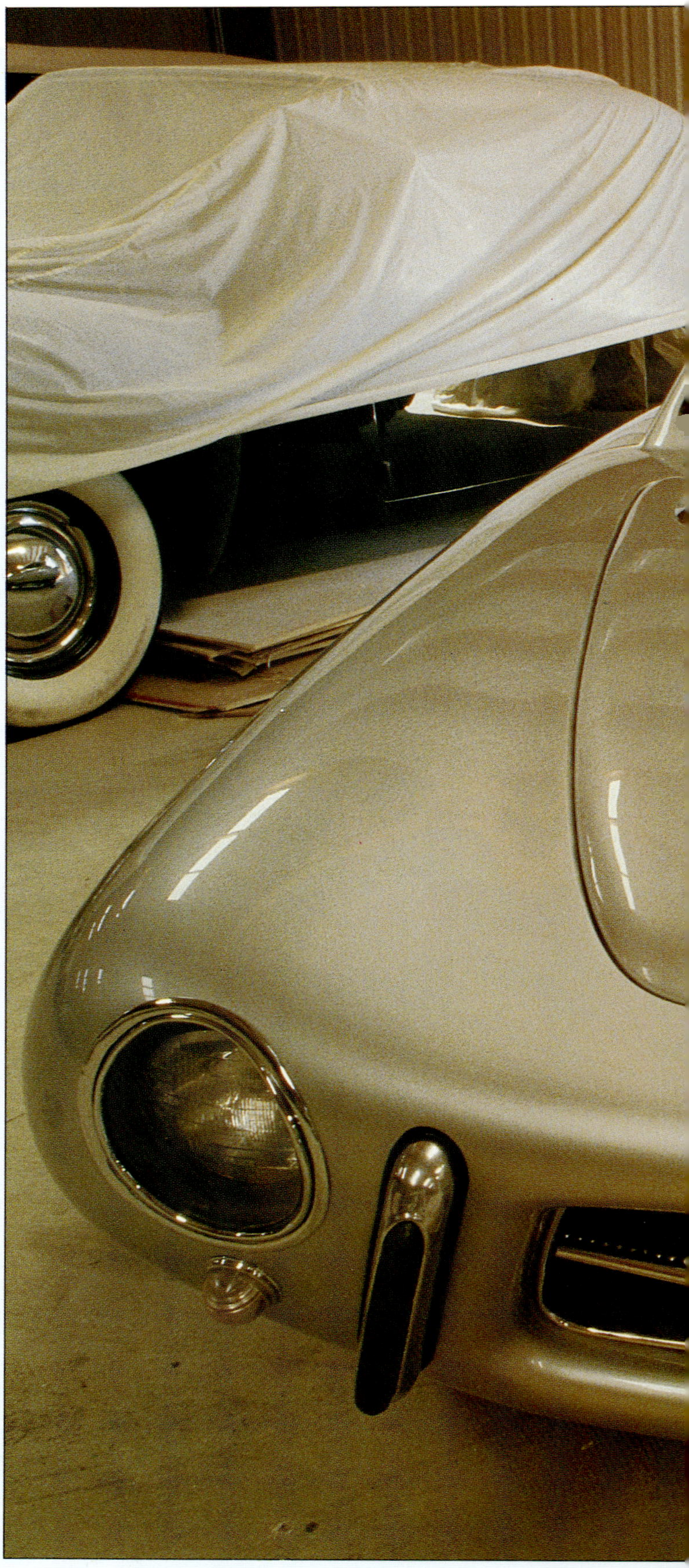

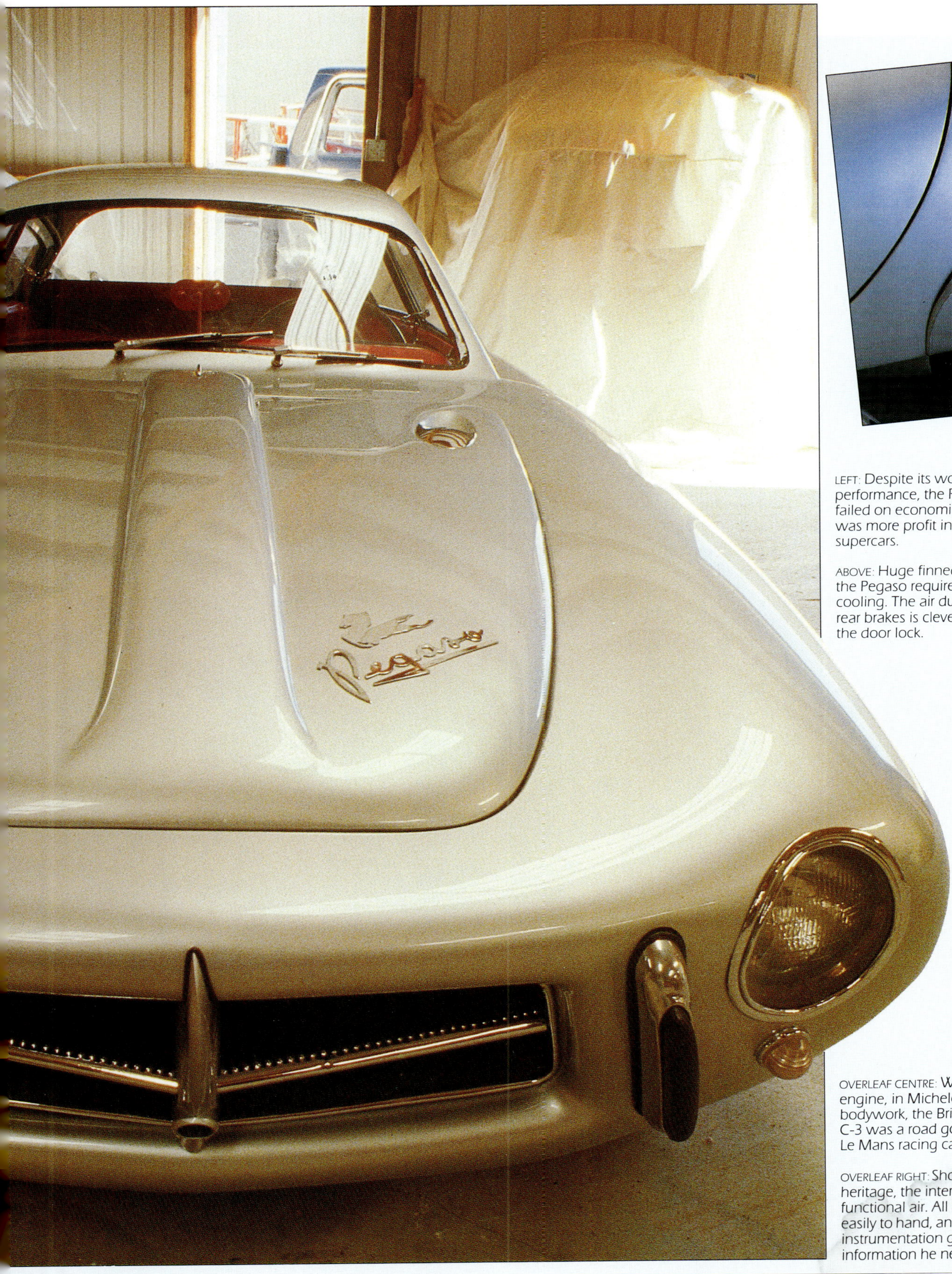


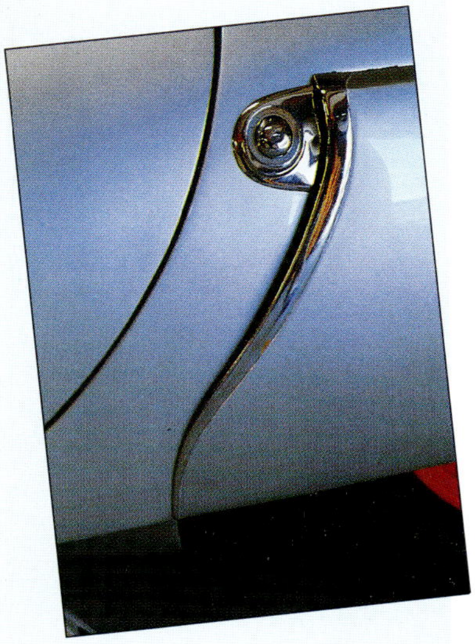

LEFT: Despite its world-beating performance, the Pegaso Z102-B failed on economic grounds—there was more profit in making trucks than supercars.

ABOVE: Huge finned drum brakes on the Pegaso require a good airflow for cooling. The air ducting intake for the rear brakes is cleverly blended in with the door lock.

OVERLEAF CENTRE: With its Chrysler V8 engine, in Michelotti-designed bodywork, the Briggs Cunningham C-3 was a road going version of the Le Mans racing car.

OVERLEAF RIGHT: Showing its racing heritage, the interior of the C-3 has a functional air. All the controls fall easily to hand, and the comprehensive instrumentation gives the driver all the information he needs.

Just consider for a moment the technical specification of the Pegaso, as it was to be called. There were not many full competition cars around in those days that could match it. It had a 2.8 litre V8 double overhead camshaft engine that could be ordered with any one of nine different compression ratios, three induction arrangements of either single carburettor, quadruple carburettor, or supercharger, with horsepower ranging from 140bhp to over 200bhp (at the end of 1954 a larger 3.2 litre engine was introduced, and with the single carburettor this unit produced 225bhp!) depending on which induction system was used. The 5-speed gearbox was built in units with the differential and located at the rear of the car for better balance. It is of considerable interest to note that this superb gearbox had no syncromesh installed, yet was so easy in use that it was possible to change gears without recourse to the clutch pedal. Suspension was all-independent front and rear based on torsion bars, the rear arrangement following the classic DeDion principle, a method that ensured that the rear wheels remained vertical during suspension movement retaining a full, and consistent tyre contact with the ground. The Pegaso's brakes were massive finned, ventilated, drum-type components, as powerful as any fitted to the Grand Prix cars of the day. Steering was ultra-fast with no more than 1.7 turns of the steering wheel from lock to lock. All of these features were mounted on a chassis that did not dampen these components' individual qualities, and which carried one of two body styles that were stunning in their beauty, a coupé and a convertible.

The Blackhawk Collection has the coupé version and even today thirty years after it first appeared stands out from the crowd by virtue of its good looks and performance potential. Every line and curve of the Pegaso speaks of exciting, fast travel. Road tests of the day shower praise on its high levels of roadholding, braking, and safety performance, with every control being light and efficient. The Pegaso looked to be at least a match for the few other high performers that were available to the fast car customer.

To prove that it was a car that had to be taken seriously as a truly fast machine Pegaso took a Z102-B to the famous Jabbeke stretch of autoroute in Belgium in September 1953 and established world records in the flying mile and kilometre classifications, with speeds of 234km/h (146mph) and 244km/h (153mph) respectively. The car also attained an outright speed of 250km/h (156mph).

In 1957, only six years after beginning production, the factory closed down its sportscar programme and reverted to building the trucks that still dominate Spain's highways. The reasons given for this move were that it was not perceived that the high performance, high priced market could support another very expensive car. The costs involved in establishing a proper dealer network were too much for the factory to bear, and the factory in any case had enough to do in building trucks. The car production was seen as a hindrance to the profitable running of the

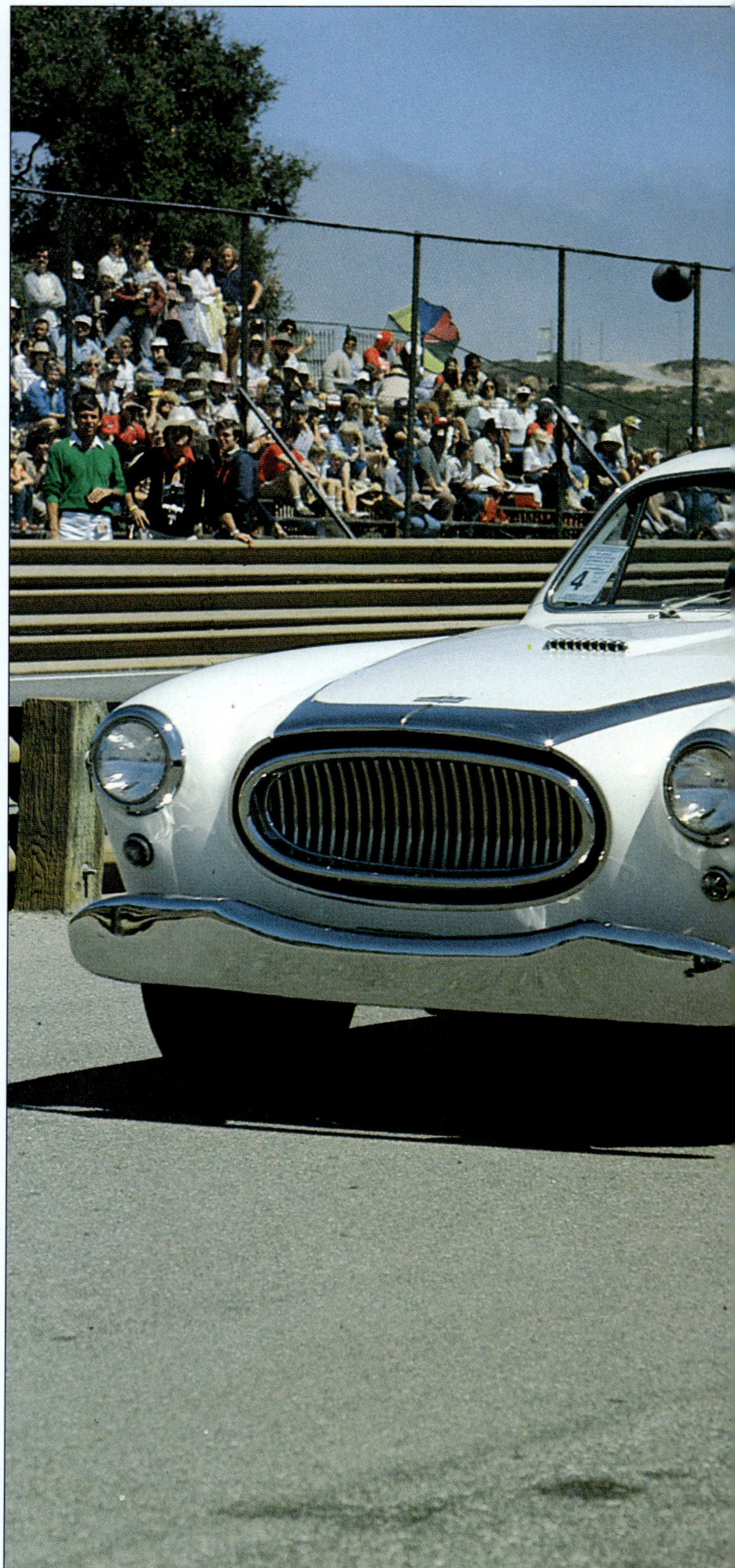

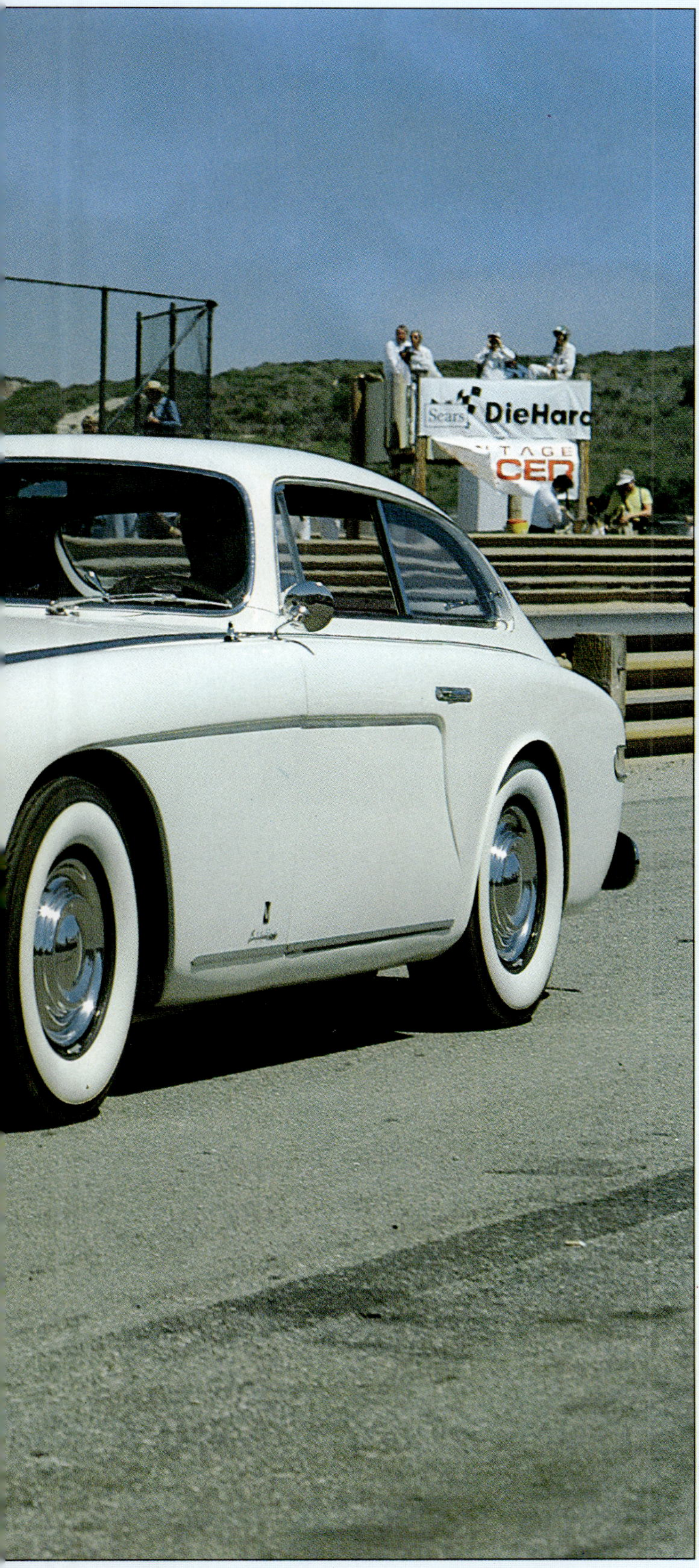


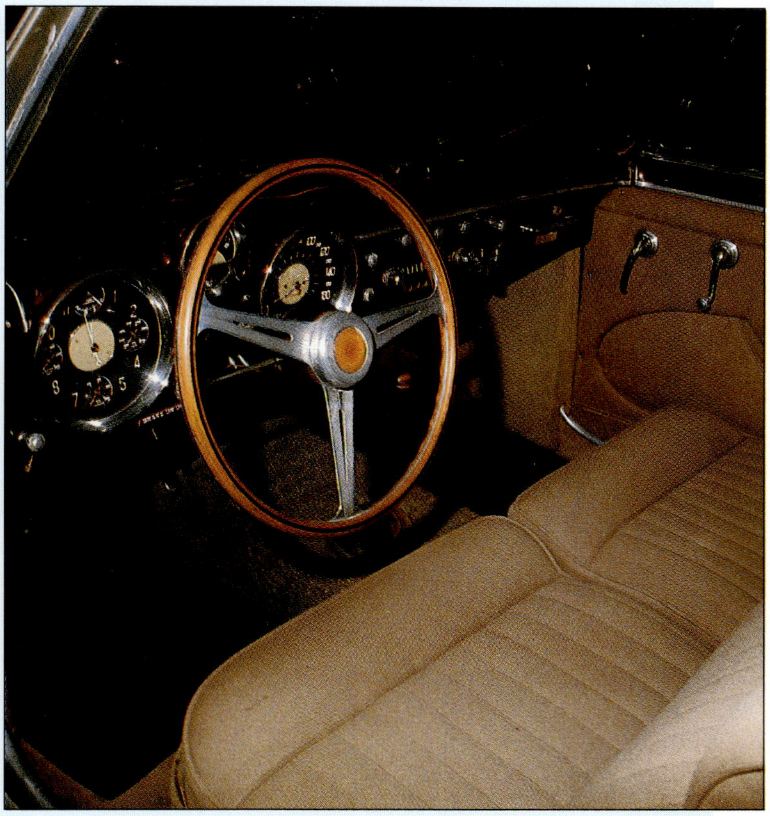

Barcelona factory, and in the commercial climate of the 1950s that was really all that was needed to stop Pegaso production once and for all.

Like its closest rival, the Mercedes-Benz 300SL, the Pegaso Z102-0 has become a much desired automobile by collectors the world over. To see one in a collection such as the Blackhawk is still a thrill but to see one being used would be even better.

That great American sportsman, Briggs Cunningham, during the five years of building sports/racing cars to win the Le Mans 24 hours race, also established a very small production line of powerful, large road-going coupé versions of his racers. He called them the C-3 coupés and adapted the best of American and European automobile techniques and parts, namely the splendid Chrysler V8 Hemi engine and Torqueflite transmission housed in a European-styled, and roadworthy chassis/body unit. Using the skills of Michelotti to design the body, and Vignale to build it resulted in a magnificent road car with a very high price tab. This model was featured in the motor-racing film 'Such men are Dangerous' starring Kirk Douglas.

The few C-3 Cunninghams are still regarded as splendid sporting coupés by their fortunate owners and reminders of the great days at the Sarthe circuit in north west France when the big Cunningham R-type racers thundered around the track from 4pm on Saturday until the same time on the Sunday, in front of 300,000 spectators.

# Modern glamorous cars

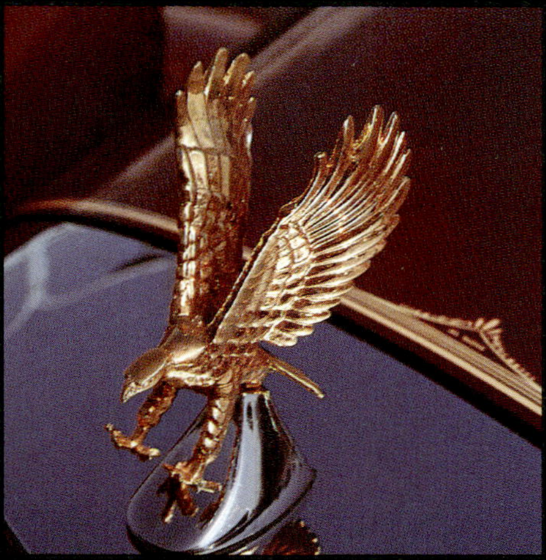

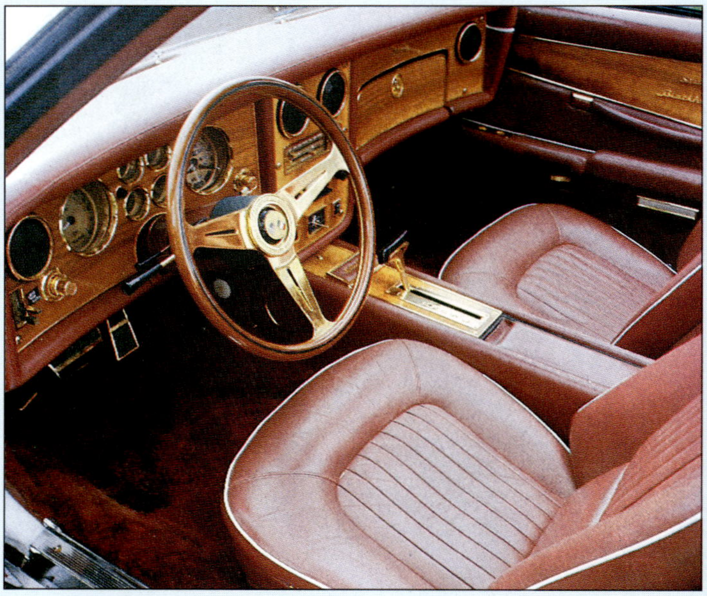

The driver of a modern Stutz Blackhawk enjoys a power hood, good seats and full instrumentation.

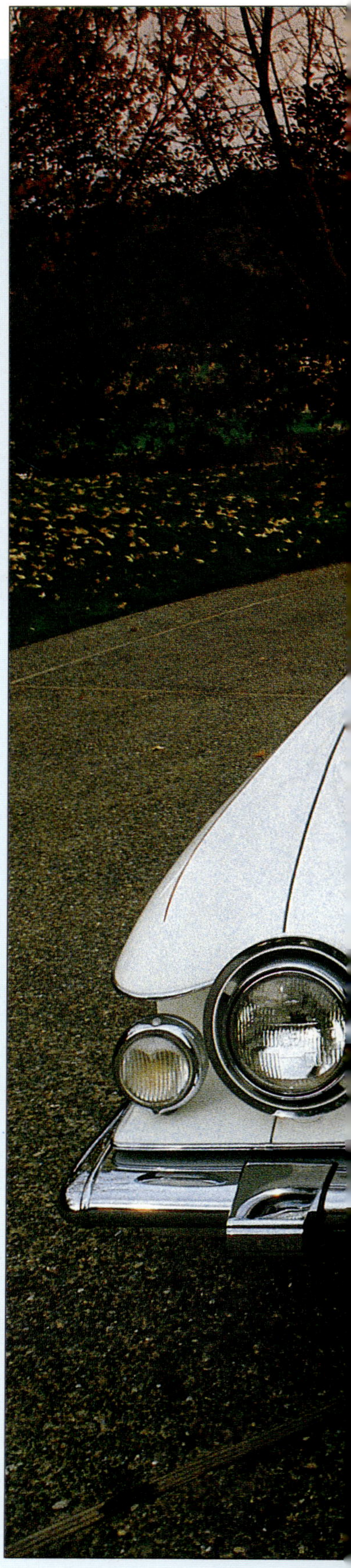

The dictionary defines 'Glamorous' as a charm on the eyes, making them see things as fairer than they really are: witchery: deceptive or alluring charm!

If that is accurate then the cars in this chapter fall very neatly into that category. Consider the first car, the 'modern' Stutz Blackhawk. A rebodied Pontiac that has pretentions to be more than that. To say that it is an example of attempting to make a silk purse out of a sow's ear, in automotive terms of course, may be an exaggeration because the base Pontiac is by no stretch of the imagination 'a sow's ear'. But that phrase, used as a simple analogy, will serve its purpose for the moment.

In 1970 the Stutz Motor Company of America was formed to produce a luxury car based on an American chassis, engine and transmission unit. They engaged Virgil Exner to style the car which was to be called the Blackhawk. The name Stutz was used because it was thought that it epitomized the best—as defined by the Stutz Company of course—that money could buy.

In 1949 Virgil Exner had left the Studebaker company to join Chrysler as chief stylist. The Chrysler corporation was engaged in an intensive sales fight with G.M. and the Ford Motor Company, and their new president, Lester 'Tex' Colbert had decreed that styling would spearhead their efforts. He gave his full blessing to Virgil Exner to develop the 'forward look' in their corporate styling programme. This was no more than a cynical, inexpensive method, and a cheap one at that (compared with a programme of real technical advance), to give their mechanical components a new suit of clothes. Virgil Exner, with the full support of Tex Colbert, did what he was noted for. He covered the Dodge and Plymouth models with acres of chromium plating, garish colours in duo-tone and tri-tone combinations, and used the greatest styling gimmick of all time, discovering the FIN. Within ten years he had equipped every Chrysler model with a set of rear fins that

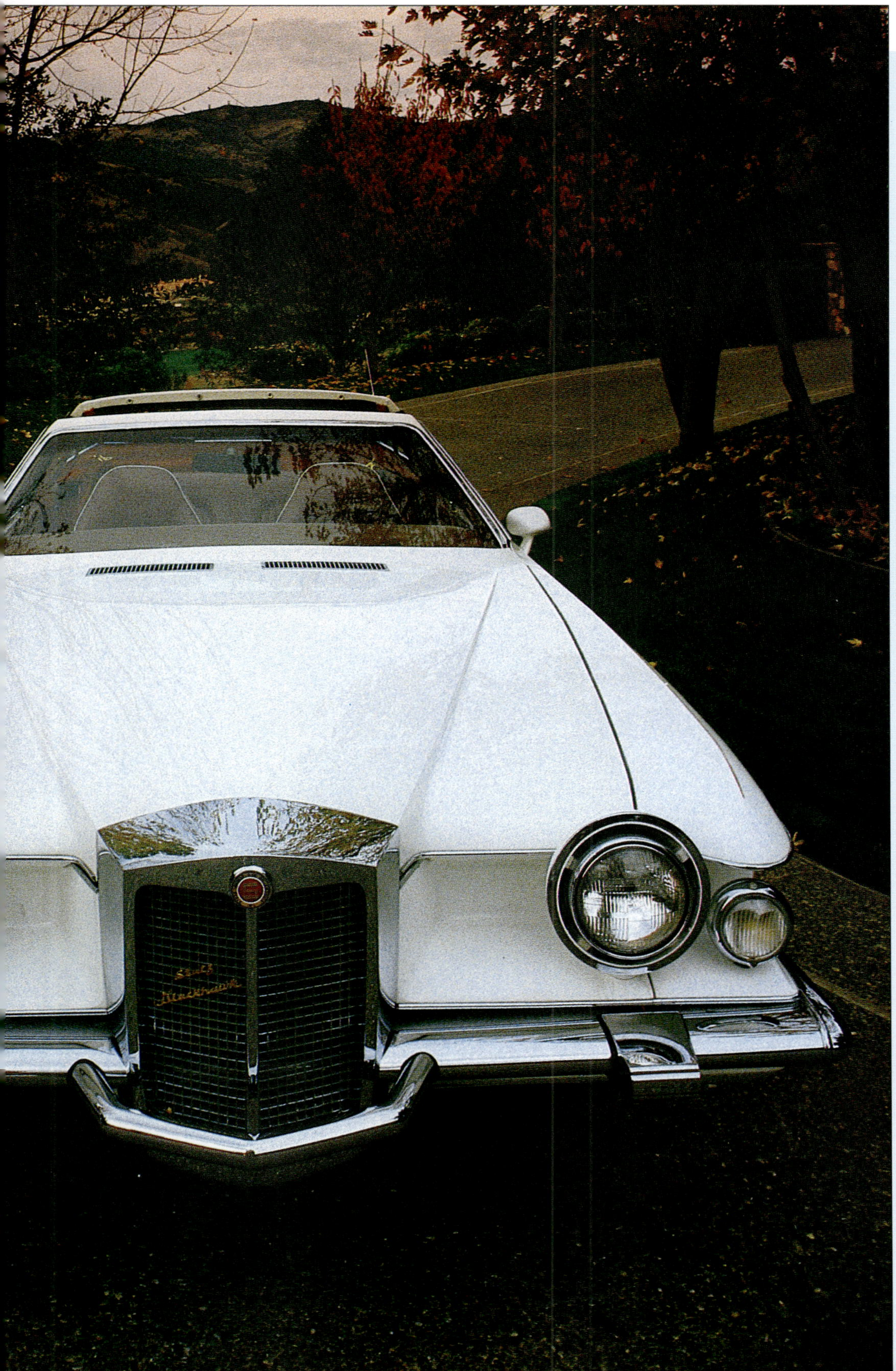

Exner's controversial styling of the Stutz Blackhawk's body conceals a humble Pontiac underneath.

The early 1930s design of the Stutz's radiator contrasts with the car's modern bodywork.

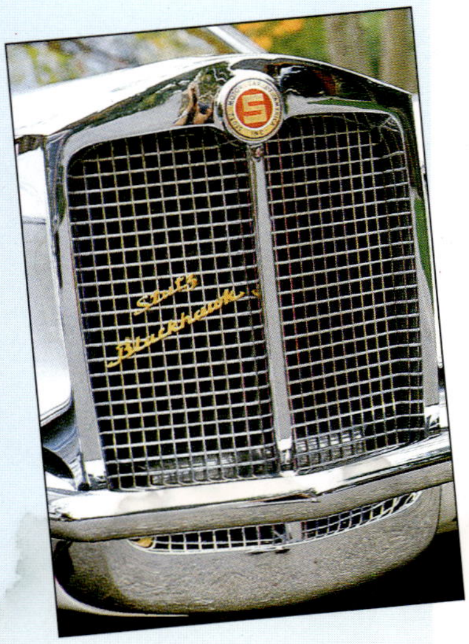

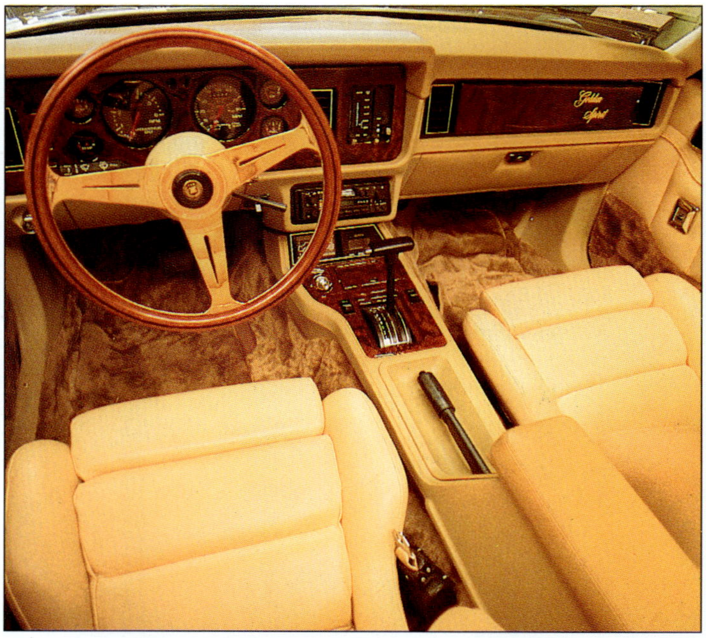

The Zimmer's interior is actually a retrimmed version of the Ford Mustang's.

were so extreme that they could almost have served as models for the Space Shuttle!

An early modern Stutz Blackhawk was in Monte Carlo on the occasion of the 1974 Monaco Grand Prix. It appeared out of the car park behind the pits, turning heads as it rolled towards the exit road leading back to the Hotel de Paris. 'Outlandish', was the general comment from all who saw it, and even without a detailed inspection it did not impress in regard to beauty of line and proportion. The gold paintwork, strange sculptured body panels, outside exhaust system that served no functional purpose, the headlight treatment, and the gold-plated interior jarred the senses of anyone who appreciates beautiful cars. Monte Carlo at the time was of course full of superb Italian and German cars. The original Stutz cars when made in Indianapolis were handsome rather than beautiful and were by no means ugly or ungraceful, unlike the 'modern' Stutz, which is surprising bearing in mind that the Pontiac components are shipped out to Italy to Carrozzeria Padana of Modena to have the body and trim finished. There has not been a really ugly Italian road car in the last fifty years, and so it is a great disappointment to learn that the modern Stutz Blackhawk is the work of Italian craftsmen.

The Zimmer Golden Spirit automobile can be described as an extreme clone of the Stutz Blackhawk. The very name gives more than a hint of its true worth. Golden . . . promising luxury and high class value. Spirit . . . a direct effort at associating the car with the Rolls-Royce model of the same name. Would it were the case, but the Zimmer is no more than an attempt at delivering a classic-looking car to customers with little real taste in such matters, but with large bank accounts, and pretensions to owning a high class car.

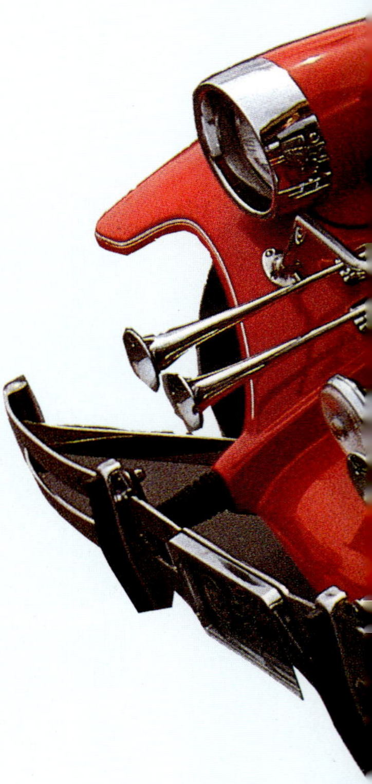

The Zimmer is produced in Pompano Beach, Florida, and is heavily based on the Ford Mustang. The centre section of the Ford is retained, as are all the mechanicals. New bodywork is

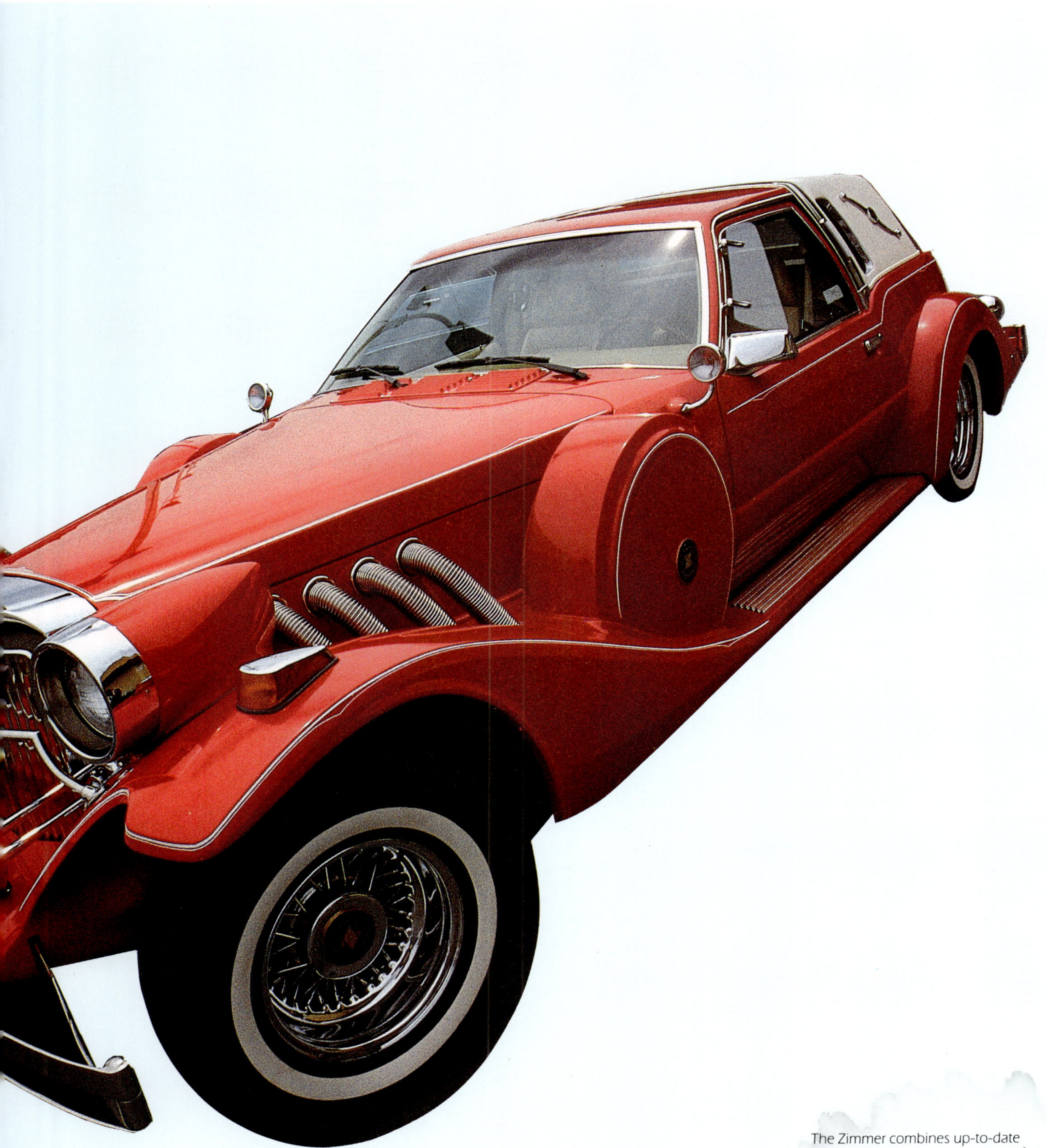

The Zimmer combines up-to-date practicality with the appearance of a 1930s classic car.

added front and rear, the interior is retrimmed, and several items of 'styling' are added to the overall package.

It is a fact that when cars of this type are laid out on the drawing board three factors are usually included, wire wheels, outside-the-bonnet exhaust with pipes of the flexible type, and separate wings at the front. In these respects the Zimmer does not disappoint; it has all of them. In the case of the exhausts they leave the bonnet side panels some four inches forwards of the actual engine location, and bear no relationship to the functional exhaust system! The wire wheels and the separate front wings are genuine, but the wheels look too small in diameter, being out of scale and out of character with the body styling as a result. The new bodywork is made in that ubiquitous material glass fibre reinforced plastic, very well molded, and of a good heavyweight quality. The sprayed-on paintwork has no more than a mass-produced quality. A Zimmer seen recently that had been in constant use for several years was holding up in the appearance department, the paint a little dulled by the intense Californian sunlight, but the plastic moldings were beginning to show signs of distortion. It is likely that before long the car will become shabby. As a poseur-mobile the Zimmer would rate a 10!

The Gatsby Griffin, like the previous two automobiles is a fake, but it does have two good things going for it, price and good looks. It is constructed in San Jose, northern California at the Gatsby Coachworks, and styled by Sky Clausen. Sky makes no secret of the fact that he designed the car, and makes it for profit only. He has no pretensions to making a classic car, simply one that in some ways resembles a classic of the 1930s.

Sky uses a stretched Ford LTD chassis on which to mount his shapely bodywork, and the car can be powered by any Ford V8 engine up to a 491cu.inch capacity. Californian traffic and speed-restricted conditions mean that the car is pleasant enough to drive. The brakes and ride could be judged as fair to good, but the steering and roadholding are no more than adequate. The suspension feels 'loose', the usual standard Ford poor shock absorber control being the main cause for this sensation, and the steering suffers from the usual over-servoed American power system, lacking in road feel and feedback. For such a large car, the view over the bonnet from the driving seat is impressive for the distance to the front of the car, and the prominent front wings allow the Griffin to be placed on the road with some accuracy. Engine response is sluggish, no doubt partly due to the strangulation effect of the Californian emission equipment with which the poor engine is saddled. These problems are further amplified by the very smooth but slow automatic gearbox performance.

The Clenet, now out of production, was again cast in the mold of the previous cars. Based on a current American production car, using plastic body panels to give it a 1930s look it was really very well made, quite expensive, and only produced in small quantities and has achieved almost star rating among collectors because used examples are in some demand in the USA,

## SKY CLAUSEN

Sky Clausen dreamed as so many engineers and mechanics do, of building and selling his own car. His many years in racing and classic car restoration, convinced him that he could produce the car he wanted. He set up his workshop in the northern Californian town of San José and was soon able to show the world his first product, the Gatsby Cabriolet, a car based on a Ford LTD chassis and running gear. It can be bought with either a glass fibre or a steel body. His second vehicle is the Griffin, less restrained in style and better looking on it's Ford LTD under-pinnings.

Sky has been forced to concentrate on re-bodying current production chassis, instead of designing complete cars from scratch. As he explained, 'One step at a time, is my motto. I'm not going to make the mistake so many others have made in this business, of running before they can walk. I intend to establish my business, get it on a firm commercial basis, then I'll get down to making my own, all mine, car!' Time only will tell if Sky can realize his ambitions.

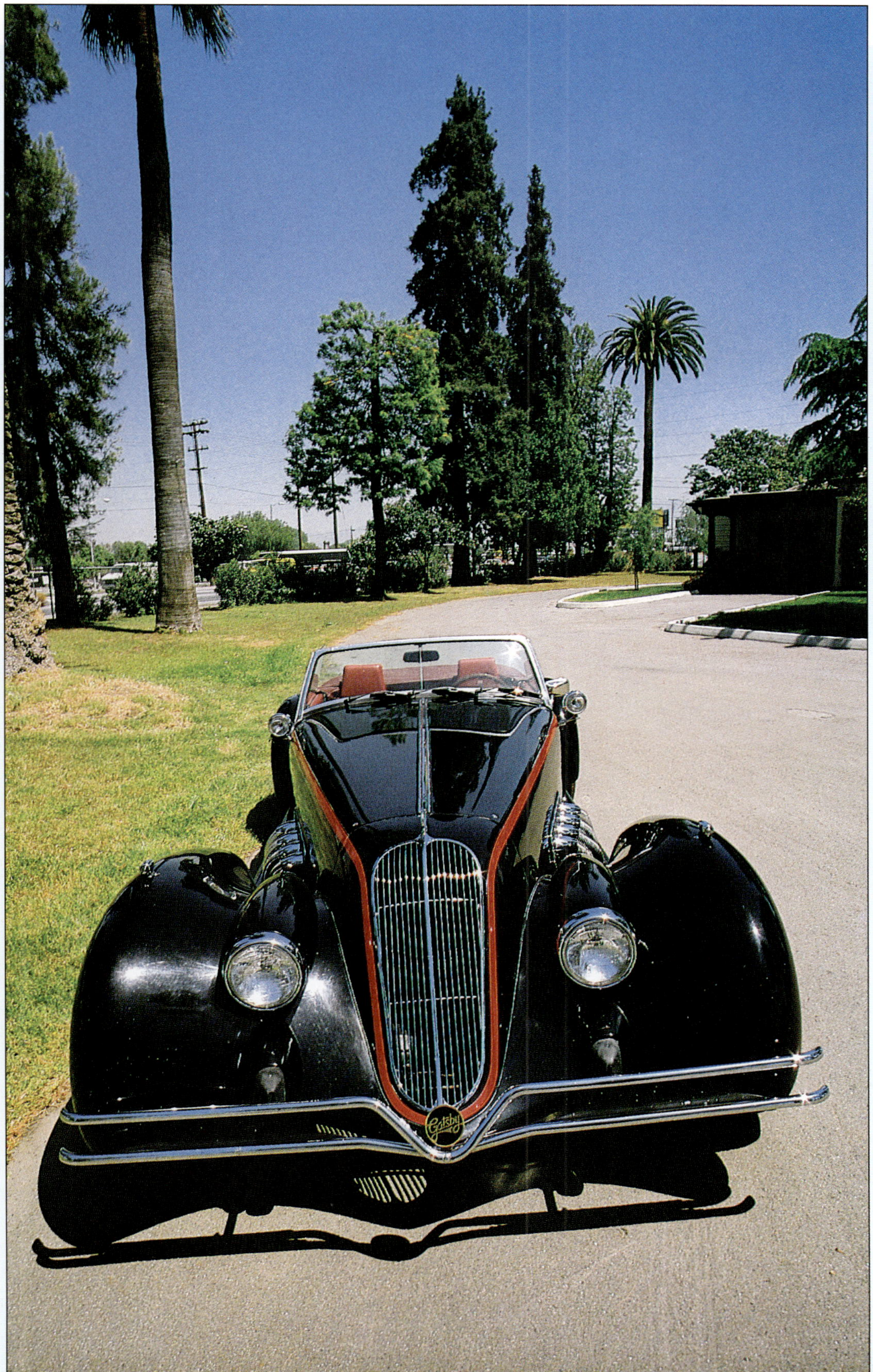

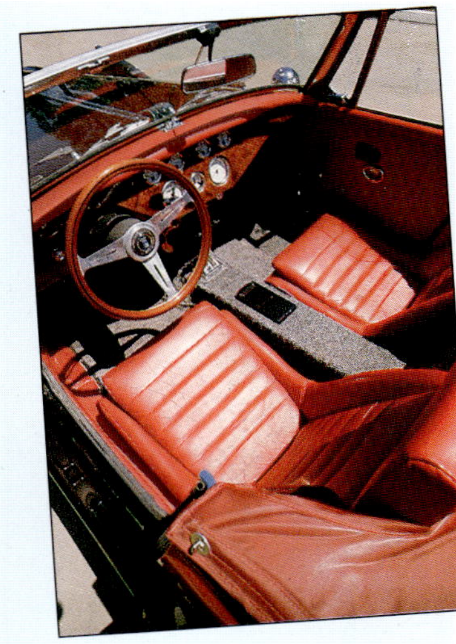

A touch of Italian class—the Nardi steering wheel graces the Griffin's rather cramped interior.

Good looks and a reasonable price have made the Gatsby Griffin a successful seller.

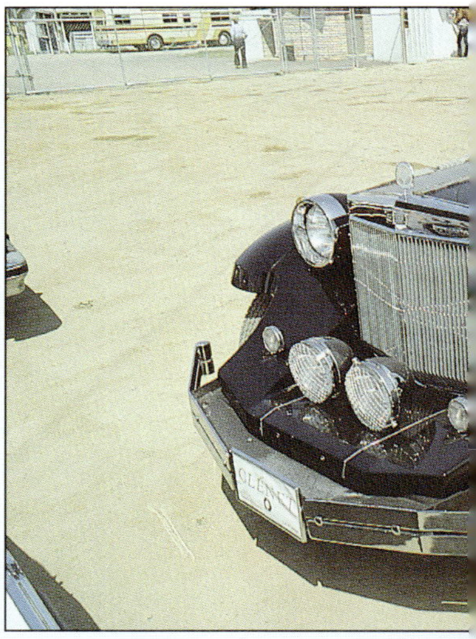

especially on the West Coast.

The Doval Shadow (again another sly reference to a Rolls-Royce model) is a little different from all the previous cars in that the body, which again goes on a Ford LTD chassis, is made by ex-Rolls-Royce and Aston Martin craftsmen in East Haven, Conn. It is manufactured in light alloy material, and as one would expect from craftsmen of this experience, is beautifully constructed. Like the Clenet and the Griffin, the Doval has rather cramped accommodation in the tiny driving compartment; although the trim and seats are excellently made and finished, it is still a struggle for a person of average American proportions to get in to and out of these cars.

Road performance, again, is just like the others. Obviously these manufacturers devote all their efforts towards the

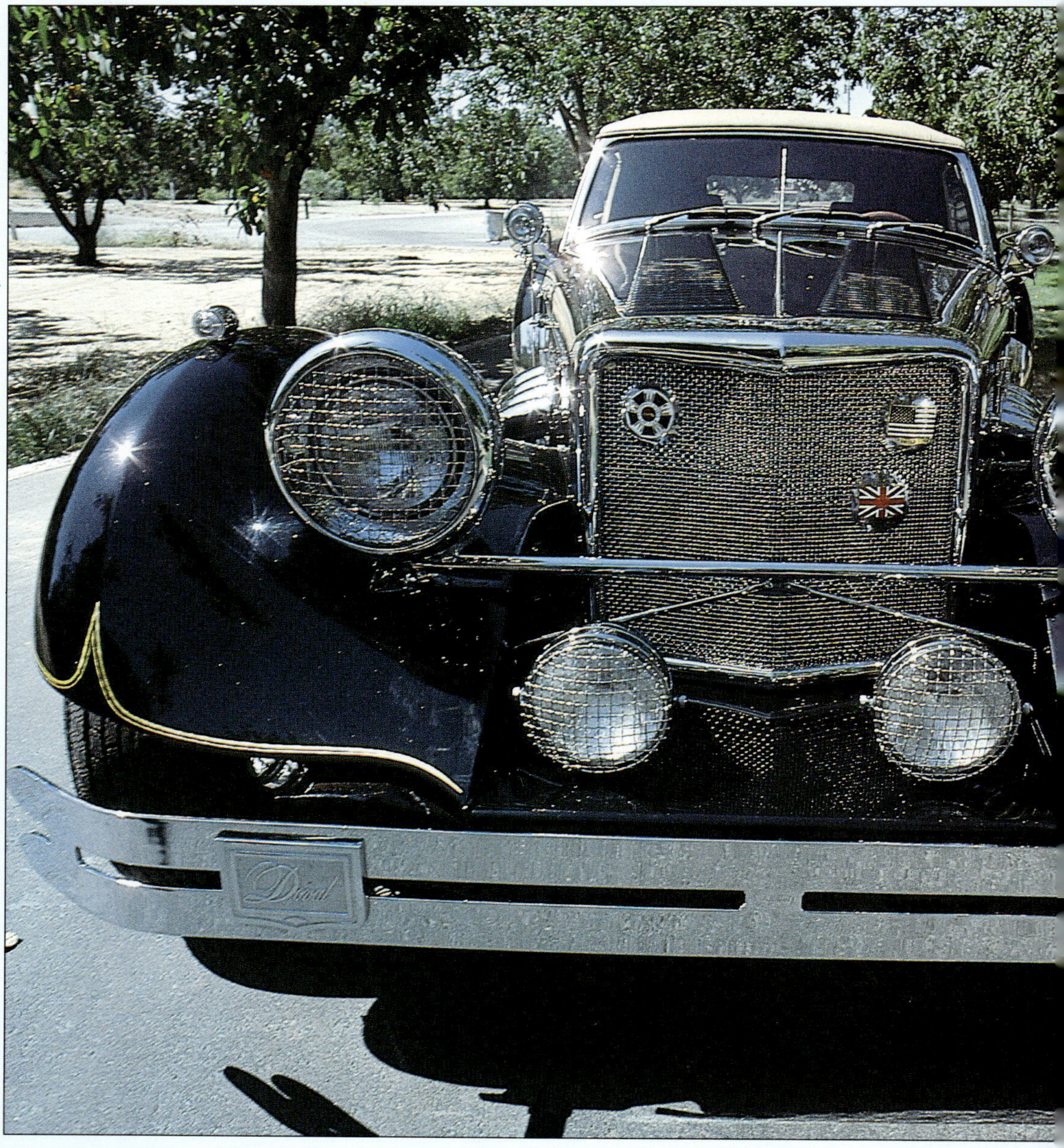

Most American custom cars have glass fibre bodies, but the Doval Shadow, built by ex-Aston Martin and Rolls-Royce craftsmen, has light alloy panels.

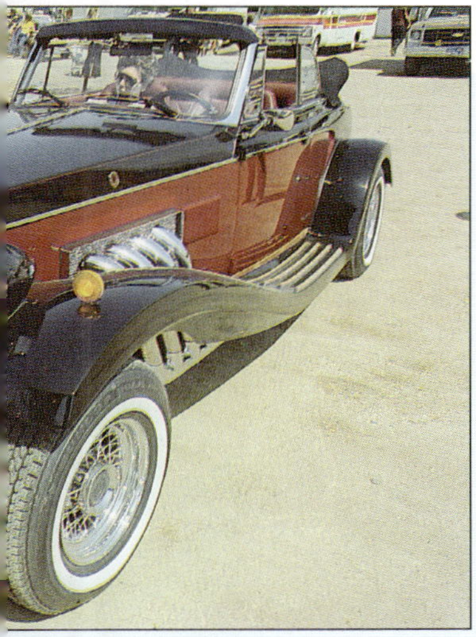

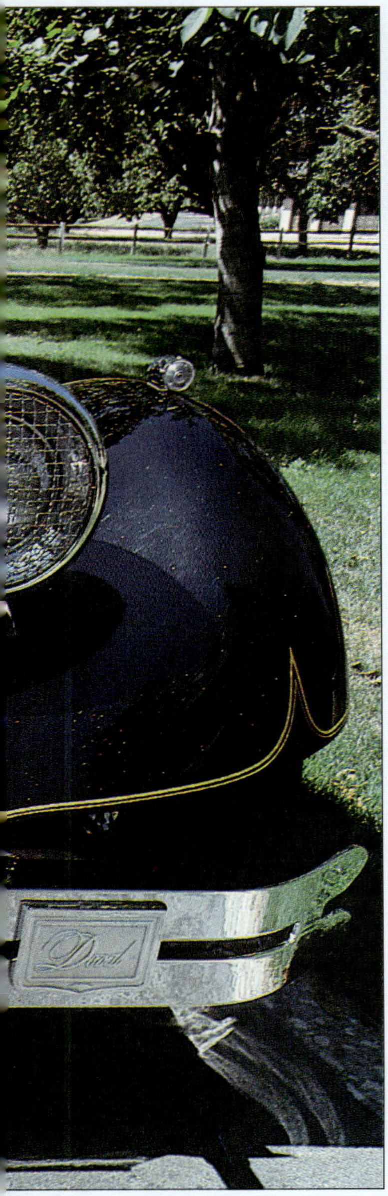

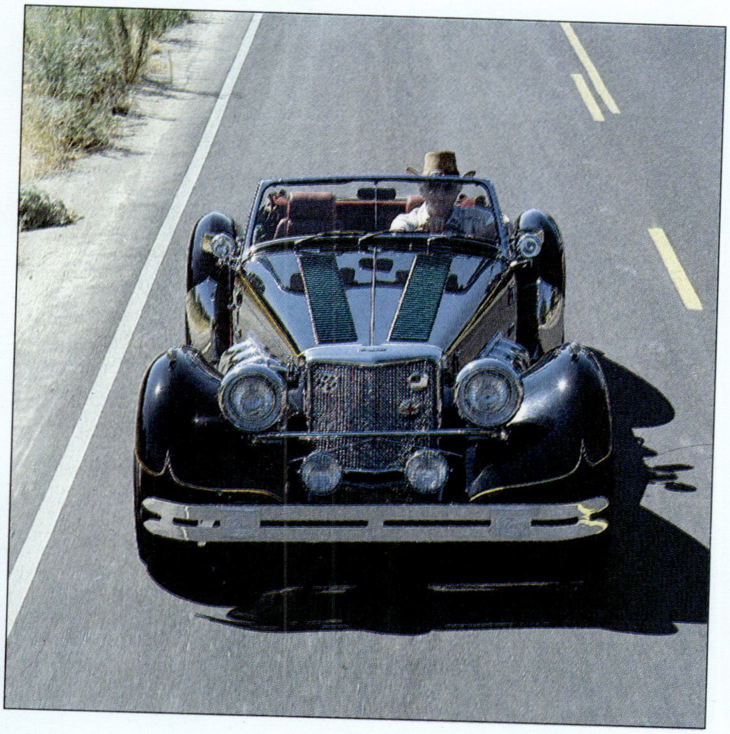

LEFT: On the road, the Doval Shadow, which is based on the Ford LTD, drives like an ordinary American car.

FAR LEFT: Alain Clenet was one of the first American custom car makers to offer a well-made, expensive vehicle that combined the comforts of a modern automobile with the appearance of a rare, classic car.

appearance of their vehicles, and virtually nothing to their dynamic qualities. The Doval, for such a large car, has no provision for carrying luggage, the large rear section to the bodywork being no more than an empty shell, without even a floor! Don Hart who operates the Doval Coachworks did confirm this fact, and added that the tail of his car would possibly get a luggage compartment soon, but few, if any, Doval Shadow customers had passed comment about this!

All of the cars in this chapter are American-financed, and styled to cash in on the nostalgia craze on the assumption that any vehicle that can be made to look like a 1930s car with an outside exhaust system, wire wheels, and separate wings can be sold. The old saying, 'You can fool some of the people, some of the time' appears to work in this area of automotive fakery, because all of these vehicles did sell. However, it would seem that even the rich, undiscriminating public are seeing through these efforts to part them from their money, and Doval and Clenet are not producing cars at the moment.

All these cars fit as standard the expensive, and superb Nardi steering wheel, which must demonstrate that the dominant profit motive behind them was not quite strong enough to prevent just a little real class from getting through to the paying customer.

There is a place for such vehicles in the automobile market, and there always has been, but the buyer, without experience and knowledge, should beware, and not be taken in by surface gloss and skilful advertising.

CHAPTER FIVE

# The Packard

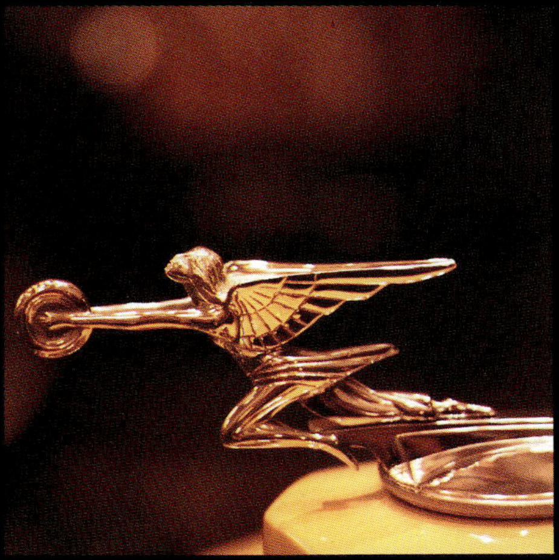

Although the Packard Model L's artillery-style wheels look delicate, their quality of construction gave them ample strength.

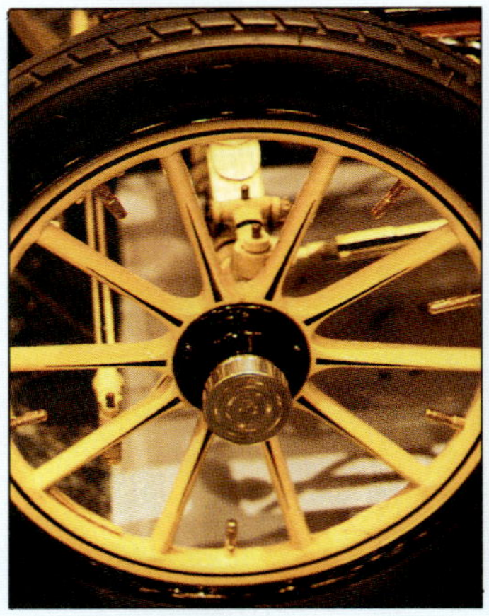

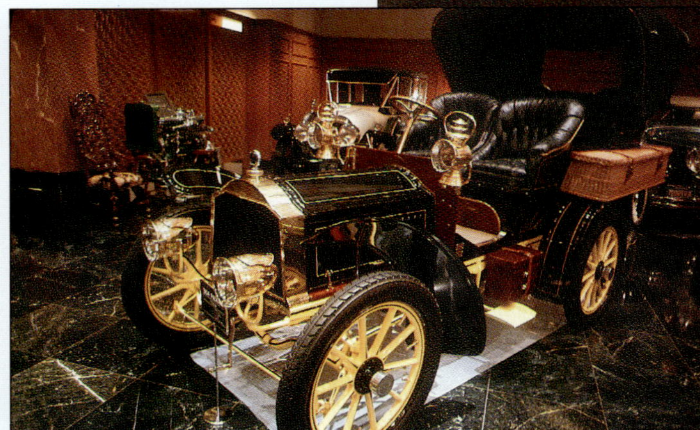

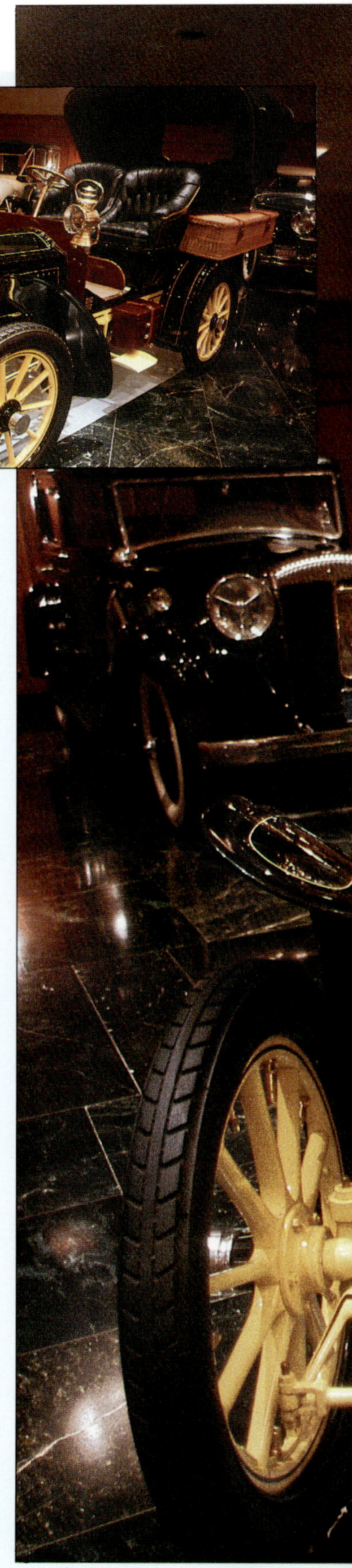

Ask the Man who Owns One', for years this was the advertising slogan used by the Packard Motor Company to sell its cars. By today's standards it is a rather low key headline for a major automobile manufacturer to use, but it says a great deal about Packard and its products. The slogan hints that the Packard car is so good, so reliable, of such high quality that all the potential buyer need do is to ask a Packard owner to confirm what he already knows, that the Packard is the best that money can buy.

Like Rolls-Royce, the Packard company came into being after some years as an electrical equipment manufacturer, placing a very high value on good design, careful construction and great durability. These values remained with the Packard company until almost the very end of its life. James Ward Packard began making cars in 1899, but was bought out by a Detroit businessman, Henry B. Joy, in 1901. The new Packard company introduced a four cylinder 12 litre engine into the model L Packard in 1904. A splendid example of the model L in the Nethercutt Collection is housed in the most spectacular style in the Tower of Beauty in Sylmar, California.

However, it was not until 1912 when Jesse Gurney Vincent joined Packard as chief engineer that the company really began to make its mark as a manufacturer of luxury, high class cars. Jesse Vincent designed the first V12 engine to go into mass-production for use in an American automobile. He called his car the Twin-6; the engine was a V12 side valve unit, with a 60° angle between the cylinder banks of 6.9 litre capacity, and was among the first with alloy pistons as part of Vincent's search for lightness and strength. This power unit gave the Twin-6 the necessary refinement and performance that the luxury class customer demanded.

It was so successful that in its first year 3,606 examples of the Twin-6 were built and sold. In 1917 4,140 Twin-6s reached happy customers. In that year Packard made more V12-engined cars, of the highest quality, than the total production of similar vehicles produced by all of Europe's luxury car makers combined!

When Warren G. Harding became the first President of the United States of America to ride to his inauguration by car, he

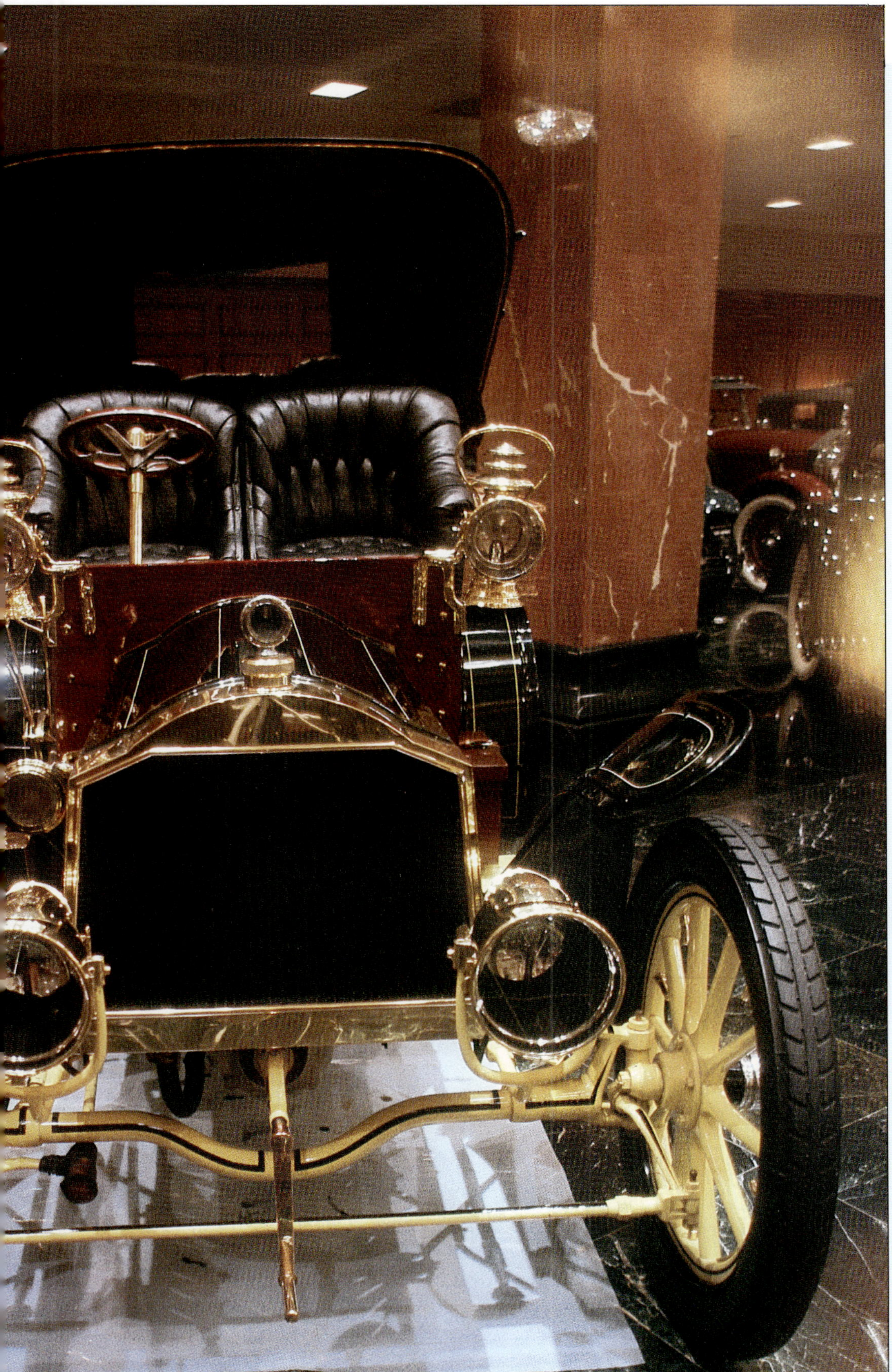

LEFT AND CENTRE: The Packard Model L equalled the quality of any European rival and set the standard for a long line of top-class American cars.

Phil Hill owns this Packard Twin 6—the first car to have a mass-produced V12 engine.

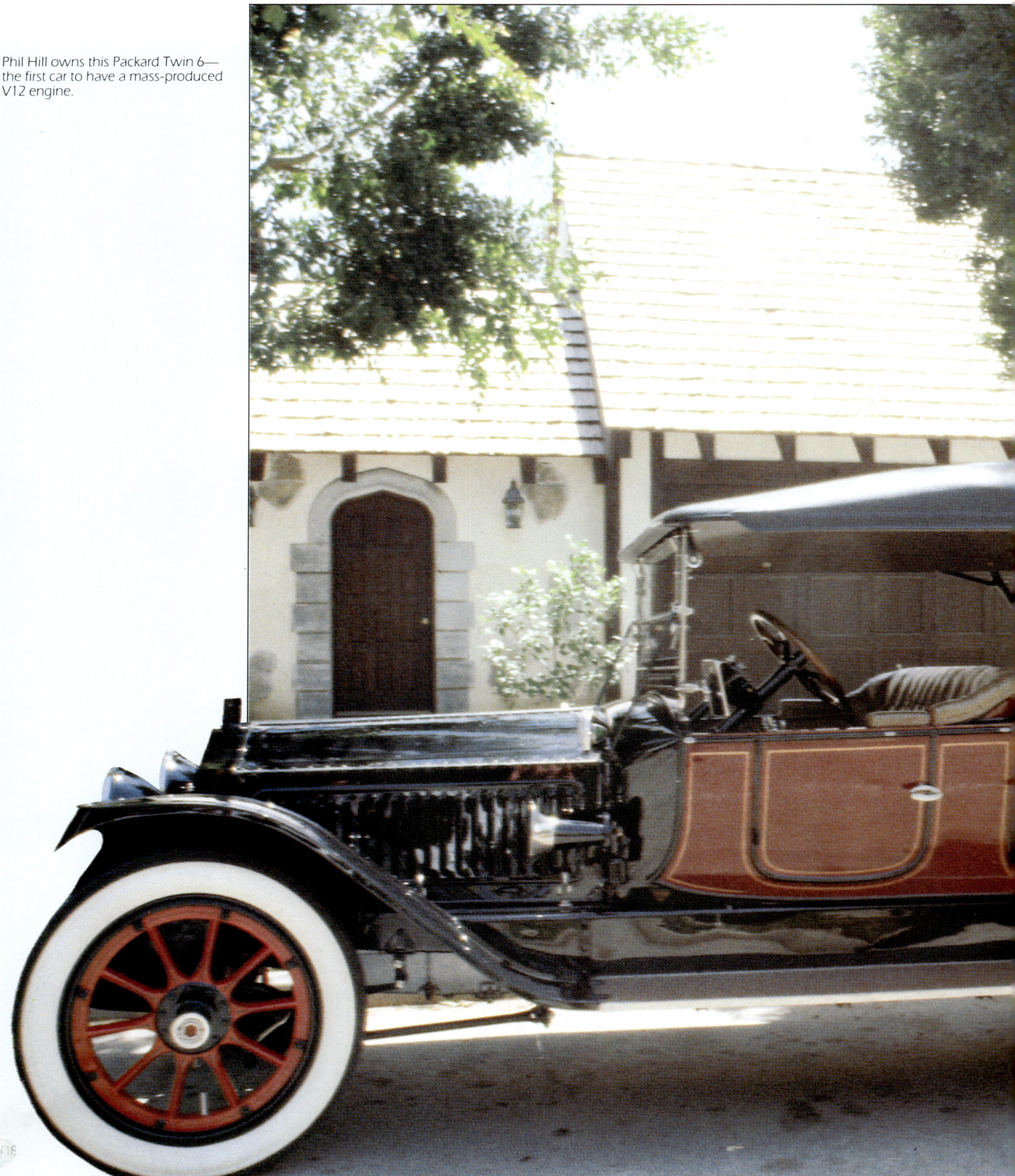

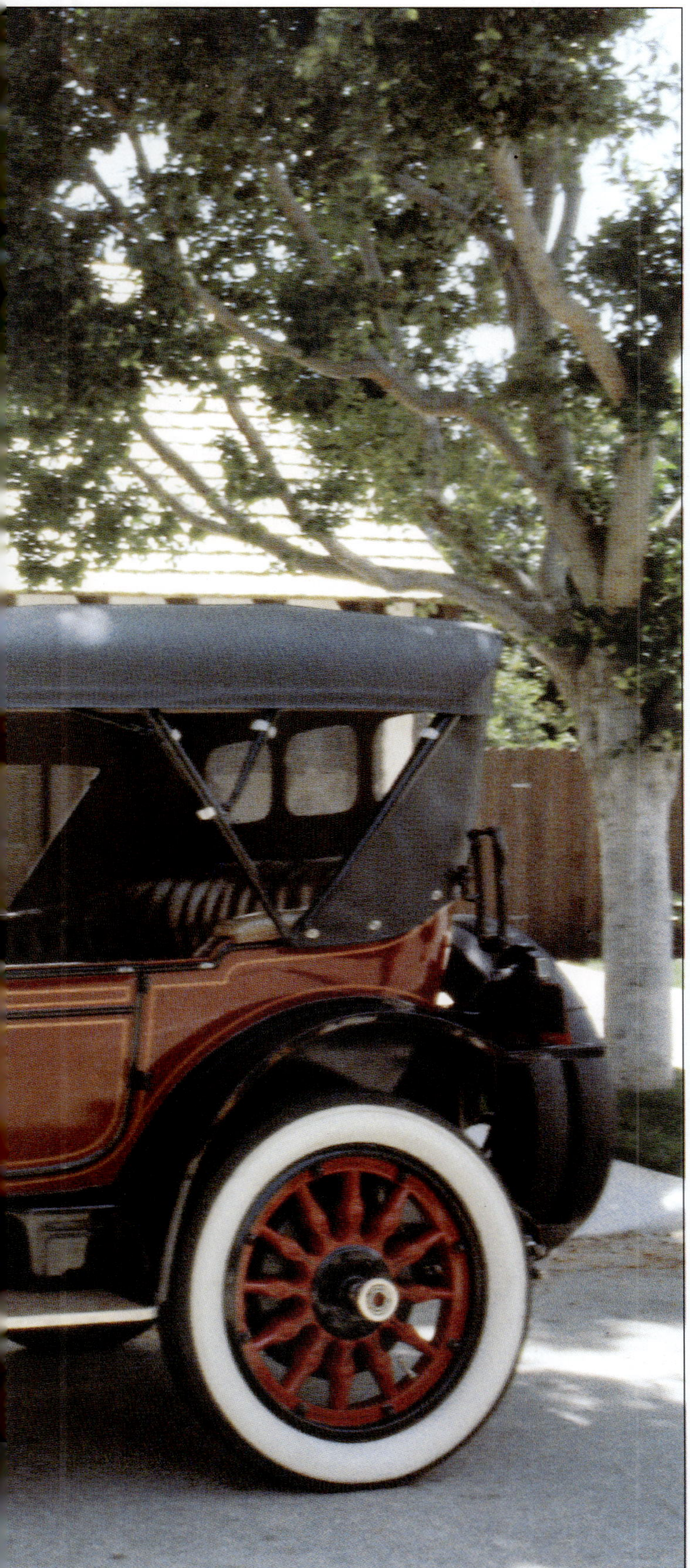

used a Packard Twin-6.

In 1923 the Twin-6 was replaced by the single-8 model, when over 35,000 examples of the V12-powered car had been made. The new car served further to establish Packard as the name for a top quality automobile, and the company went from strength to strength.

Phil Hill, the first American to win a Formula One Driver's World Championship, in 1961, is an avowed Packard enthusiast. He has a Twin-6 at home and wished to demonstrate it.

He drove the car out of his garage, checked it for fuel, took up some adjustment on the rear brakes (the only brakes the car has) and made ready to take the car for a run.

He quickly drove down to the Santa Monica Freeway, and thrusting his precious car into the crowded road he proceeded to put the Packard through its paces, giving the machinery no mercy. In his day as a top racer Phil always drove hard with 101 percent effort. Now, taking maximum revolutions in first and second gears, gearchanging with lightning speed he quickly reached a cruising speed on the freeway of 75mph. At this speed, which is well over the national speed limit of 55mph, the big car sat on the road as solid as a rock, the high placed seats giving marvellous visibility in all directions, and in spite of the author's concern about the car having only rear brakes, Phil's driving ability, anticipation, and reflexes ensured that the car invariably slowed smoothly and without panic. All the time Phil kept up a commentary on the car's abilities and after 30 minutes of practical demonstration there was no doubting Packard quality and Phil's competence behind the steering wheel.

Phil said, almost as an aside, that he considers that his Twin-6 would make the perfect vehicle in which to take his family back to New York during the summer. 'It will cruise at a very happy 60-65mph all day, there is enough room for the rest of the family to stretch out in the back without getting in each other's way, and the suspension would make for a very comfortable journey! And he was serious, as he is about all motoring matters.

When in 1923 Packard introduced four-wheel brakes, and four- speed gear boxes, they continued to make that masterpiece of automotive power units the V12, this time yet another Jesse Vincent design, but of 7.3 litre capacity. This engine remained in production, with updating modifications, until 1939.

Two Packards that featured this engine were the Le Baron Towncar, and one of the most covetable cars in the world, the V12 convertible by Dietrich, known as the 'Orello', and, like the model L, to be found in the Nethercutt Collection. For sheer style and glamour these two cars must rank with the best.

This latter car is known as the 'Orello' because although it is a model 1108 Packard its colour is a combination of yellow and orange, specially selected by Jack Nethercutt to match the famous Packard advertisement in Fortune magazine which ran in 1934, the year the 'Orello' was built. The car is a four-door convertible sedan by Dietrich, one of the very best of America coachbuilders. It is a model of quiet good looks and proportions, yet because of its splendid V12 engine, fast, comfortable, and able to cover long distances at high speed. Maintained in mint condition by the restoration staff at the Nethercutt Collection it is, like all the cars at Sylmar, ready for the road at short notice, requiring no more than fuel and a battery to run. Unlike so many desirable and rare cars these days, the 'Orello' Packard could be put to everyday use now, without any concern from the driver at using such a vehicle in today's traffic conditions. To be able to say that about a fifty-year-old motor-car speaks volumes about the Packard's design and construction. For a convertible the 'Orello' looks just as impressive and handsome with the top up as with it down, a truly magnificent automobile.

If the 'Orello' has glamour it is because of its striking good looks, beautiful finish, performance, and sheer class, the Le Baron Towncar scores in the glamour stakes with its aura of grand style. To anyone who thinks of the typical American car as a flashy, chromium plated, extravagance on wheels, then the first sight of the Packard Le Baron would quickly effect a change of opinion. The Le Baron towncar is quite simply a superb carriage for the grandest occasions. Travelling in the grand manner is the sole reason for its existence. It is a sober, stately vehicle in the best possible taste.

The 7,298cc V12 engine sighs into life at no more than a touch of the starter button, and remains quiet and unobtrusive throughout its working range, giving the heavy car a performance quite out of keeping with its appearance. The steering, brakes, and ride are all perfectly matched to the engine,

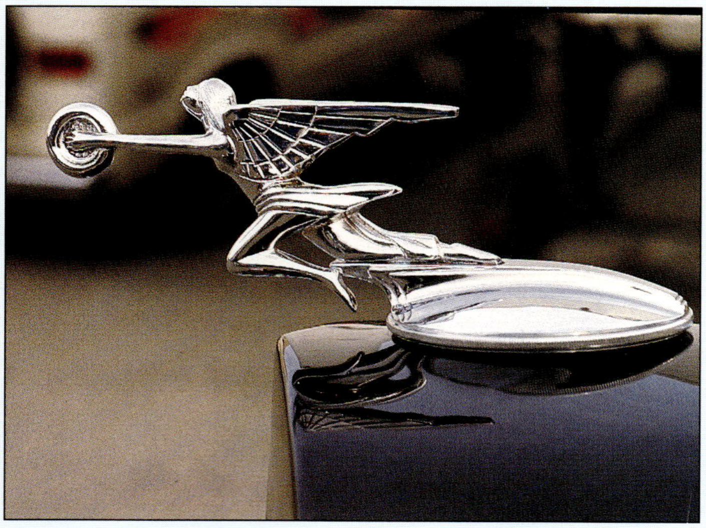

The Packard radiator mascot, just like the car itself, is distinctive, simple and attractive.

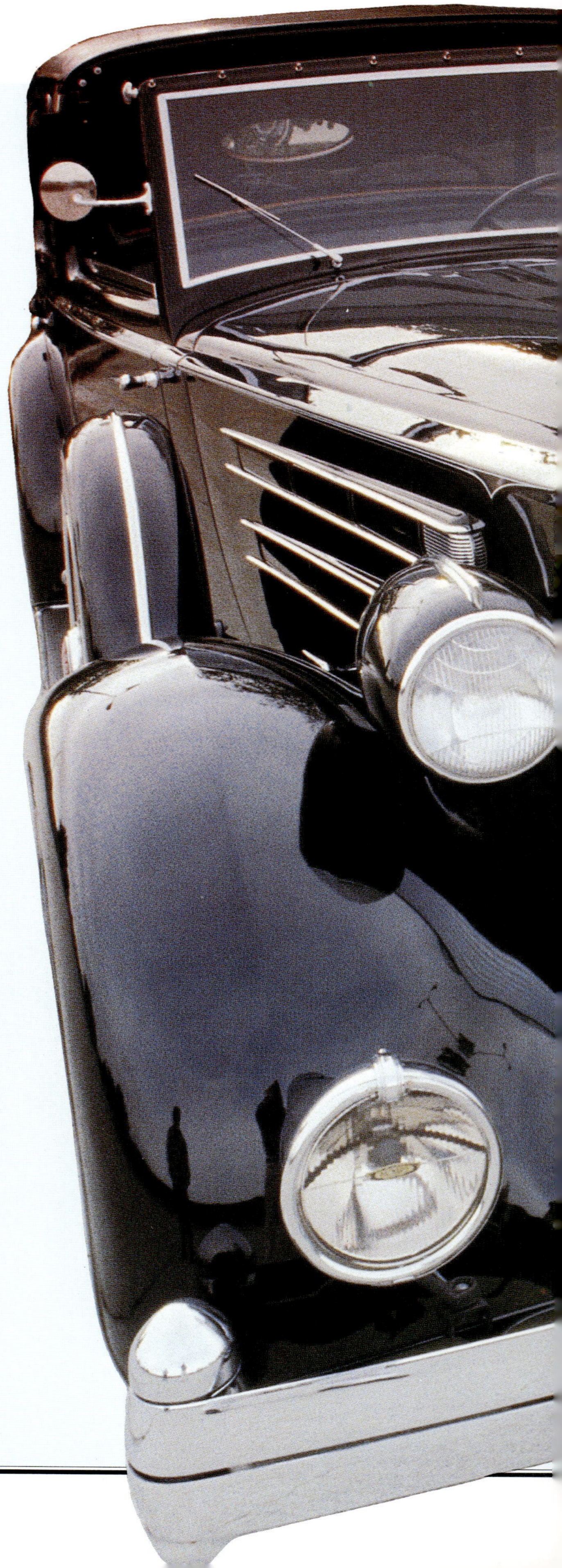

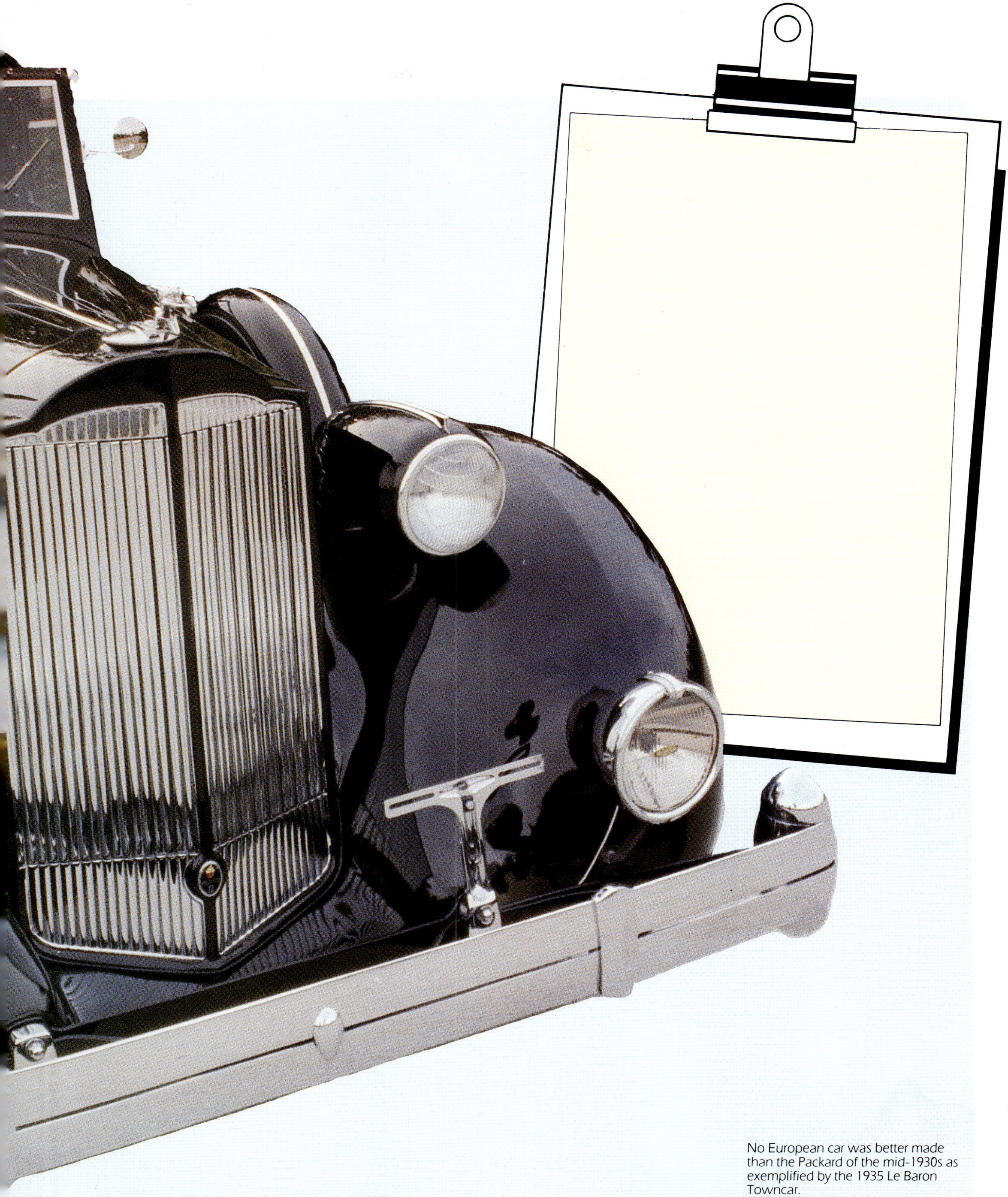

No European car was better made than the Packard of the mid-1930s as exemplified by the 1935 Le Baron Towncar.

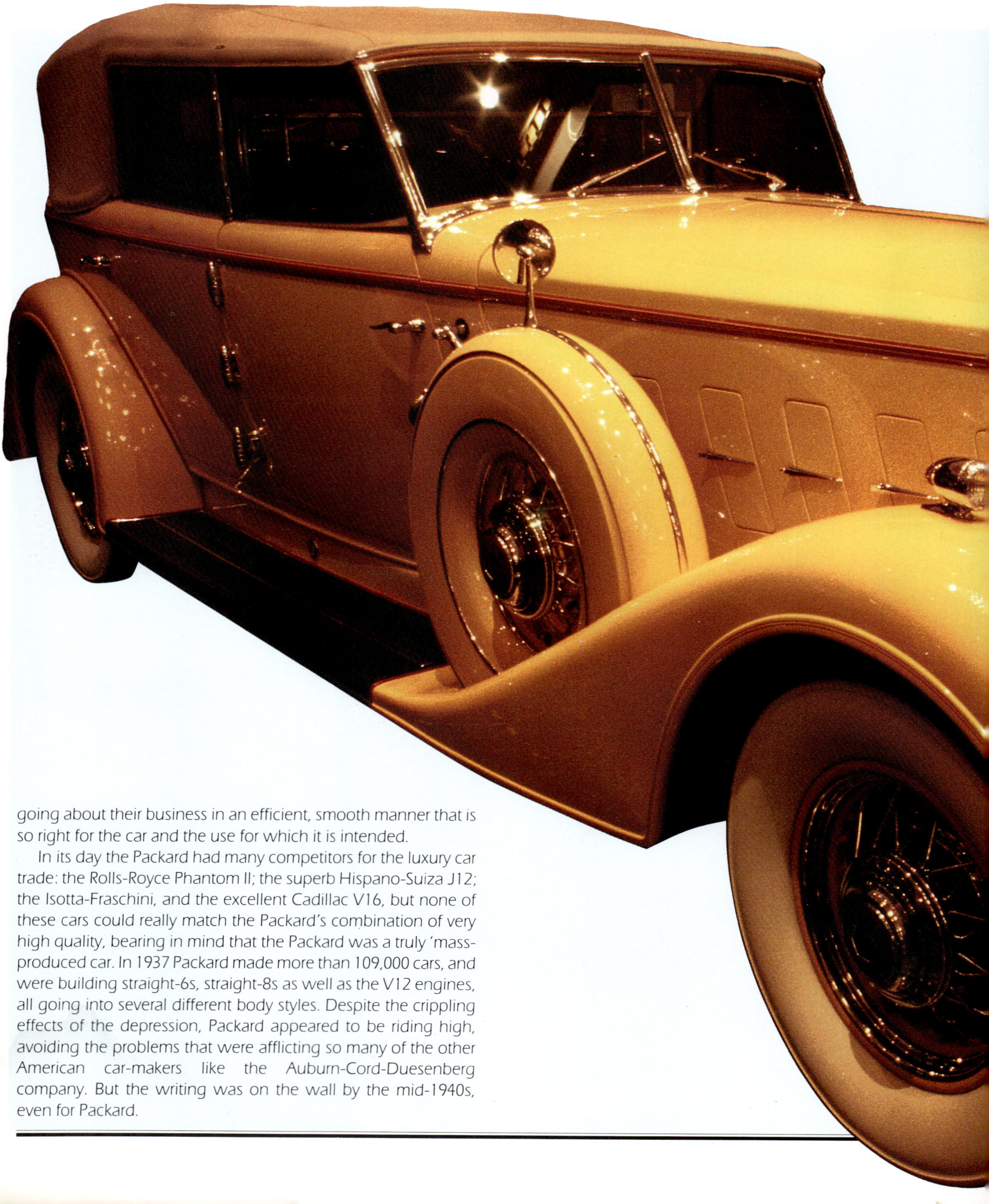

going about their business in an efficient, smooth manner that is so right for the car and the use for which it is intended.

In its day the Packard had many competitors for the luxury car trade: the Rolls-Royce Phantom II; the superb Hispano-Suiza J12; the Isotta-Fraschini, and the excellent Cadillac V16, but none of these cars could really match the Packard's combination of very high quality, bearing in mind that the Packard was a truly 'mass-produced car. In 1937 Packard made more than 109,000 cars, and were building straight-6s, straight-8s as well as the V12 engines, all going into several different body styles. Despite the crippling effects of the depression, Packard appeared to be riding high, avoiding the problems that were afflicting so many of the other American car-makers like the Auburn-Cord-Duesenberg company. But the writing was on the wall by the mid-1940s, even for Packard.

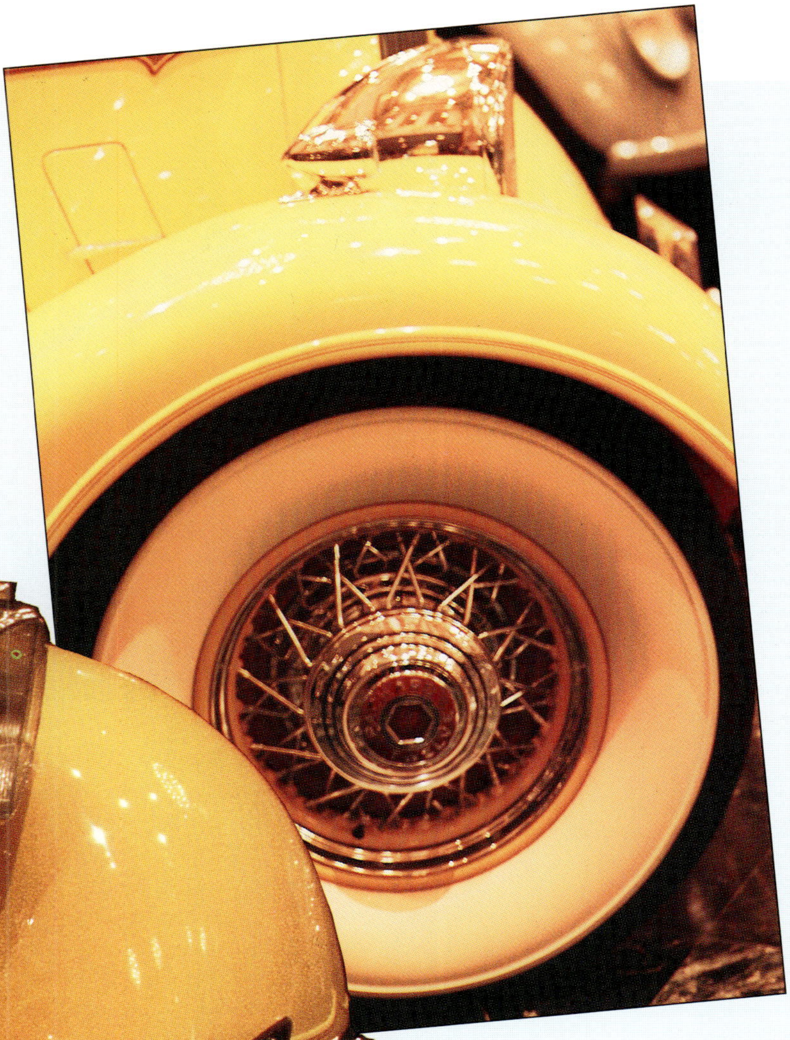

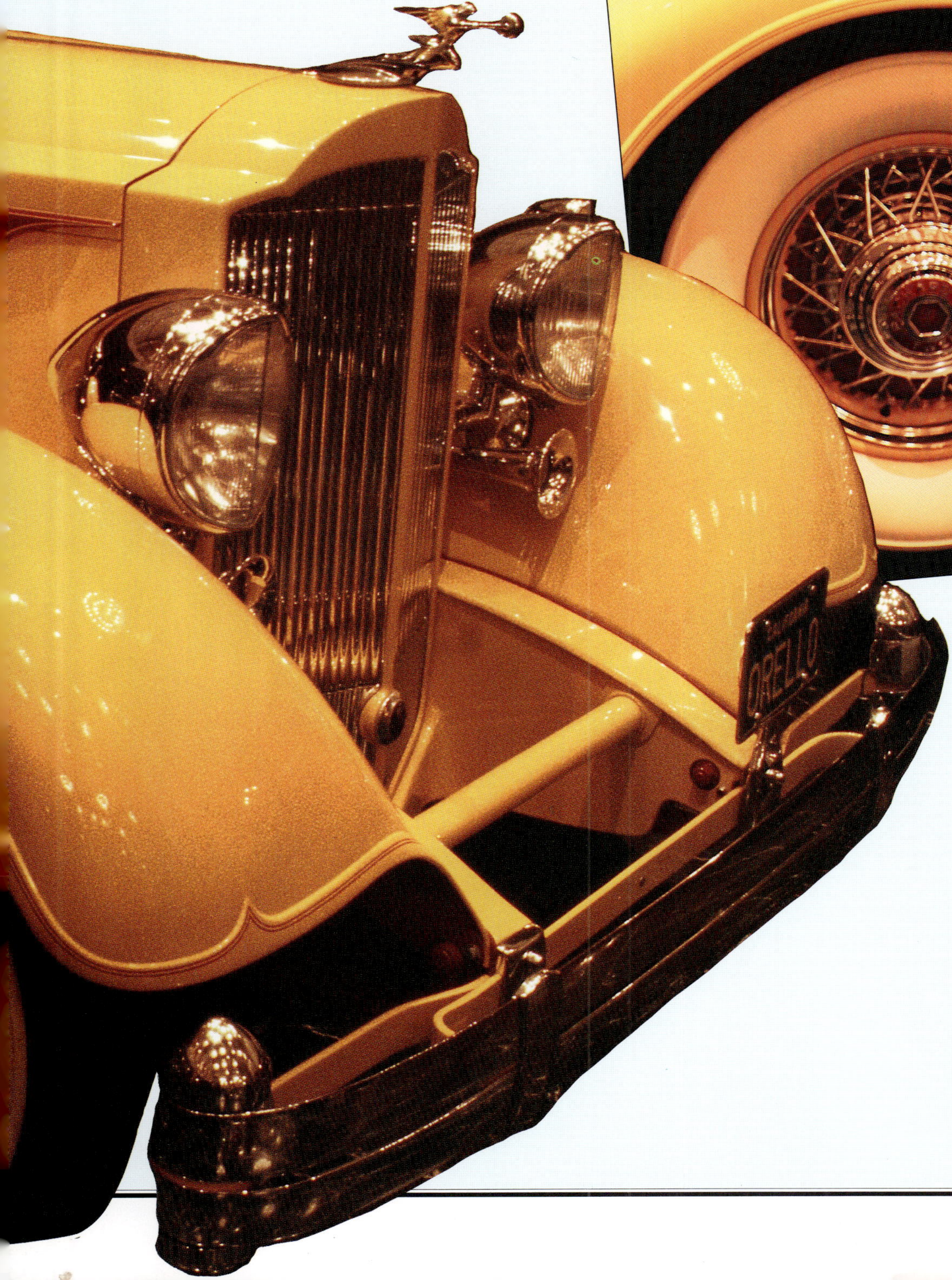


Packard used independent front suspension and low-pressure tyres (above) to give their cars a comfortable ride.

Even today, this 1934 Packard V12 'Orello' (left) is a pleasure to drive, on the open road or in traffic.

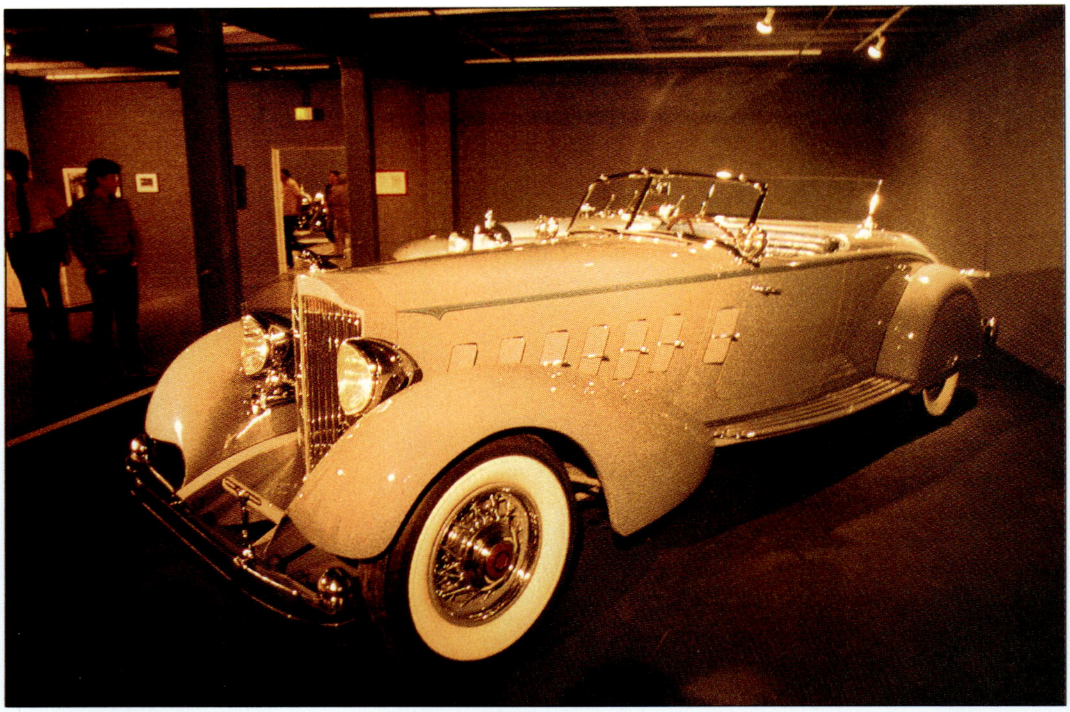

During World War Two, Packard had further enhanced their engineering reputation by manufacturing aero-engines, possibly the most famous being the Rolls-Royce Merlin engine that made such a major contribution to British victory in the Battle of Britain. Packard quality was built into it, and this earned warm praise from the pilots and maintenance crews in all the theatres of war where Merlin-powered aircraft flew, and even Rolls-Royce themselves. At the end of the War Packard had been persuaded to sell the body dies for their luxury model, the Senior Series 8-cylinder car, to the Russians in a forlorn gesture of American/Soviet goodwill, a move that left Packard with no true luxury car for the post-war period. The Russians went on to make their version of the Packard for many years, calling it the ZIS-110 model, but it was only available to members of the Politburo.

Packard returned to making cars after 1945 with the wrong class of automobile, and with a new president, James J. Nance, who wanted desperately to return to luxury car manufacture. Packard was faced by a buoyant General Motors Corporation intent on holding on to their preeminent position in the domestic market, and a hungry Chrysler Corporation equally keen on retaining their reputation for the finest mass production engineering. The Ford Motor Company were in dire straits, beset with internal conflict that nearly destroyed them. Even so, Packard never really regained their position in the market place. Their problems increased further when they purchased the dying Studebaker company in 1954 in a desperate attempt at broadening their market appeal, but as one might have supposed, two dying companies can never really restore each other's fortunes. The shrinking luxury car segment of the market only made life even more difficult for Packard; besides, Cadillac and Lincoln had that piece of the action firmly in their tight grip,

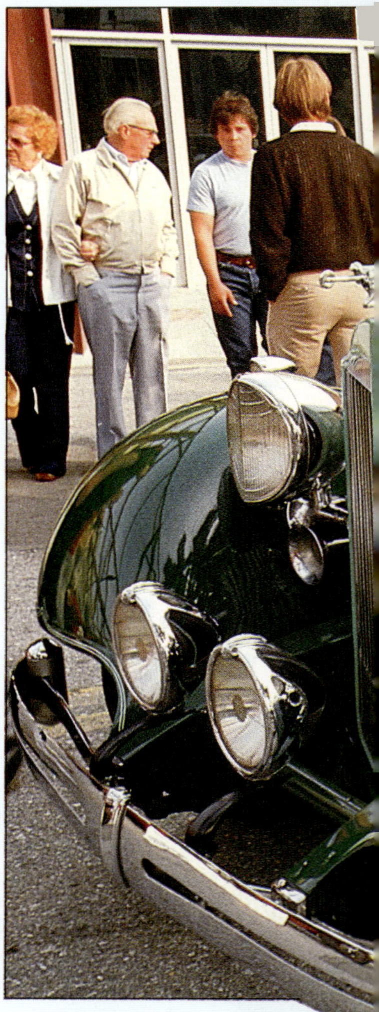

so Packard were frozen out of even their special area of operation. Within four years of making the disastrous merger with Studebaker, the famous and prestigious name of Packard had gone for ever from the lists of great American car makers. That year, 1958, was a sad year for lovers of grand luxury cars, and you have only to see examples of the best of the Packard range to fully appreciate what has been lost.

Carefully designed and built, and carrying some of the most beautiful bodies made by such names as Dietrich, Le Baron, Murphy, and Darrin, the Packard effortlessly covered the market for high quality cars. Whether the customer was a head of state, a film star, a socialite, a country doctor or simply someone who fully appreciated fine automobiles, there was a Packard in the range for them. Just take a look at the Packard Super-8 of 1932, which the company entitled the Phaeton. Introduced to a public at the height of the Depression, it demonstrated that Packard was capable and willing to fight on against the odds with quality cars. Offered with a choice of two engines, the straight-8 with 135hp, the new V12 with 160hp, the car delivered stunning good looks with reliability, durability, and performance. The Super-8 could

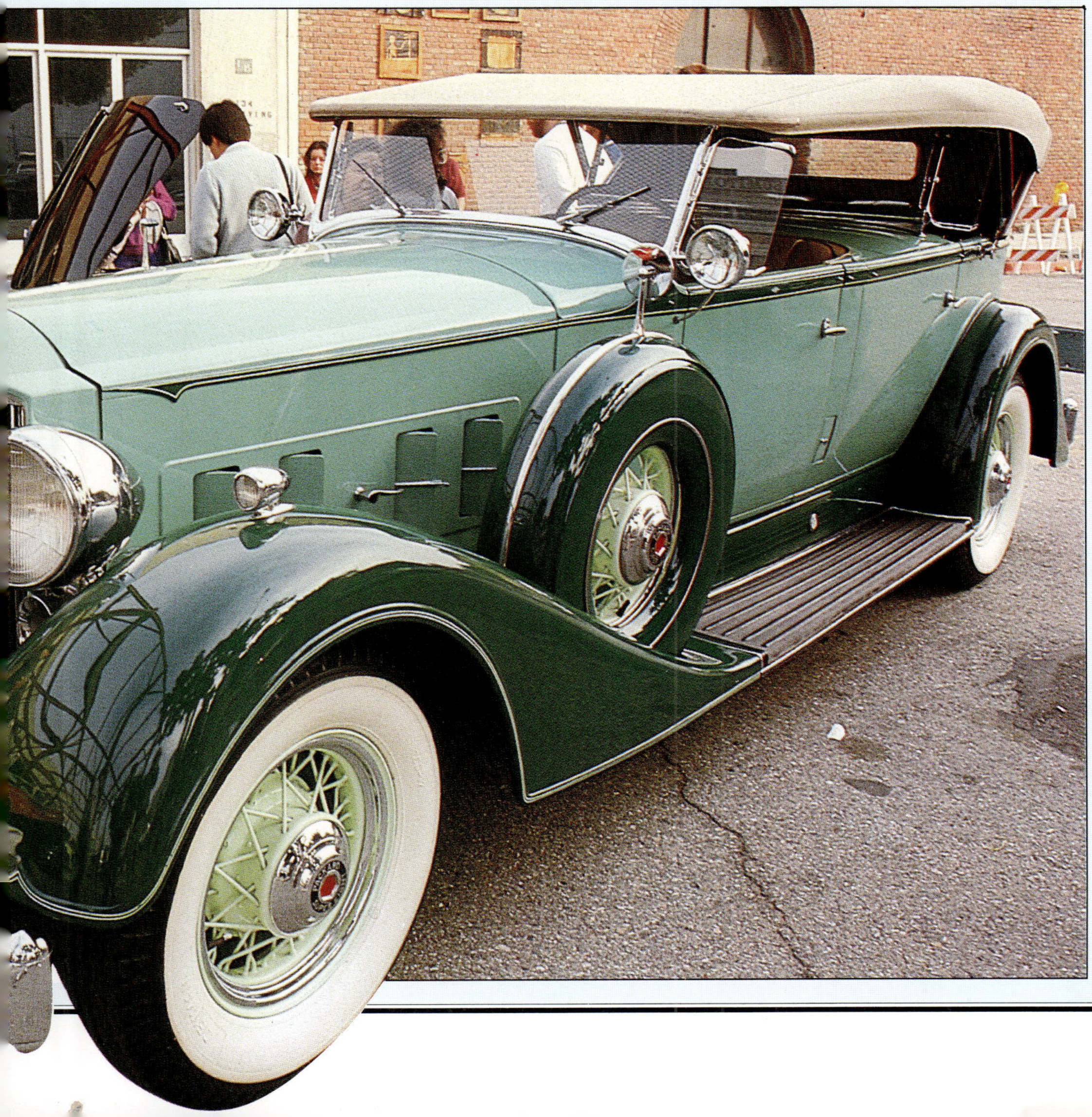

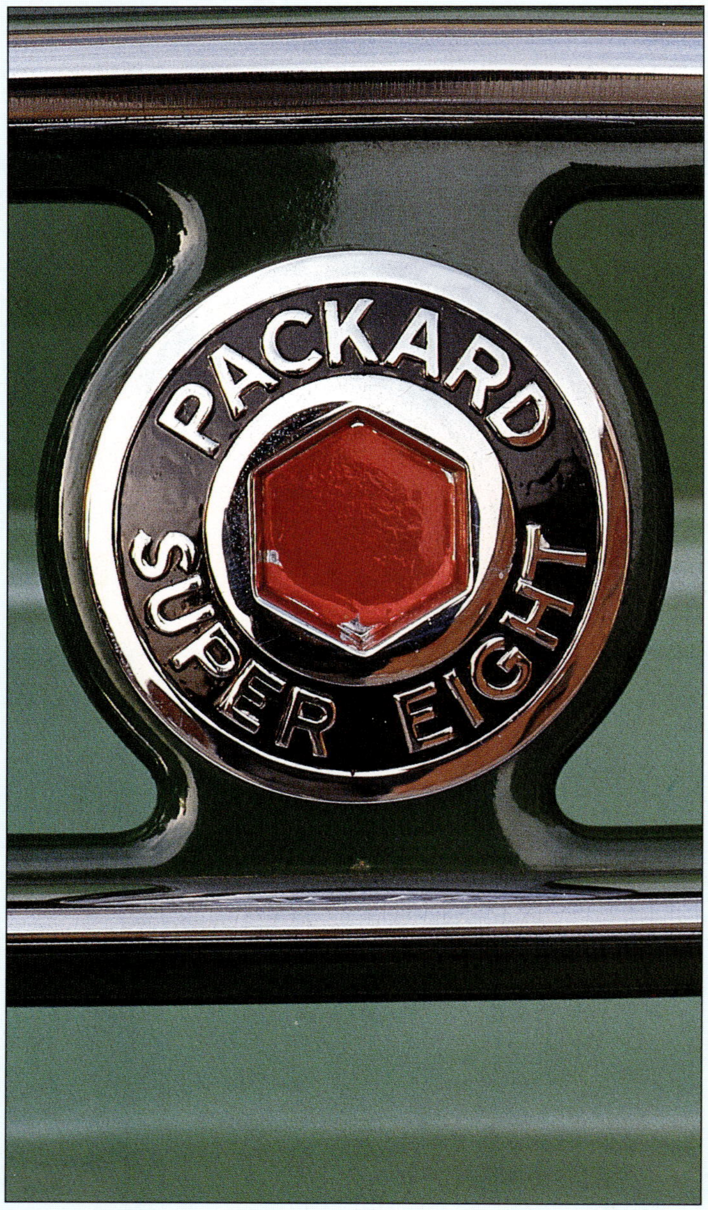


cruise at 85mph, and the V12 could easily attain a speed of over 110mph. The green Super-8 in the photographs was spotted in Los Angeles this year outside the Museum of Contemporary Art. It is in regular use, yet it looks so good that that it ought to be on display inside the Museum! However, inside the Museum there is a Packard Super-12 Phaeton occupying a stand in the exhibition of classic cars.

The Packard story could be described as one of riches to rags in only 59 years. Thankfully they left behind a dynamic record of many good cars and several really excellent ones, and an aero-engine that was a positive factor in victory in the Second World War; there cannot be many other automobile manufacturers who have as good a claim to fame.

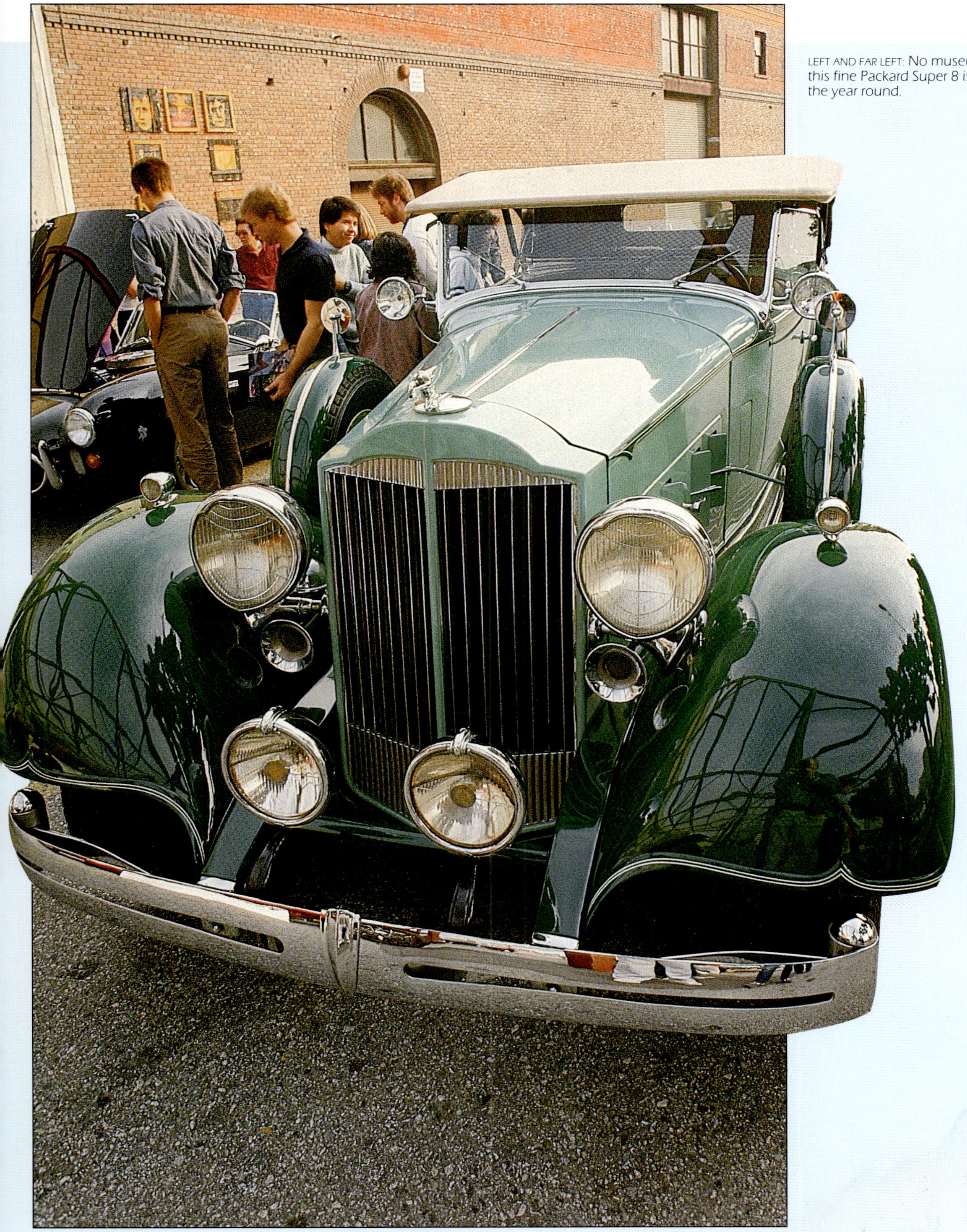

LEFT AND FAR LEFT: No museum piece, this fine Packard Super 8 is used all the year round.

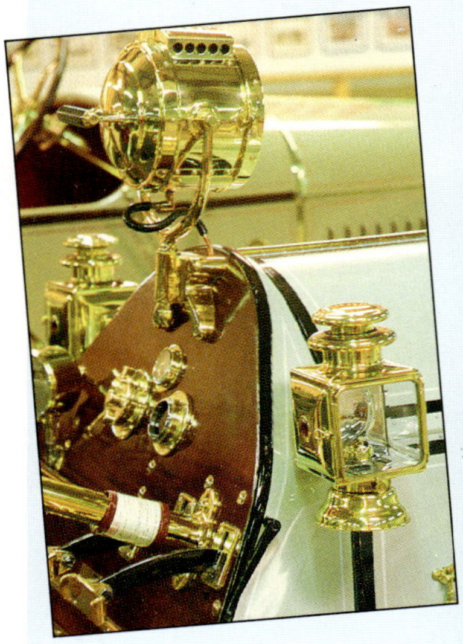

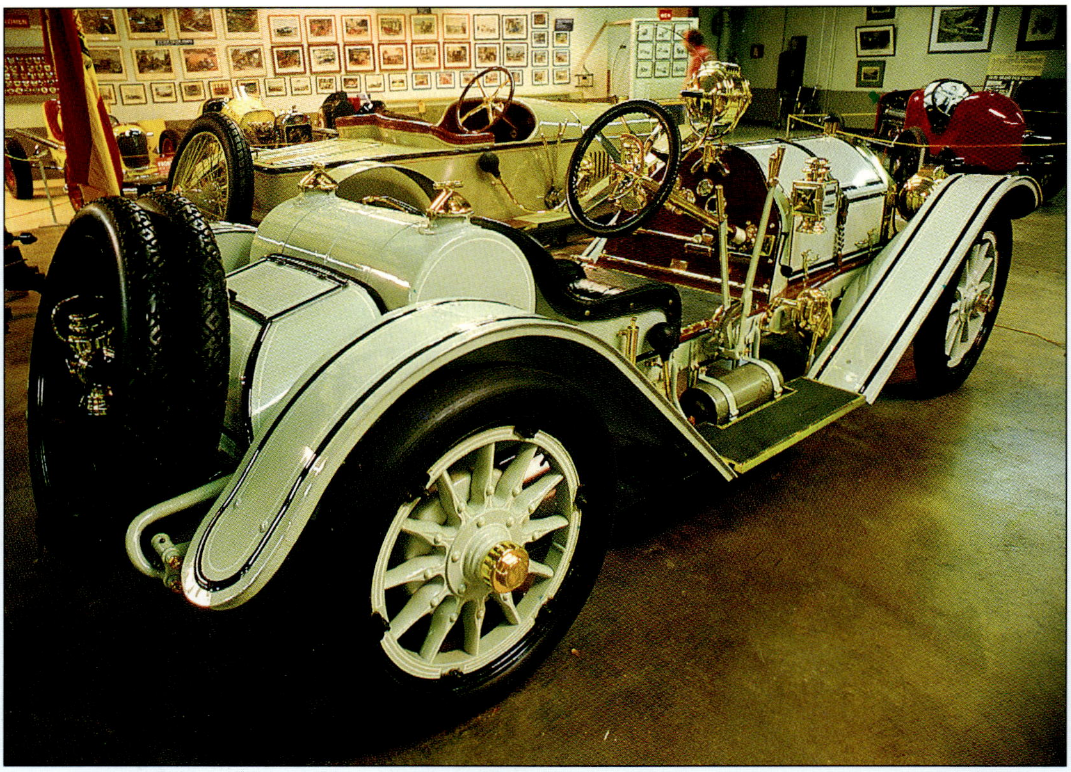

ABOVE AND RIGHT: The Mercer Raceabout 35C could be called the first American hot-rod. A simple, well-made car, it offered little more than pure performance with little concern for the driver's comfort.

It is generally held by the public that motor-racing is glamorous. To those directly involved in the activity, racing is simply very hard work under difficult conditions, usually hundreds of miles away from the home-base. It is also dangerous and exciting, and at times is frustrating, inconvenient, noisy, dirty, and always very, very expensive. Sir Thomas Lipton once said that racing a yacht in the America's Cup can be accurately compared with standing under a cold shower for hours on end, and tearing up £5 notes at the same time! The same thought must have entered every motoring journalist's head when covering some motor-racing events.

Yet to the occasional spectator any mention of being involved, even on the very edge of the sport, brings a gleam of envy into their eyes. Throw in a hint that the next race to be visited will be the Monaco Grand Prix, or the Italian G.P. at Monza, and their immediate response will be to exclaim, 'You lucky so-and-so!' Although a car race itself is very glamorous, one must not forget that, were it not for the machinery involved, the event would not happen.

The Mercer Raceabout was built in Trenton, New Jersey in the early days of this century. Mercer stopped producing cars as early as 1925, but their great days were those prior to 1915 when the Raceabout was in production. The Raceabout was, in fact, probably the best car that they ever made and certainly the most famous.

By 1910 their fastest car was the Speedster, but in that year Mercer's chief engineer, Finlay Robertson Porter, designed a road-going version of the Type 30-M racing car, and called it the Raceabout. It was an instant success, guaranteed to be safe at

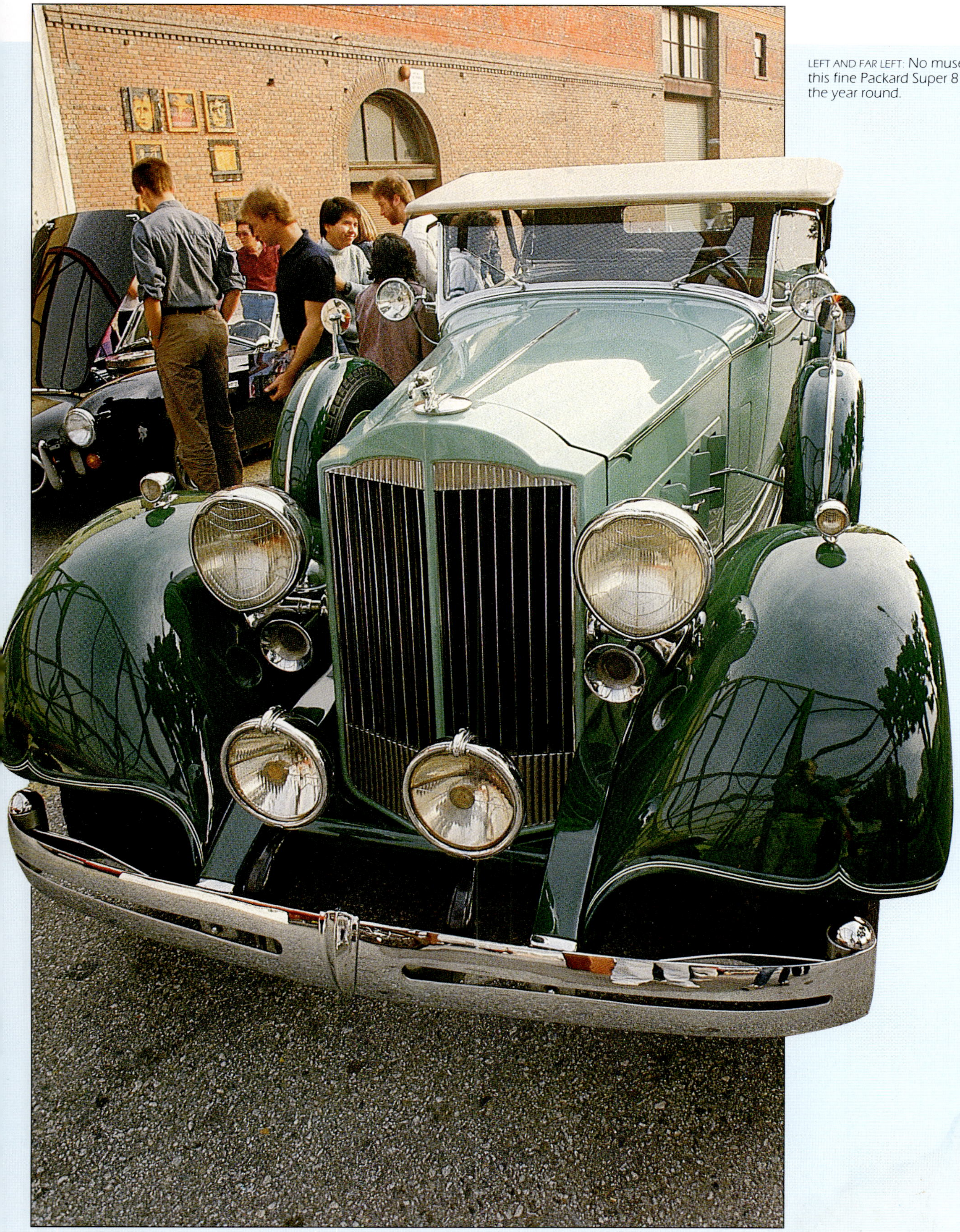

LEFT AND FAR LEFT: No museum piece, this fine Packard Super 8 is used all the year round.

CHAPTER SIX

# Racers

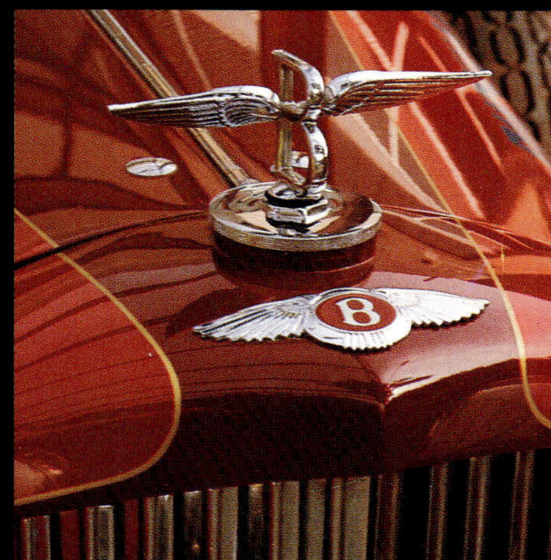

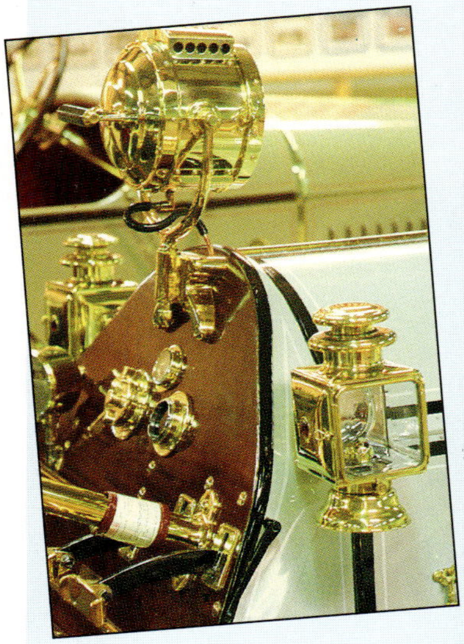

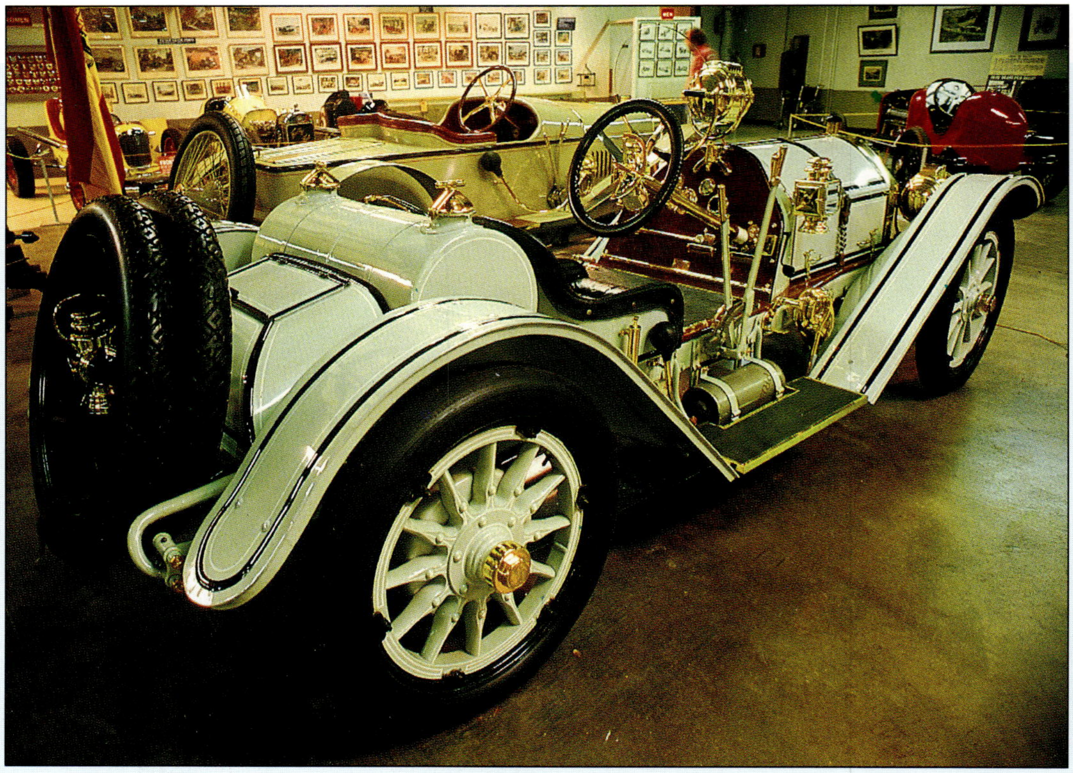

ABOVE AND RIGHT: The Mercer Raceabout 35C could be called the first American hot-rod. A simple, well-made car, it offered little more than pure performance with little concern for the driver's comfort.

It is generally held by the public that motor-racing is glamorous. To those directly involved in the activity, racing is simply very hard work under difficult conditions, usually hundreds of miles away from the home-base. It is also dangerous and exciting, and at times is frustrating, inconvenient, noisy, dirty, and always very, very expensive. Sir Thomas Lipton once said that racing a yacht in the America's Cup can be accurately compared with standing under a cold shower for hours on end, and tearing up £5 notes at the same time! The same thought must have entered every motoring journalist's head when covering some motor-racing events.

Yet to the occasional spectator any mention of being involved, even on the very edge of the sport, brings a gleam of envy into their eyes. Throw in a hint that the next race to be visited will be the Monaco Grand Prix, or the Italian G.P. at Monza, and their immediate response will be to exclaim, 'You lucky so-and-so!' Although a car race itself is very glamorous, one must not forget that, were it not for the machinery involved, the event would not happen.

The Mercer Raceabout was built in Trenton, New Jersey in the early days of this century. Mercer stopped producing cars as early as 1925, but their great days were those prior to 1915 when the Raceabout was in production. The Raceabout was, in fact, probably the best car that they ever made and certainly the most famous.

By 1910 their fastest car was the Speedster, but in that year Mercer's chief engineer, Finlay Robertson Porter, designed a road-going version of the Type 30-M racing car, and called it the Raceabout. It was an instant success, guaranteed to be safe at over 70mph, which was a remarkable speed for a roadster in those days. It looked the part of a racing car, its mechanicals barely covered by the bodywork—this gave the car a purposeful, uncompromising appearance. The engine, a four cylinder, T-headed Continental unit of 5 litres capacity had a revolution limit of 1700rpm, and produced a meagre 50hp. This large, but low powered engine endowed the Mercer with shattering performance which was helped by a primitive lightweight chassis. The monocle windscreen was just one example of weight-saving by the factory at the expense of comfort. Only the Stutz Bearcat could approach the Raceabout on the roads of America in the four years before the Great War.

After the death of the Roebling family of Brooklyn Bridge fame, and the founders of the Mercer company, Emlem Hare acquired the concern. In the ten years to 1925, after production of the Raceabout ceased, Mercer were still to make a few good cars, but as their cars became more civilized they became more conventional and of less interest to potential buyers. By 1925 the Mercer company had been reduced to just another small-time, underfinanced American car maker, under attack from the giants of the industry. They closed their doors that year never to make another sportscar again. But the Raceabout lives on in people's memories. The author saw an elderly gentleman in a wheelchair explaining the intricacies of the Raceabout next to him in the Briggs Cunningham Museum. His enthusiasm was plain to see, and it was clear that he had had more than a little experience of the car. His eyes shone with delight as he talked his son through the starting procedures, and how the car had to be controlled at speed on the rutted, dirt roads of pre-1914 California.

The mighty Daimler-Benz company of Germany, producers of Mercedes-Benz automobiles, have always used auto-racing for one purpose only, to sell their roadcars. In 1968 a graph in the export department demonstrated the success of this policy: after every period of factory racing activity sales of Mercedes-Benz cars increased. This may well be the reason for their not returning to Grand Prix racing; as their cars are always in demand, they may have no need to go back to the race tracks of the world.

But the situation was far different after World War 1, the German economy was in a very bad way, and industry was desperate to earn foreign currency and prestige. Auto-racing has always provided publicity, and success for one company was seen to reflect glory on to other German industries. It was a marvellous shopwindow for the whole German nation after the battering it had taken during the four years of the Great War, and the internal conflict that was taking place afterwards.

At the Berlin Auto Show of 1921 Mercedes-Benz introduced two new cars, the 6/25/40 and the 10/40/65. It is the former car that we are concerned with here. The designation refers to the fiscal horse-power rating of 6 taxable horse-power, the 25 to the maximum horse-power produced without the supercharger, and the 40 to the power produced with the blower. The engine of this car had a capacity of 1.5 litres. The supercharger was of the Roots-type, an American invention which used twin rotors in a sealed compartment mounted on the front of the engine, and driven by the crankshaft. This is a more efficient method of supercharging an engine than the centrifugal method as it provides boost from very low engine revolutions. It was brought into operation at the fullest extent of the throttle movement, when a multi-plate clutch operated the supercharger. In other words, when the accelerator was pressed to the floorboards the blower cut in!

The author once experienced this effect during a memorable drive in a Mercedes-Benz 540K across London when aged about 15. A doctor friend of the family owned the 540K and offered a ride one Sunday afternoon late in the summer of 1948. In those days there was very little traffic using London's roads, and we made good time to the Blackwall Tunnel under the river Thames. This old tunnel was (and still is) lined with white tiles, and these have an amplifying effect on sound. Halfway through the tunnel the good doctor floored the accelerator in second gear, and with a scream the blower engaged, the walls of the tunnel reflected the sound, amplifying it to an almost unbearable level, and with a rush we stormed out on the other side. To anyone outside the Blackwall Tunnel on that summer's day it must have sounded as though the Hounds of Hell were coming!

This was the device that Mercedes-Benz would use in all their competition cars, and many of their road cars right up to 1939. It was first used in their 1922 Targa Florio racing car. The cars for the Sicilian race were heavily modified, and carried the first twin overhead camshaft cylinder heads fitted to any Mercedes-Benz car. The engines were fitted into three converted 1914 Grand Prix chassis, given mudguards and windshields to make them look like sportscars, as the Targa Florio is for sportscars, and not G.P. machines! Count Masseti won the race in front of two French Ballots, using one of these supercharged Mercedes.

The 38/250 Mercedes-Benz sportscar of 1928 may be worthily described as one of the greatest sportscars ever built. It combined in the one vehicle high performance, superb good looks and a level of construction for which the Stuttgart factory had always been famous. The 38/250 in the Blackhawk collection looks today as if it had just left the factory, being quite immaculate in all respects. It exudes an aura of power and speed that can be felt almost as a physical thing. The engine, the heart of any car, is a 7,069 cc, six-cylinder, single overhead cam unit providing the driver with 140bhp in unsupercharged form, and 200bhp when using the blower. The supercharger was not to be used for periods of more than 20 seconds—in other words it was an overtaking device, definitely *not* to be used on long fast stretches of autobahn for mile after mile, unless frequent engine rebuilds were to be undertaken!

Even without the aid of the supercharger the Mercedes-Benz SS 38/250 could be cruised at over 110mph for hours on end. The car remained in production until 1933 as the standard sportscar made by the company, although only 111 examples were built in that time.

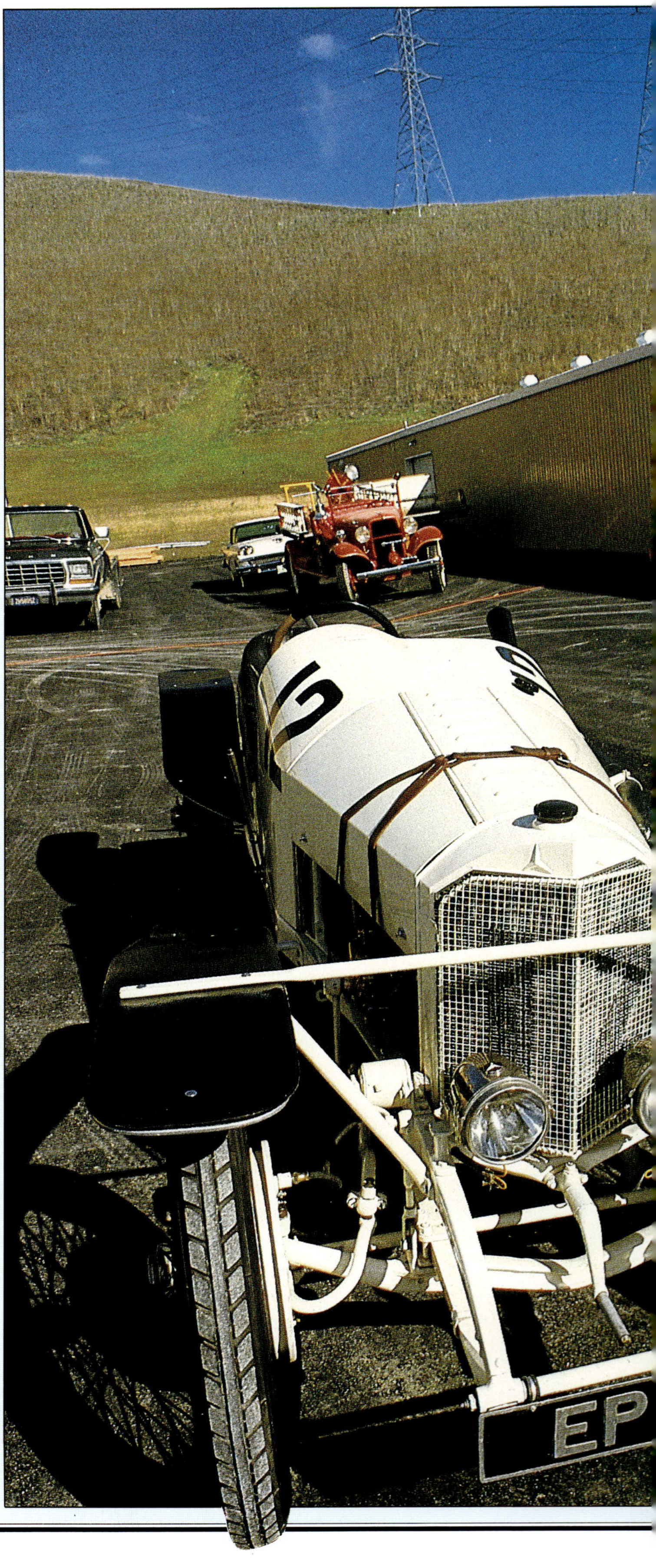

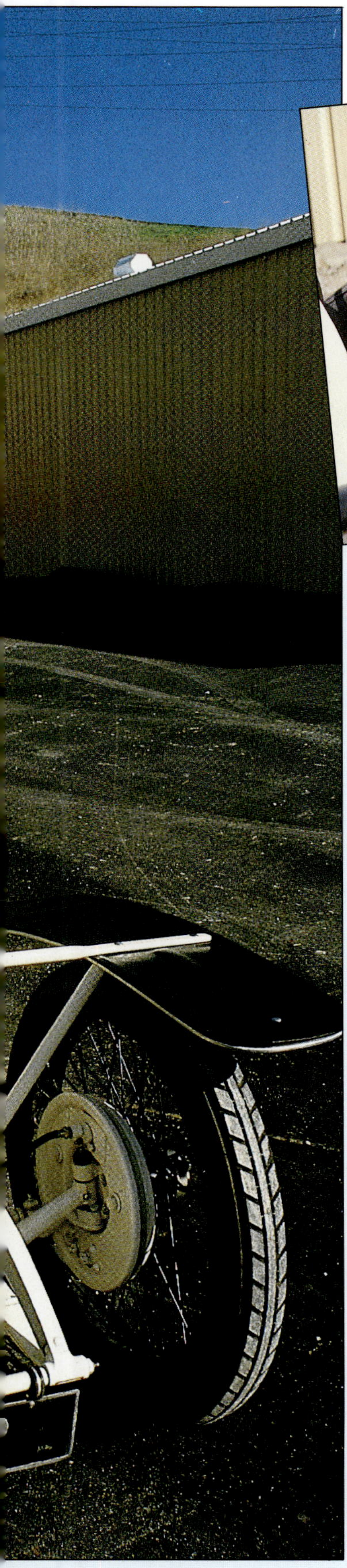

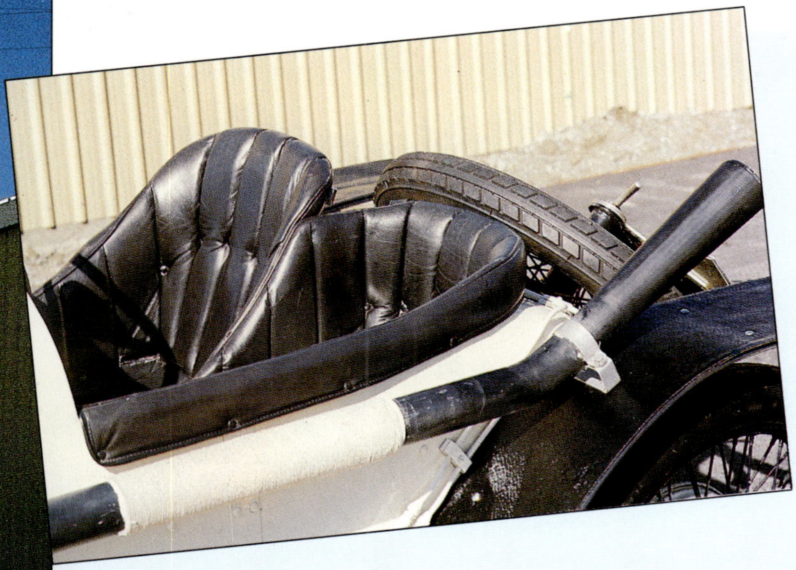

LEFT AND FAR LEFT: Mercedes-Benz have always used motor racing to develop their cars and to stimulate sales. One of their cars won the 1922 Targa Florio in Sicily by a handsome margin.

Delage Grand Prix cars for the 1926 formula were very few in number, only 7 being constructed in all. The 1.5 litre supercharged straight-8 Delage has been labelled the most beautiful Grand Prix car ever built and it was successful to boot! In one of these lovely cars, Robert Benoist won the 1926 British G.P. at the Brooklands Track.

The Delage engine contained 60 roller and ball bearings, and was recognized as being 'bulletproof'. John Burgess, the Cunningham Museum's director told of when he used to demonstrate some of the collection's cars in the Museum car park (which was very large at the time). He remembers taking out the Delage, and as a very experienced racing driver he was able to show the car off, putting it through its paces in a very thorough manner. It had rained the night before and although the hot southern Californian sun had dried up most of the car park there were still several damp patches under some trees. In crossing one of these wet areas in second gear John was astonished to get wheel spin with the revolution counter flashing round to 9,300rpm! Up to that day previous drives had seen 7,000rpm used as the maximum safe rev. limit. This figure had been calculated when the car had become part of the Cunningham Collection without any details regarding safe engine speeds. 7,000rpm was reckoned to be about right for a car that was over 50 years old. The Delage was rushed into the well-equipped Cunningham workshops, stripped down and checked for valve bounce and any other mechanical derangement. Nothing appeared to be amiss with the engine, and it was reassembled and returned to its place in the hall of the Museum. Later that year John took it to Laguna Seca for the annual Historic Car Races held there every September. He was to put on a driving display on the track of about five quick laps. Before he went out on the track, and still mindful of what had happened in the car park, John was approached by an elderly Frenchman who introduced himself as one of the Delage mechanics from the factory racing days. John

RIGHT AND FAR RIGHT: The 1927 Delage Grand Prix car has been called the perfect racing car. Even when competing against more up-to-date machinery, it still set records.

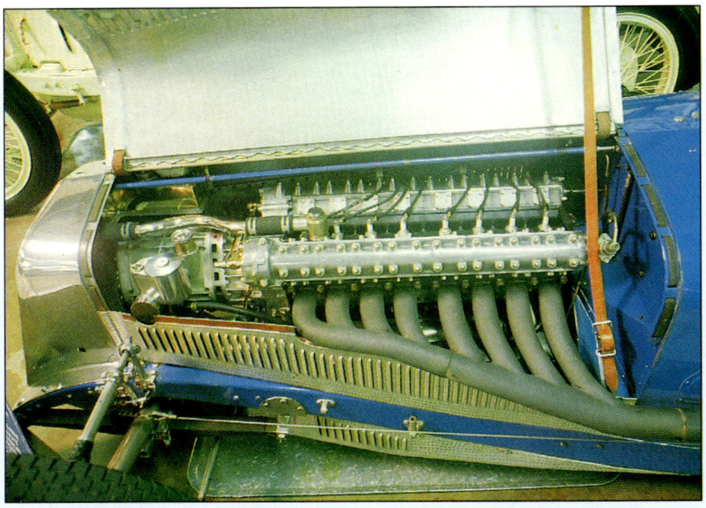

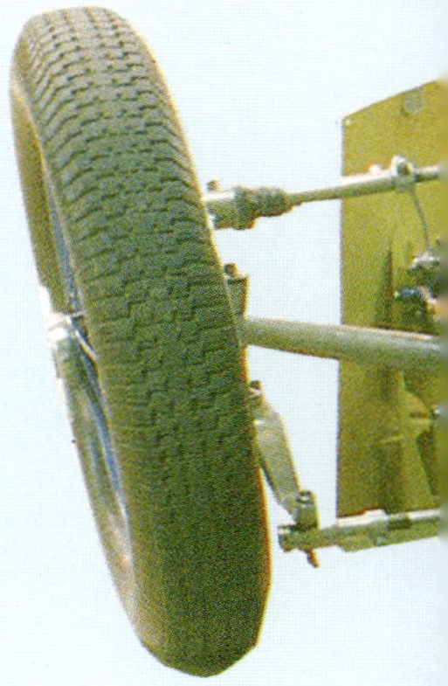

immediately asked him about rev limits for the engine. The reply was that 10,000rpm was regularly used by all the team drivers, and 9,300rpm was perfectly O.K.!! The Delage company really knew what they were doing when they designed and built these marvellous engines at 140, Avenue des Champs Elysées, Paris, back in 1926.

The Talbot Lago could be described as a racing Cinderella. A tough, French racing car of the 1950s, it carried the French colours with some distinction across Europe, competing in the Grand Prix racing programme against the might of Alfa Romeo, Ferrari and Maserati. It used an overhead valve six-cylinder engine mated to a Wilson pre-selector gearbox. What success it achieved, 1st, 2nd and 3rd in the 1937 French G.P. and 1st in the French G.P. of 1947 was largely due to its inherent durability, and its frugal fuel consumption. The car was often able to go through a full race without needing to make a pit stop for fuel. Talbot Lagos are still to be seen in the historic car races now held in many countries of the world.

The 1937 Rolls Bentley can more accurately be described as a two-seater, open Rolls-Royce. It was a much more civilized car that the vehicle made by W. O. Bentley, but lost a great deal of excitement and driver interest as a result. It will never have quite the same appeal as a W. O. Bentley car, or the same financial value. However, it is still a delightful car of the mid-1930s, and the one featured in this chapter has one special claim of interest. It was entered in the 1984 Great American Race, from Los Angeles to Indianapolis. It went on to win this new event on the public highway, and in doing so it secured for its owner a cheque for $100,000!

The Bentley is for sale as this is written, with a price tab of $100,000.

The story of the Arnolt-Bristol is very much more the story of Stanley Harold Arnolt III than that of just an automobile.

'Wacky' Arnolt was born in Chicago in 1907 into a family of bookbinders, not poor, but not wealthy either. The young Arnolt attended the University of Wisconsin and took a degree in mechanical engineering, but when it was time for him to find a

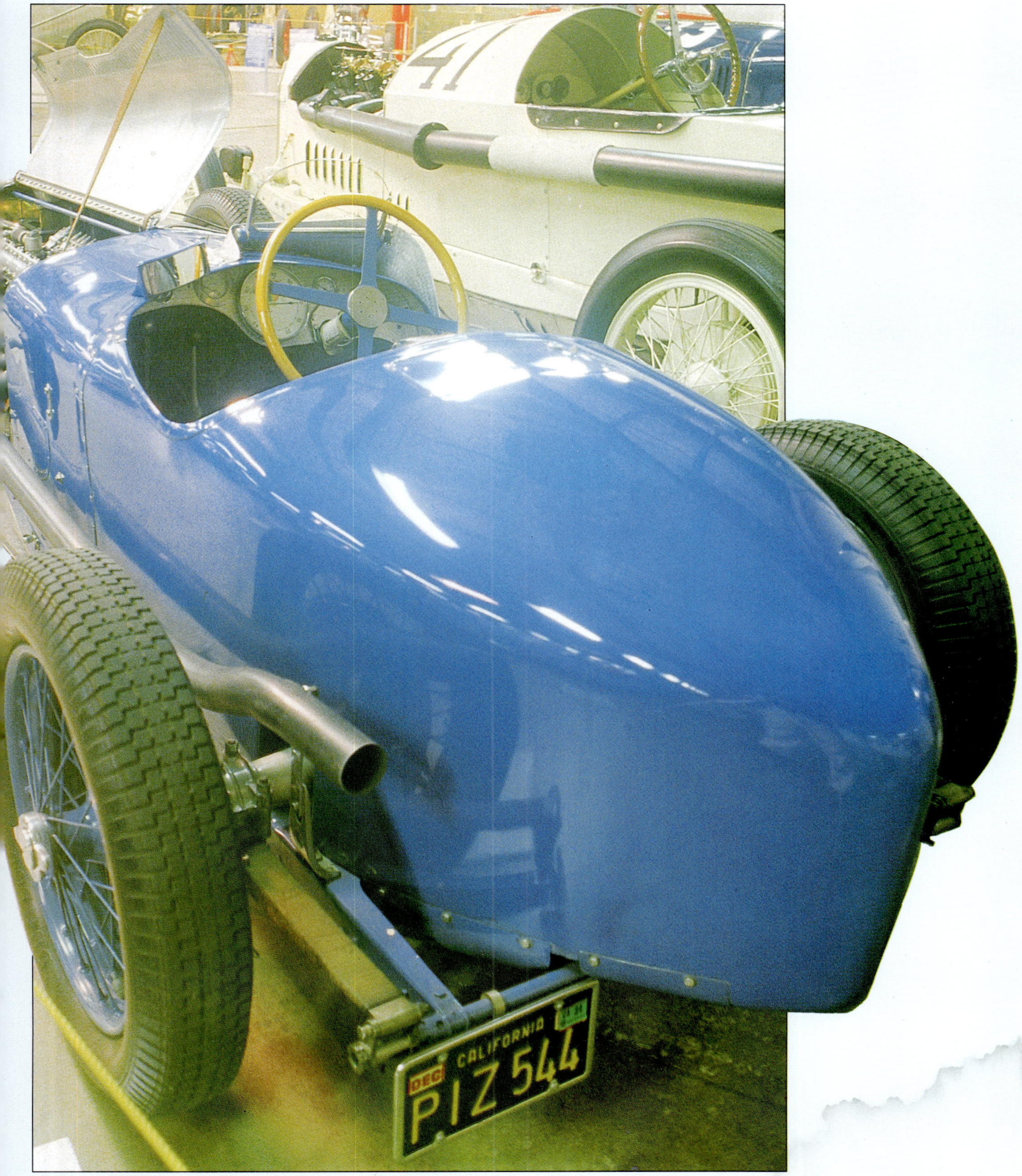
41
CALIFORNIA
PIZ 544

RIGHT AND FAR RIGHT: The Talbot Lago was a French racing car of the 1950s. Although its design was already out of date when the car was new, its fuel economy and durability brought it some success.

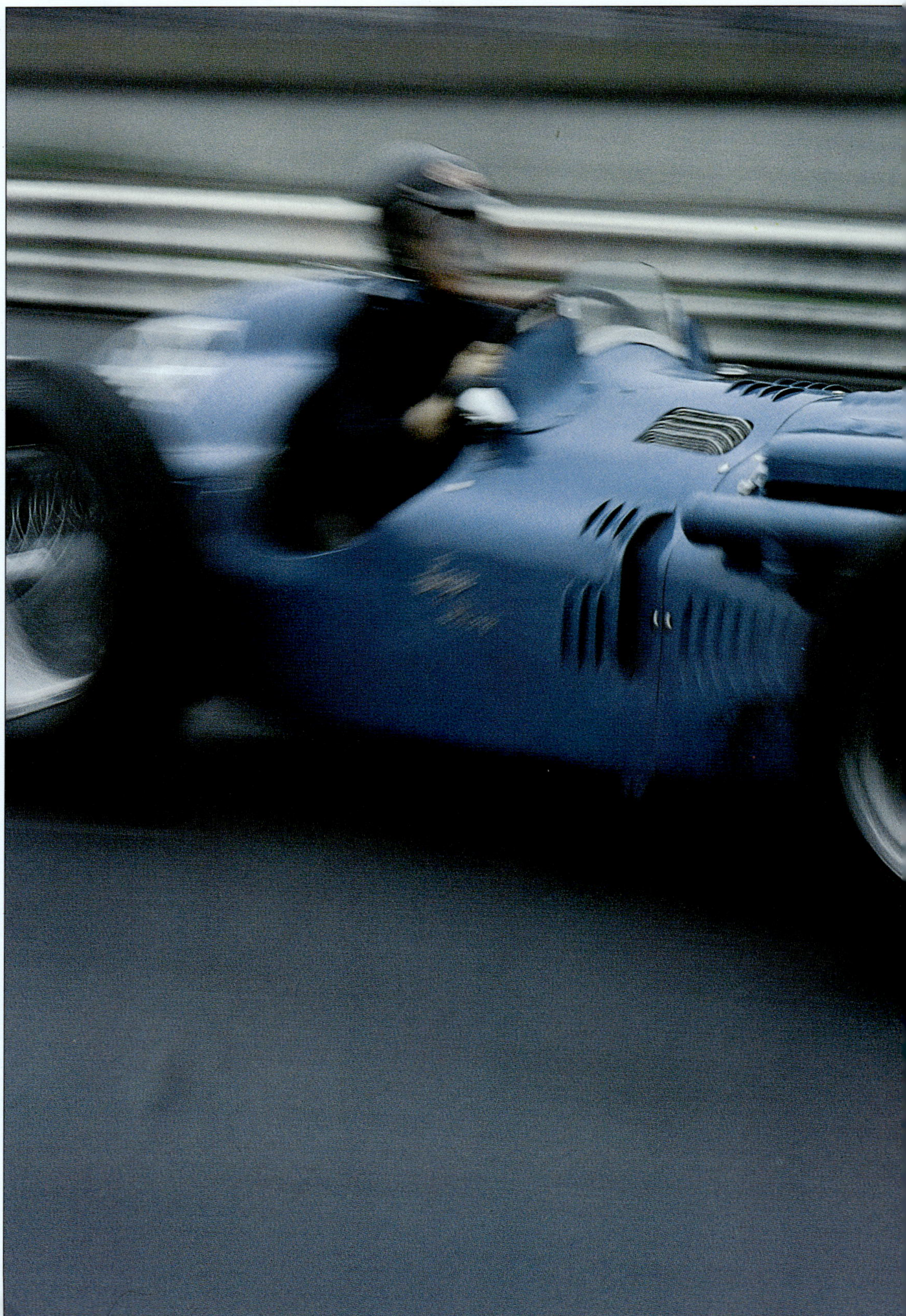

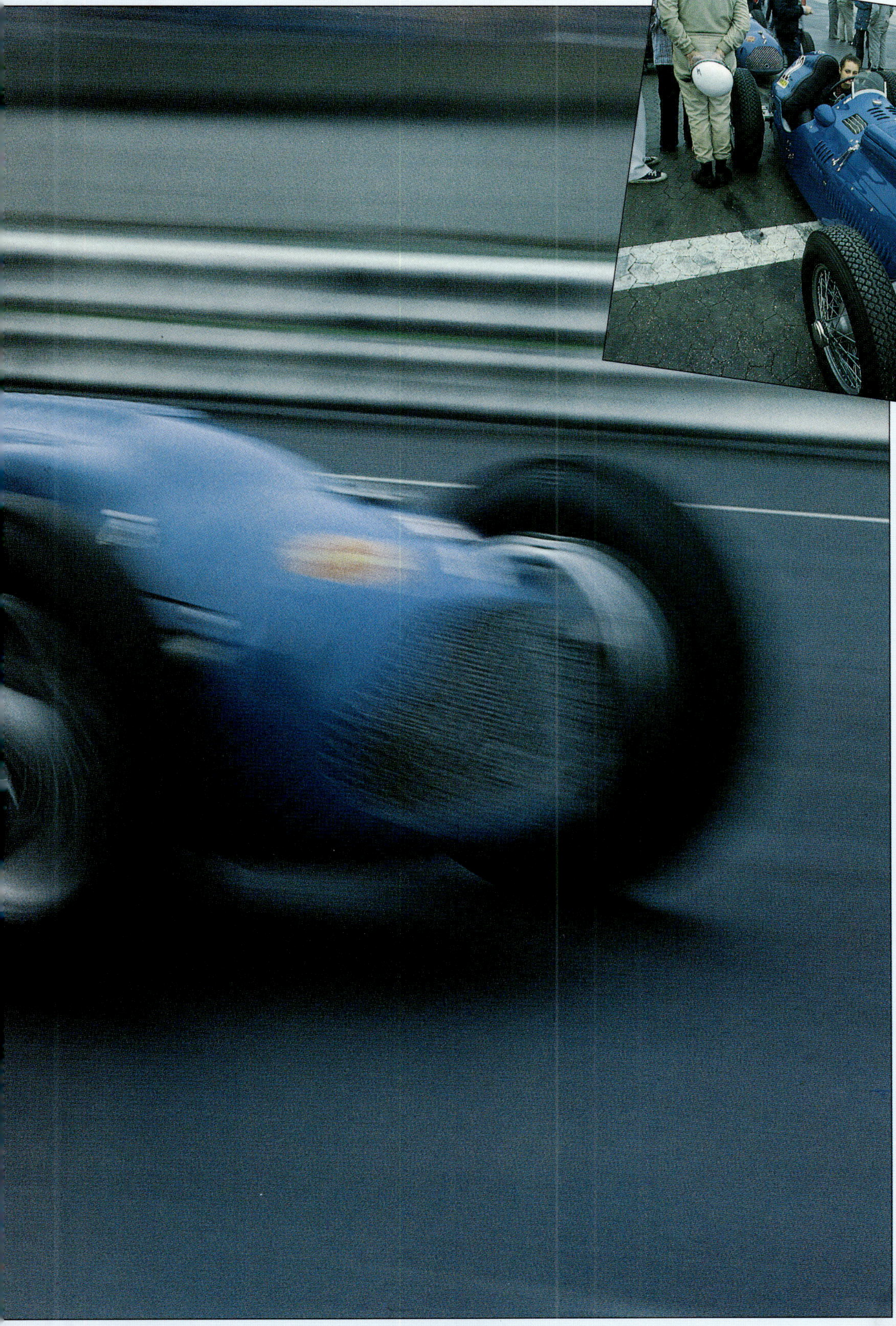

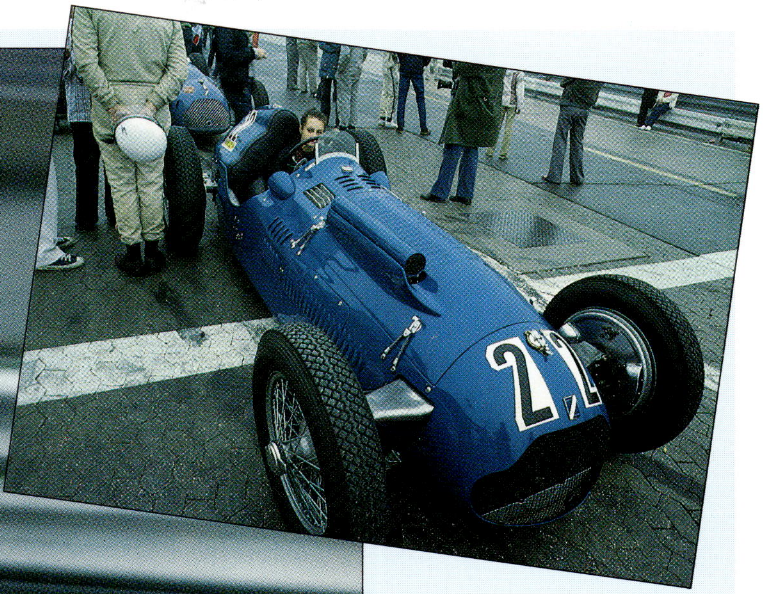
2

## TONY CROOK

Tony Crook, the managing director of the Bristol Company, can be variously described as a gentleman, businessman, racing driver, salesman, and test-driver.

It was as a racing driver that he first came to the notice of the general public, having the distinction of never having been beaten by another driver in a car of equal performance. His greatest success was as a driver of a Frazer Nash sportscar in the race that supported the Monaco Grand Prix. He had a tremendous tussle with the Lancia of Valenzano before taking the lead, and holding it to the line. From 1946 to 1955 he drove Bristol-engined cars in more than 400 races all over Europe.

With the then Mr George White, and two other directors he took over the car making part of the Bristol Aeroplane Company in 1956 when the parent company split it off to become Bristol Cars Ltd. In 1960, with Sir George White, he bought up the company separating it from any further control of Bristol Aeroplane. It is no coincidence that it was in this year that the first V-8 engined Bristol appeared, the 407 model.

His company has full order books, a world-wide reputation for excellence and yet is run in the most friendly, easy manner. Tony apparently knows each and every owner (and car) made and sold over the last thirty years.

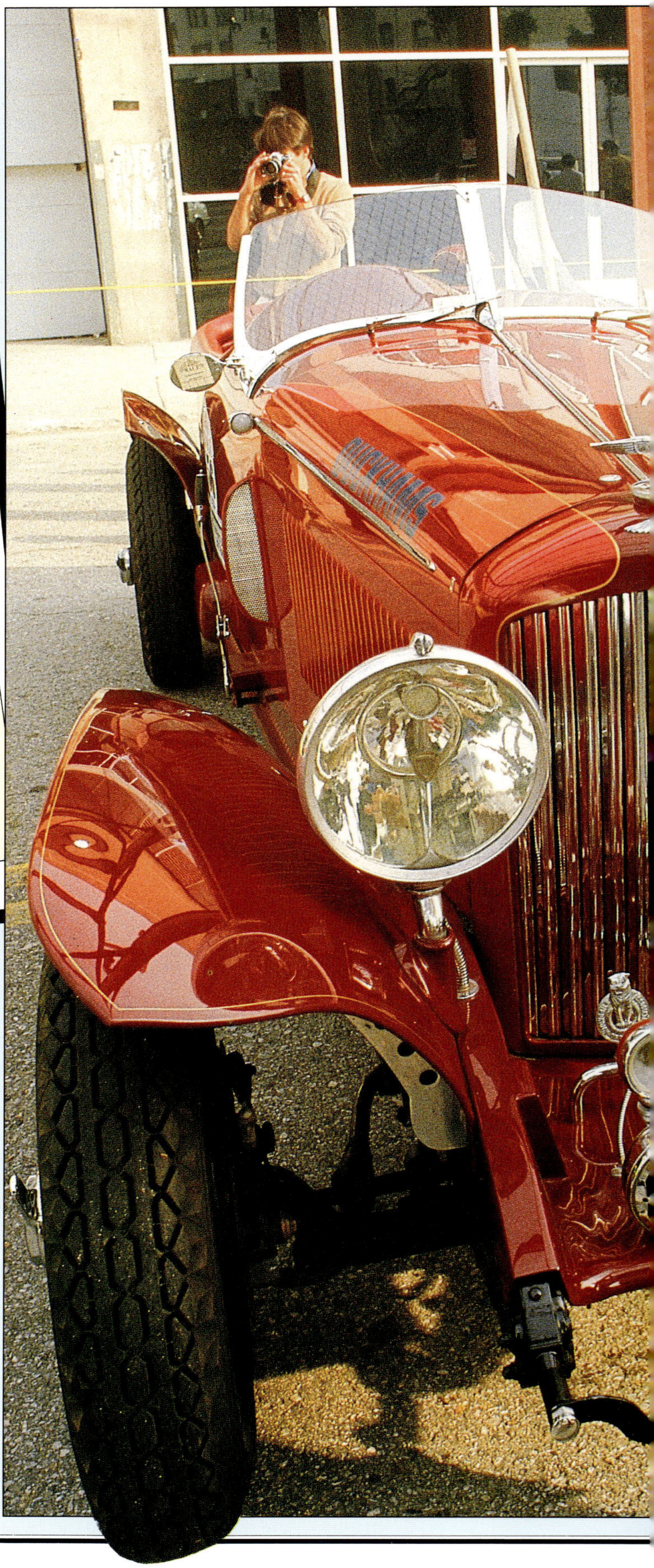

job the Depression was well under way in the USA, and jobs for young mechanical engineers were in short supply.

For the next seven years Wacky, like millions of his countrymen got by, but it was a struggle for someone so eager to make his mark in the world. Then in early 1939 the big chance came along—Arnolt was offered the full manufacturing rights to a small marine engine, the Sea-mite. Scraping together the small amount of necessary capital to buy up the complete company, Wacky moved into ownership of the concern that was to make his fortune. The secret was in his timing; within months of his take-over, Word War Two had broken out, and for the next six years the USA was to be the free world's shipbuilder. Every one of the thousands of American-built ships needed a whole host of small powered craft such as lifeboats and tenders. Luckily for Arnolt, nearly all of these small boats were powered by a Sea-mite. The Arnolt Sea-mite factories expanded to service the government contracts, and in doing so allowed Wacky to move into other products. Very soon the Arnolt enterprise was a coast to coast conglomerate, and making lots of money.

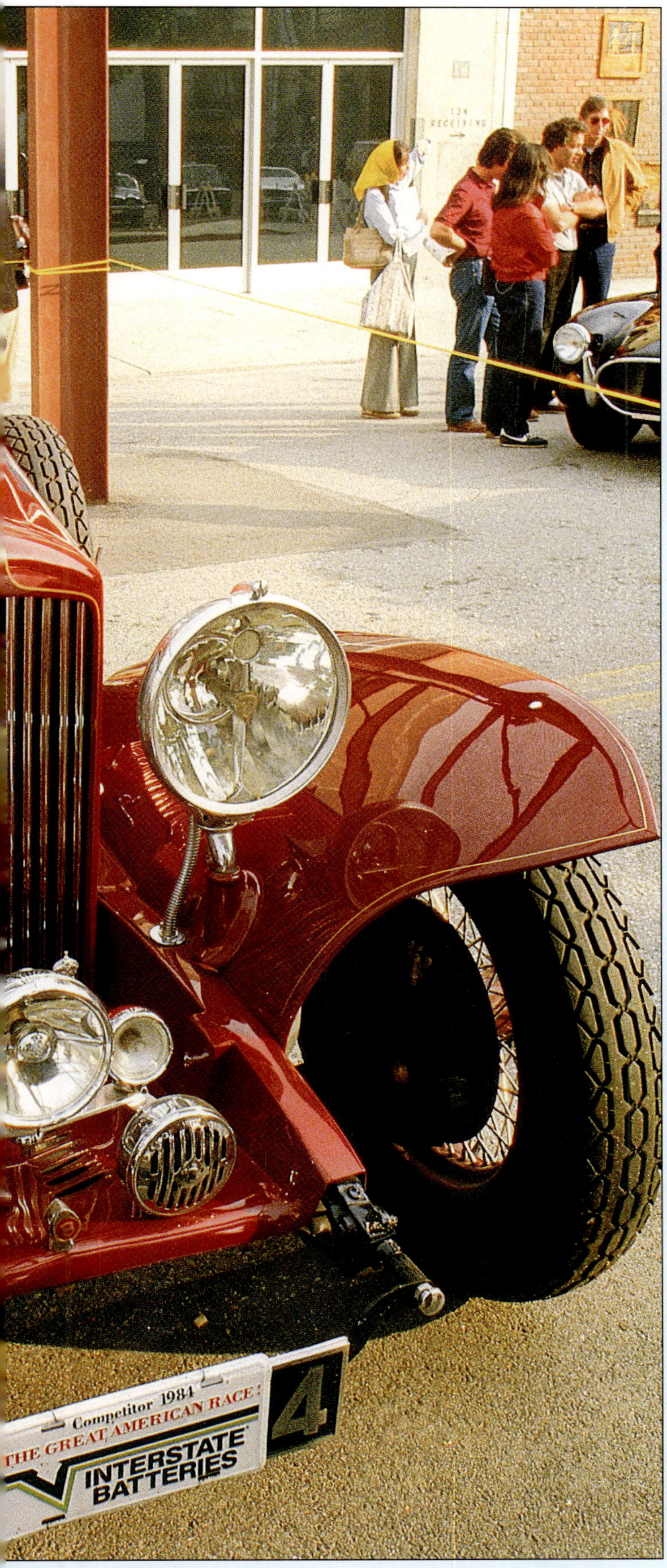


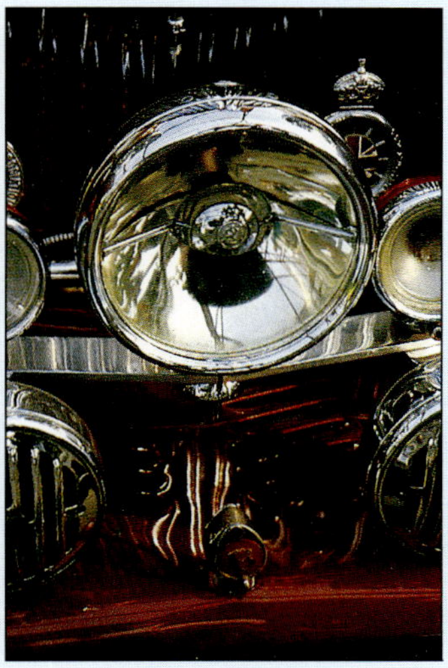

In 1931, Rolls-Royce took over the bankrupt Bentley company. Bentleys of the early 1930s were refined cars that lacked real performance. This American-owned 3½-litre example competed in the 1984 Great American Race.

At the 1952 Turin Motor Show Wacky appeared in his Stetson hat and Texas cowboy boots looking every inch the European's idea of the typical American millionaire. On the Bertone stand he noticed two very attractive M.G.-based sportscars that Nuccio Bertone had produced in a last minute attempt to stave off the collapse of his company. Bertone was hoping to persuade a major car-maker of his enormous talents as a coachbuilder, and was bowled over when this American giant ordered 200 finished Bertone-M.G.s, a move that saved the Bertone company. When two years later he saw the Bristol 404 sports coupé, it increased his desire to go in to motor-racing, but the 404 as it came from the Bristol company was too heavy to be really competitive, so Arnolt turned to Bertone for the answer. With the help of one of Bristol's best engineers, Jim Watt, Bertone produced the sensational looking Arnolt-Bristol coupé. Nuccio built a steel body on to the Bristol chassis as the lines of the car could be duplicated only in this material, alloy plainly ruling out the possibility of following the Bertone lines. It is interesting to note that the alloy-bodied Bristol 404 as it came from the factory weighed 300lbs more than the steel-bodied Arnolt-Bristol! Not only was the Arnolt-Bristol lighter, but in 1954 it was almost half the price of the Bristol 404; $4645 against the $9946 of the 404!

Using the brakes from the Bristol 403 helped to keep costs down, as did using Italian craftsmen, but even so it is remarkable that Wacky could make and sell his version of the Bristol so much more cheaply than the original model.

In all Arnolt sold 130 out of a total of 142 cars built—the remaining 12 were destroyed in a warehouse fire. The film star Lee Marvin owned one, as did Air Force General Curtis Le May, and the model labelled the 'Bolide' was raced all over the USA with some success. But probably the car, and Wacky's, greatest success came in 1955 when he persuaded the retired French racing driver René Dreyfus to lead a team of Bolides in the Sebring International Sportscar Race in Florida. The team did rather well finishing in 1st, 2nd and 4th positions!

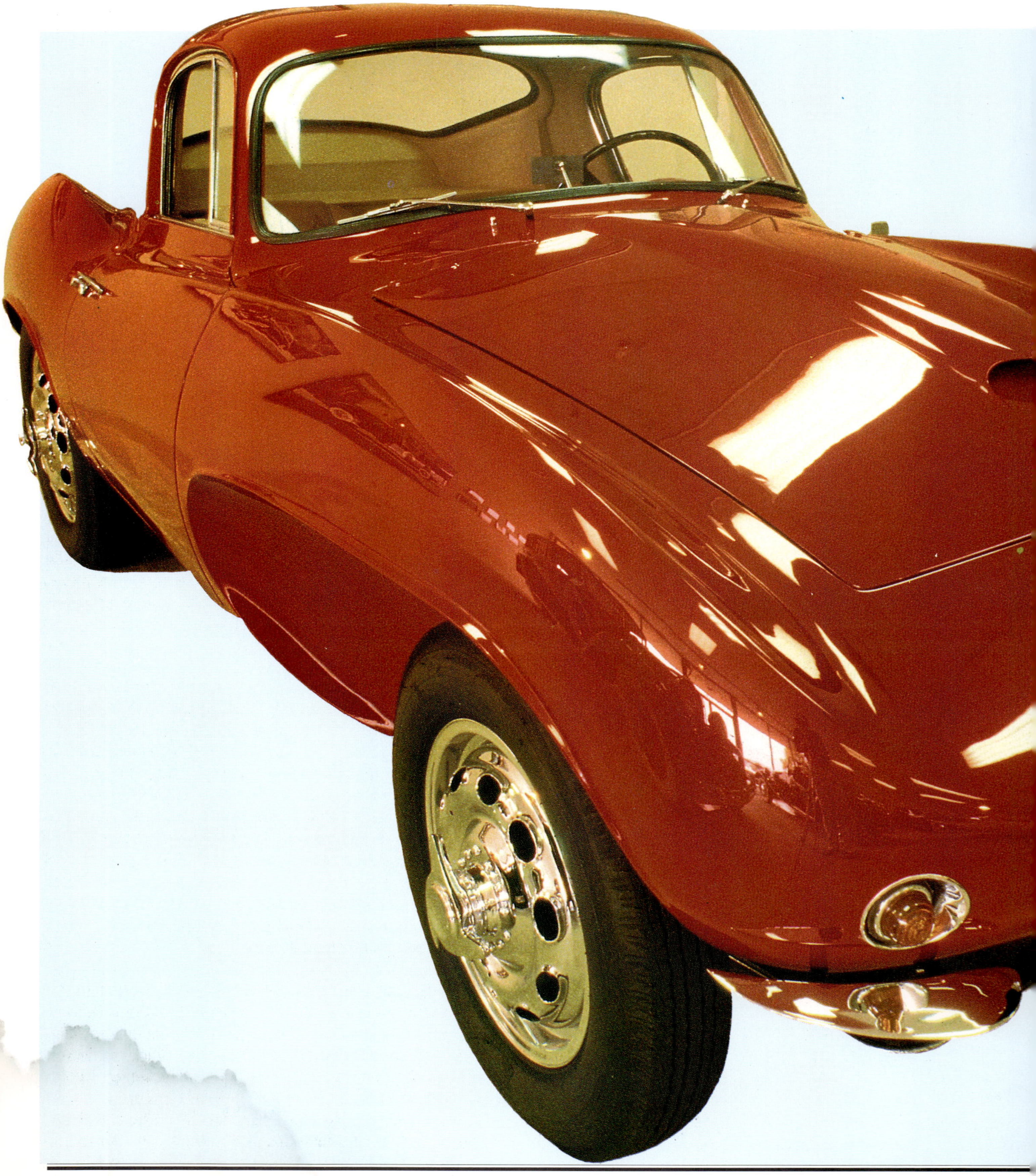

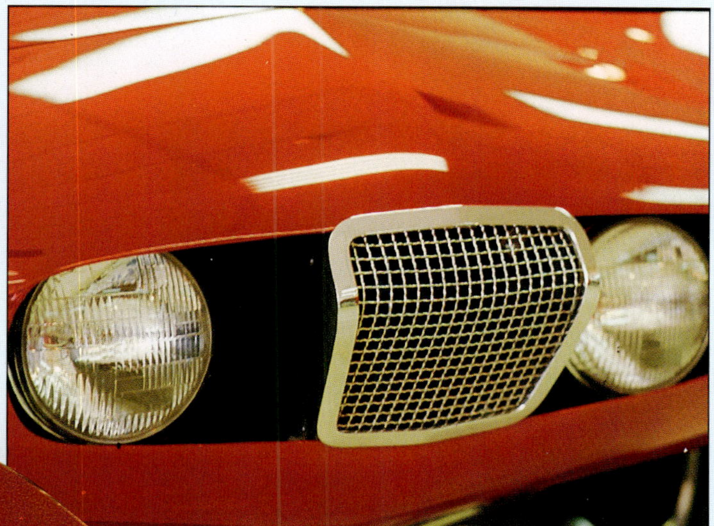

American money, an Italian body and a British chassis and engine were the formula for the Arnolt-Bristol. Its fantastic handling often helped it to beat more powerful cars.

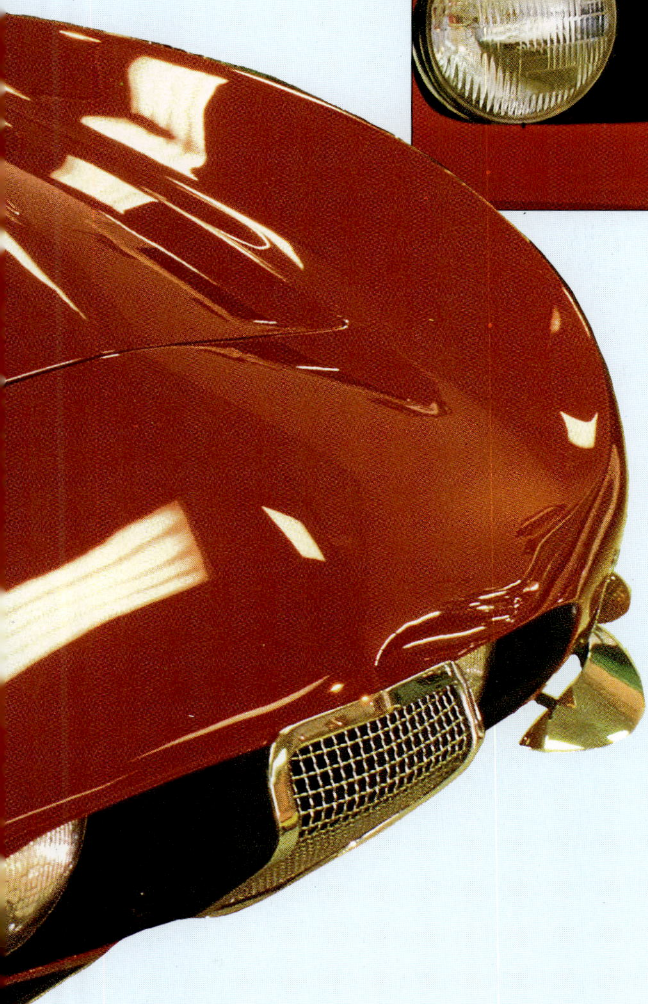

Even by the standards of the day the Arnolt-Bristol was not a really high performance car, not having a great deal of horse power. However, the car was balanced by agility and good roadholding, together with fine braking and steering characteristics. The Arnolt-Bristol team worked on the basic racing principle of, 'To finish First, first one has to Finish'.

As it came from Wacky's showrooms, the Bolide could only boast a top speed of 112mph, and a standing-start quarter mile in 17 seconds, with a 0-60mph time of 10.1 seconds. The model was last raced in 1960, by which time there were many other cars that were cheaper and faster. The beauty of the car, its racing history, and the story of its founder all make it a candidate for a glamorous car.

Stanley Harold Arnolt III died in 1963, and because he made no allowance for anyone to properly succeed him, the Arnolt car died with him.

Briggs Cunningham is the other face of the Wacky Arnolt coin, a wealthy man in his own right, and an established hero in the view of the American public by virtue of his exploits as a successful yachtsman before he turned to racing car production and driving. He manufactured cars for a very short period, only five years. Briggs was quite successful on the race tracks of America and Europe, then at the height of his fame he closed down his Florida factory and returned to California to establish his excellent Automobile Museum at Costa Mesa.

Briggs' racing programme began in 1949 with a modified Cadillac sedan at Le Mans with a Frick-Tappet modified engine. This apparently unsuitable car finished 10th! In the same race that year Briggs entered another Cadillac-engined special which was so big and ugly that the French dubbed it 'Le Monstre'. The alloy body might have been aerodynamically sound, but it really was awful to look at. Even so it finished the punishing race just behind his other car, in 11th place.

For the 1952 Le Mans race Cunningham developed and entered his most successful sports/racing car the C-4R model. This

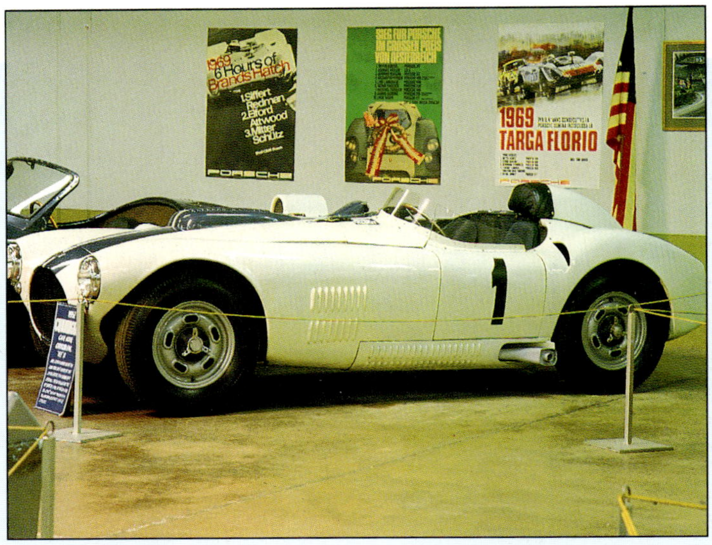


Briggs Cunningham was a rich amateur racing driver who wanted to win the Le Mans 24-hour race in a car bearing his own name. He almost succeeded in this Cunningham C-4R (right), finishing in 4th place.

was powered by a 300hp Chrysler V8 engine driving through a ZF four-speed gearbox. The whole car, like all the Cunninghams, was most beautifully crafted—the brakes, of the drum variety, were so elegant that a set has been mounted on a wall plaque in the Museum and looks like a piece of modern sculpture. However, beautiful as they undoubtedly were, they suffered from heat fade because they were too large in diameter, and too narrow in width! These two factors meant that the peripheral speed of the drums was so great that the heat build-up could not be dissipated quickly enough. Smaller, wider drums would have handled the problem much more easily, but at the time of the French classic the problem had been neither located nor rectified.

But despite this braking deficiency the C-4R gave Briggs Cunningham his best Le Mans finish—he drove the car into 4th position at the end of the 24 hours. The following year saw a development of the Cunningham sports/racer with the appearance of the C-5R which, driven by Walters and Fitch got even closer to the winner's circle finishing in 3rd position.

At this point it was becoming obvious that with the involvement of the massively financed Mercedes-Benz racing programme, small-scale efforts such as those of the Cunningham team stood virtually no chance in international racing, and Briggs ran his car operation down, finally closing the Palm Beach factory in 1955.

1966 was the year that the Ford sportscar racing effort finally, after immense expenditure of men, materials, and money, achieved success at the one race that really counts, the Le Mans 24 Hours race.

In 1962, the Ford company had made approaches to Enzo Ferrari with a view to buying his company. Enzo was interested, and for a few months teams of lawyers, engineers, and administrators commuted between Dearborn and Maranello. But in the end, and following delay after delay, Ferrari pulled out of the deal. Ford then scouted Europe for a car that could be developed as a Ford racing-car. In England they finally narrowed the list of possibles down to two, Lotus and Lola.

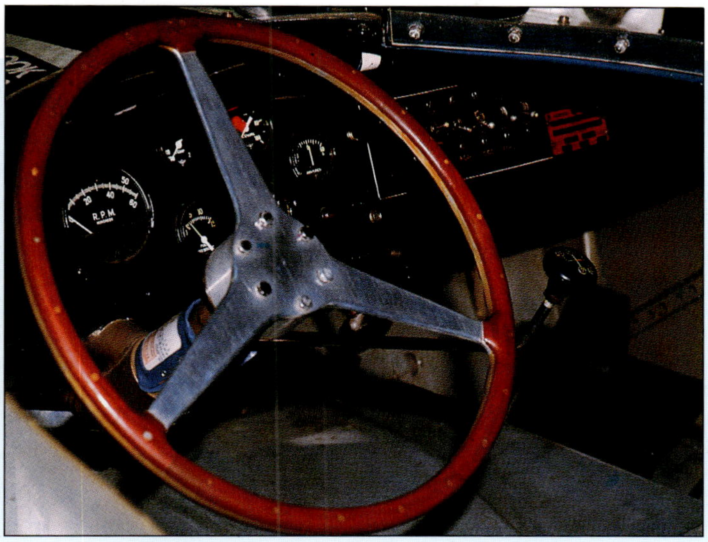

Len Terry explained how the final decision was made between these two companies. Colin Chapman the Lotus boss was confident that his company would secure the very lucrative contact with Ford, and was devastated when it was announced that Eric Broadley and his tiny Lola concern would be the ones to gain the support that Ford were offering. Broadley had shown his idea of what a modern sports/racing coupé should look like at the London Racing Car Show earlier that year—he simply called it the Lola GT, and it was beautiful. Broadley was a more amenable partner than Chapman, his car had the potential to do what Ford wanted and much of the hard work had already been done, so Broadley was the man that Ford selected.

As an aftermath to this decision Lotus rushed into producing their Type 30 sports/racing car, with Colin Chapman swearing to use it to blow the Ford/Lola car off the race tracks of the world. The Type 30, and its successor the Type 40, were probably the worst Lotus competition cars ever built; most drivers hated them as on the track they were obviously very difficult to drive competitively, only the genius of Jim Clark ever succeeding in keeping the Type 30 on the road and over the line at the finish. Eric Broadley signed a two-year contract with Ford, John Wyer was engaged to manage the racing operation, and Carroll Shelby would handle the Ford GT racing team. In June 1963 the Ford Advanced Vehicle Operation was formed to research, build, and develop the ex-Lola GT now called the GT-40, because it stood 40 inches (actually 40½ inches!) high.

The GT-40 engine would be the Fairlane alloy-block Indy 4-cam engine of 4.2 litre capacity developing 350hp. A Colotti 4-speed gearbox was fitted and was to prove a constant source of problems from then on.

The Le Mans 24 Hours race was the target for the Ford effort, as it is the most prestigious race in the sportscar racing world. Ford had ten months to prepare, and after a period of intense activity entered the 1964 season with high hopes.

Of their efforts in this, their first year in this highly competitive class of international motor-racing all that need be said is that

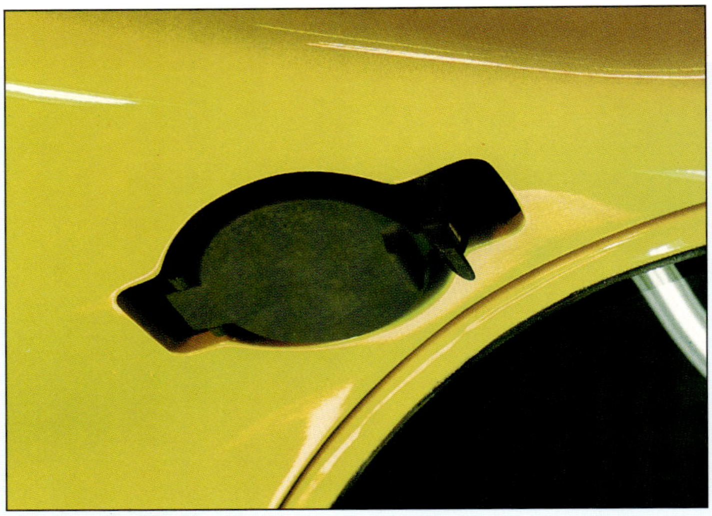

they entered ten races, and failed to finish in any of them!!

Eric Broadley did not renew the offered extension to his contract, and left after the 1964 season.

Ford contracted the Shelby-American organization to take over the preparation and development of the GT-40 programme. Phil Remington and the Englishman, Ken Miles, were given the task of making the car competitive, and with Carroll Shelby they set about this task. One improvement made was to replace the Fairlane Indy engine with a race-proven Cobra 289cu. inch unit. New ZF gearboxes were substituted for the unreliable Colotti that had been the cause of so many breakdowns in 1964. The engine cooling system was improved, aerodynamics sorted out, cast magnesium Halibrand wheels replaced the Borrani wire wheels, and bigger, better brakes were installed.

As a result the new GT-40s won the first two races of 1965 at Daytona and Sebring. But the Ferrari threat was getting stronger all the time, and the pressure from them meant that no more races were won by Ford that year, the failure to win Le Mans being the ultimate bitter blow. They withdrew from the remaining races after Le Mans that year!

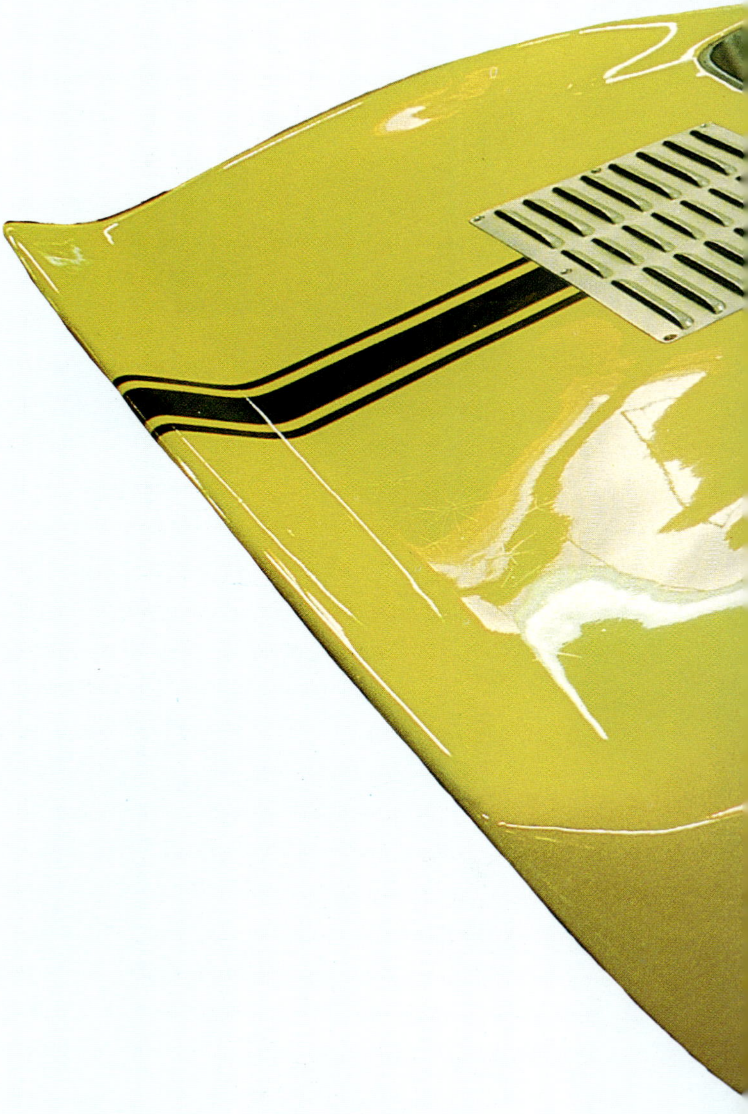

During the 1965 season a bigger 427 cu. inch engine had been tried out since it delivered a reliable 500plus horsepower, and this was obviously the way forward in the 1966 season. With this engine the GT-40 became known as the Mark II.

1966 and 1967 saw the Ford racing effort finally gain the coveted win at Le Mans, in 1967 by the greatest margin over the previous race record in history. Gurney and Foyt drove the winning GT-40 Mark IV covering 3249.6 miles in the 24 hours period, at an average speed of 135.48mph. Nobody will ever know the final cost to Ford of winning those two Le Mans races—one can only guess at the number of zeros on the balance sheet.

When Phil Hill was asked which racing cars he most liked driving, his answer was just a little surprising; he listed only two cars, the Ford GT-40, and the Chaparral—the highest accolade any racing car racing car manufacturer could wish for. In the Briggs Cunningham Auto Museum there is a yellow GT-40 on display. It is there on loan from Jim Toensing of Newport Beach, close by the Museum. Jim is a remarkably fine machinist, and he has restored the GT-40 to its original specification, that is with the Fairlane 4-OH Camshaft engine. In view of the problems that Shelby-American had with this engine, even with the fullest backing from the giant Ford company. Jim Toensing might have been suspected of going about his restoration the wrong way. However the Toensing touch was good enough to convert the fractious engine into a docile, well behaved unit that is not only immensely powerful, but can be driven on the public highway without any problems. The whole car is as beautifully turned out as the engine, and looking at it in the Cunningham Museum makes one wish it could be demonstrated by John Burgess around the car park at the side of the Museum building. A very great competition car in splendid condition.

By using its almost unlimited resources, the Ford Motor Company developed the Le Mans-winning GT40. After victories in the 1966 and '67 races, the car became an instant classic.

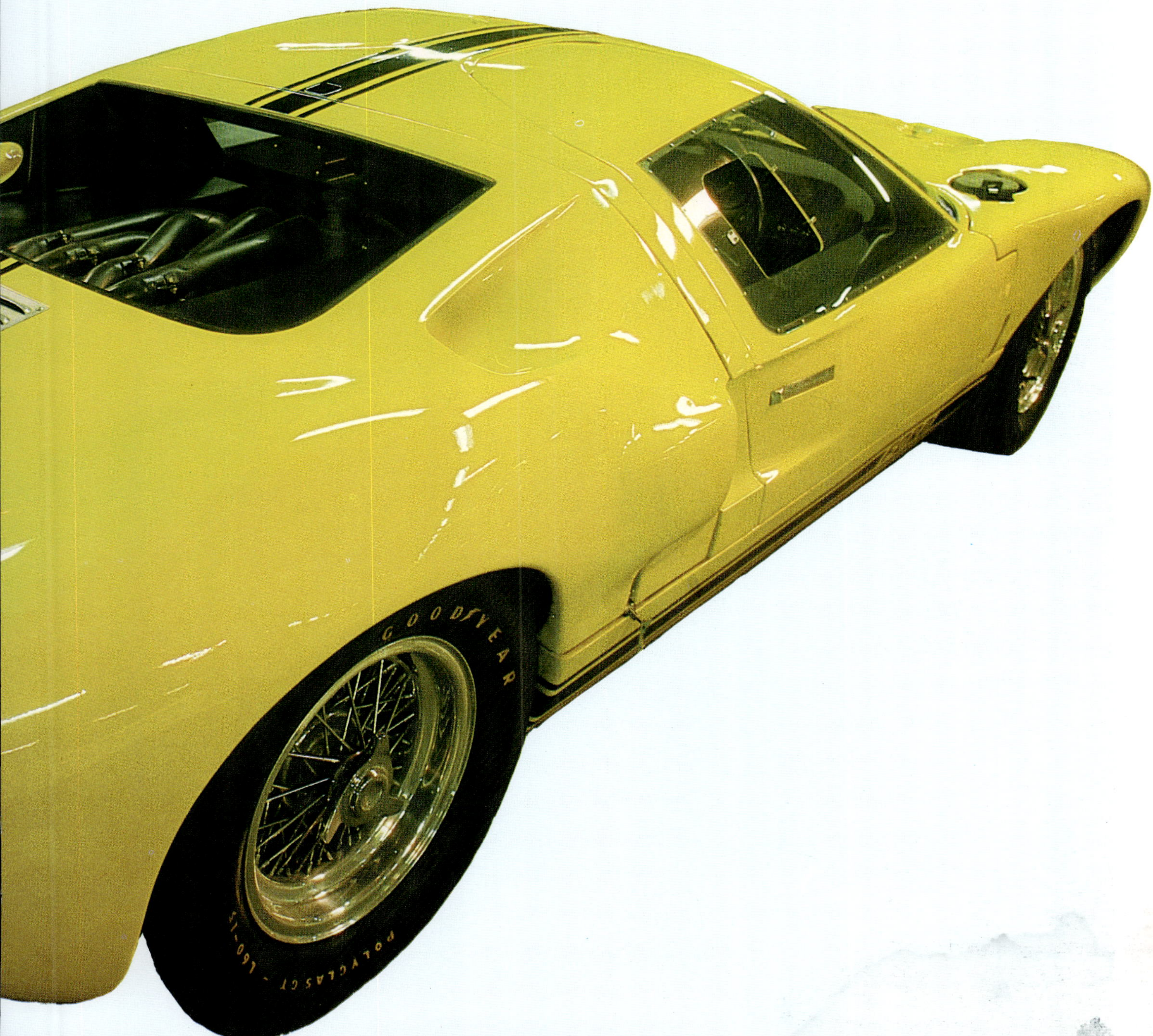

The Bucciali was a complex machine that was never marketed with any real conviction; its constructors were already dogged by the effects of the Depression in the early 1930s.

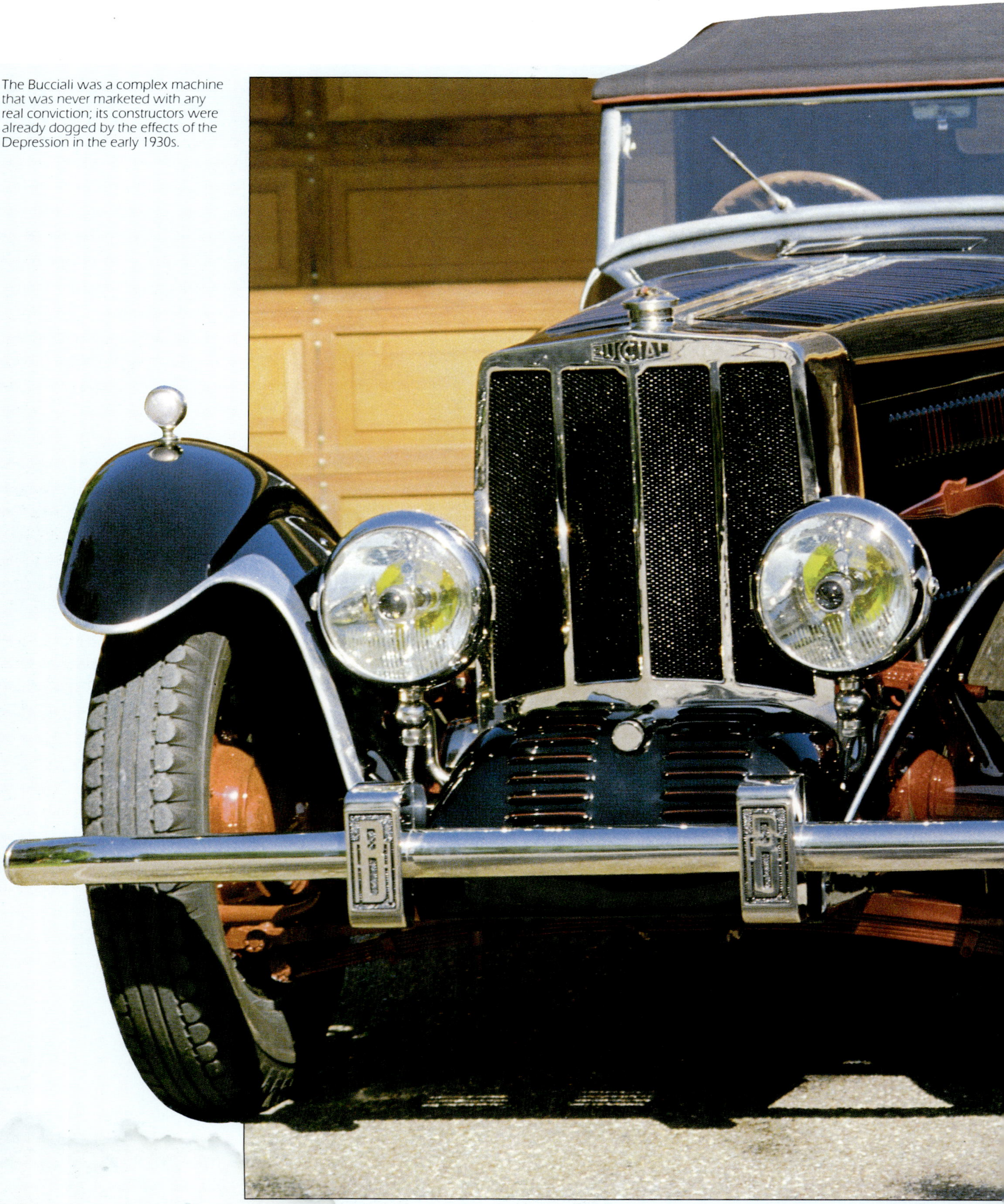

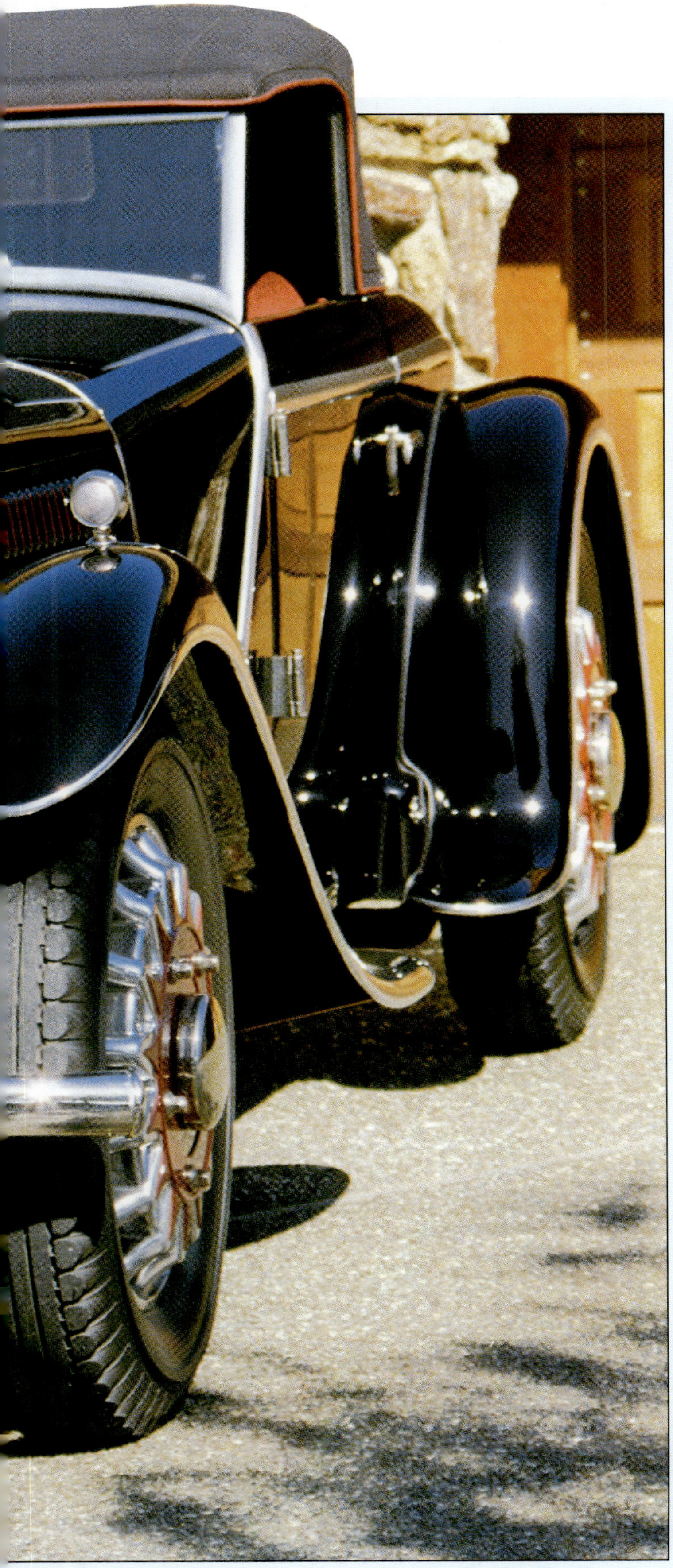

Many of the early car designers had an engineering background in steam locomotive and railroad work, or in heavy electrical equipment construction. However, one make of automobile can claim a musical design history on the part of its designer and constructor. This vehicle is the Bucciali, made by the Bucciali brothers, Angelo and Paul-Albert in Paris between 1922 and 1933.

Their father had been born in Corsica, but had left that island to move to Boulogne-sur-Mer to repair and build church organs. His two sons worked for some time at this profession before leaving Boulogne to go to Paris to make their fortune.

They had already turned their hand to car building, but until they got to Paris their work had not been very successful. In the capital city they established themselves, and began to construct their masterpiece, a car of very radical design. Firstly it featured front wheel drive, at the time a controversial method of driving a vehicle. They used a rather inefficient transmission system that was heavy, expensive, and made driving the car irksome in the extreme. In fact, the author's first sight of a Bucciali was seeing it at the foot of the steep hill that leads up to the garage that houses the pick of the Blackhawk Collection. The large car was sitting there, the side valve straight-8 Continental engine rumbling away as the driver searched for first gear so as to be able to tackle the hill. It took him several minutes before he located the right slot, and with a mighty jolt the selector went home, and the Bucciali was able to ascend the hill.

During the short life of the Bucciali company, the two brothers stayed in business by the skin of their teeth, full of very interesting ideas, but there was never enough money to realize their full potential, and the times were not the right ones for launching radical approaches to automotive problems.

In their TAV-8 and Double Huit series of designs the Buccialis came up with such features as front-wheel drive, electrical operation of the front brakes, servo-assistance for the mechanical rear brakes, and the oddball transmission system that had step-

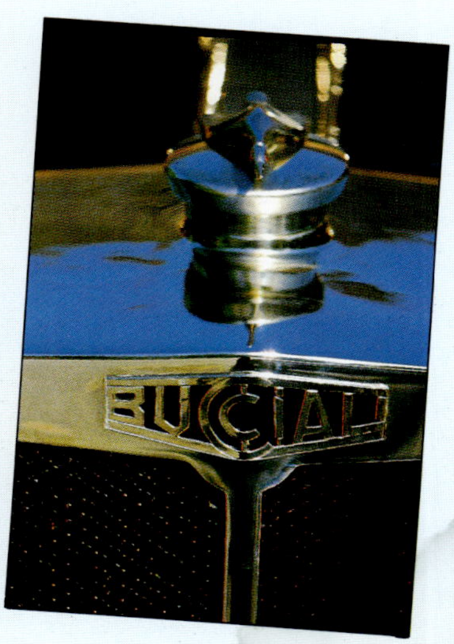

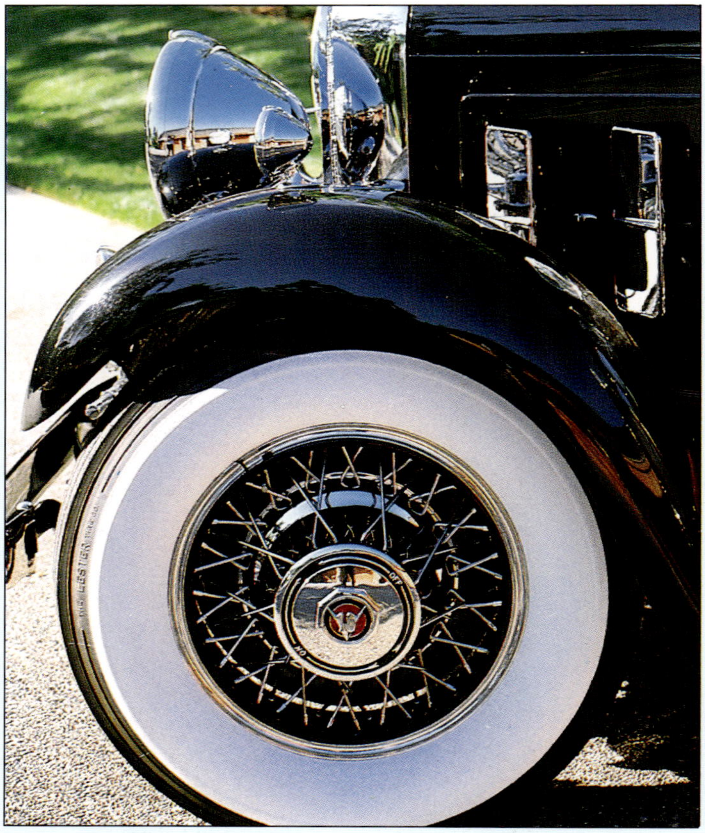

down gears between engine and road wheels before the clutch, which imposed a four times increased loading on the gearbox which component consequently had to be very much heavier, with bigger and stronger internals than would otherwise have been required. This made driving the Bucciali very difficult, and gave the driver a hard time!

For engines the Buccialis offered the Continental 3.8 litre straight-8 with 120hp, and a remarkable V16 side-valve unit that they only claimed produced between 155 and 170hp; not a great deal of power for a 7.8 litre motor! However, the lack of same was probably an advantage as it had to drive the front wheels of the car and more would have caused extra problems. Apart from a show display chassis there seems to be no record of a Double Huit ever reaching a customer's hands and being driven on the road.

The owner of the TAV-8 shown in the photograph explains that driving a Bucciali was not one of the great motoring delights. In a nutshell, it was very slow, very expensive, difficult to stop and had an awkward gear change, and its fuel consumption was never better than 10-12mpg. However, the stork emblem on the bonnet a reminder of Paul-Albert's service in the French Air Force during World War One in the Squadron Cigogne (Stork)—its sensational looks—set the car apart. With a Saoutchik body, a Bucciali could cost over $50,000 in 1930, a very substantial sum of money.

Just before the Bucciali factory closed down in 1933, the two brothers accompanied Coldwell S. Johnson, an American

Cadillac, in the 1930s, built some of the best quality mass-produced cars ever made. This example was used for many years in India for hunting tigers.

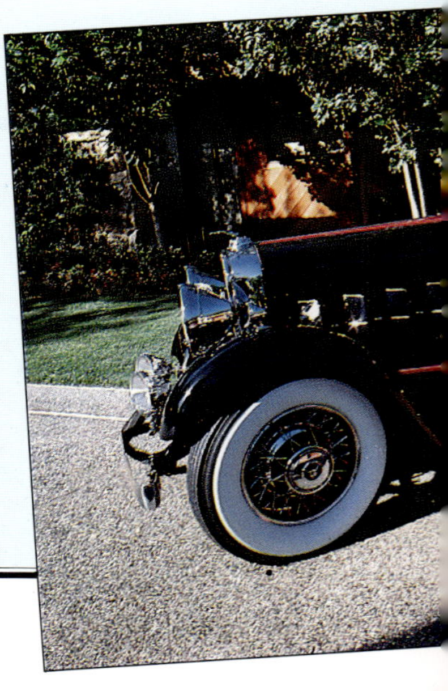

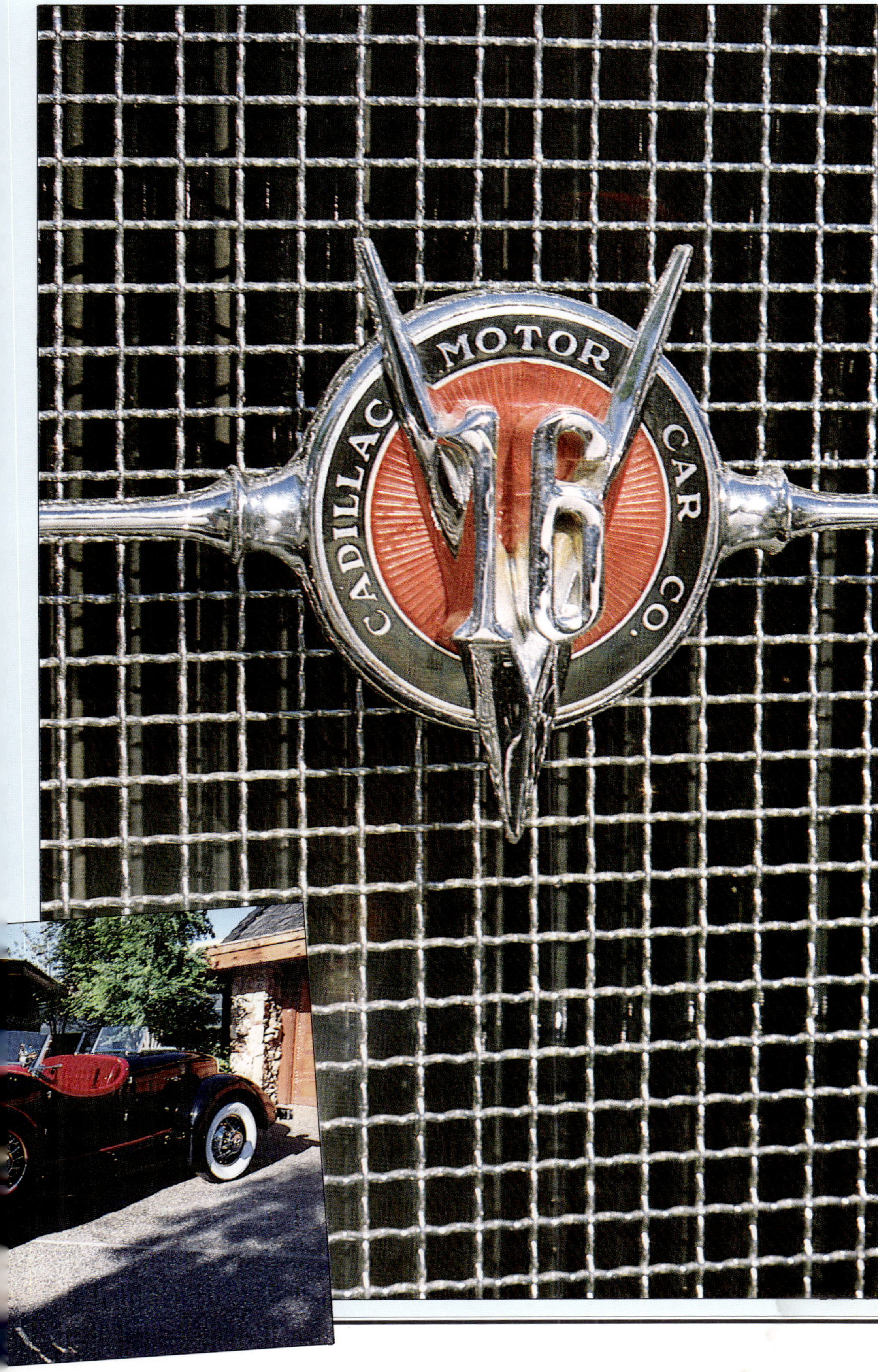
CADILLAC MOTOR CAR CO.
16

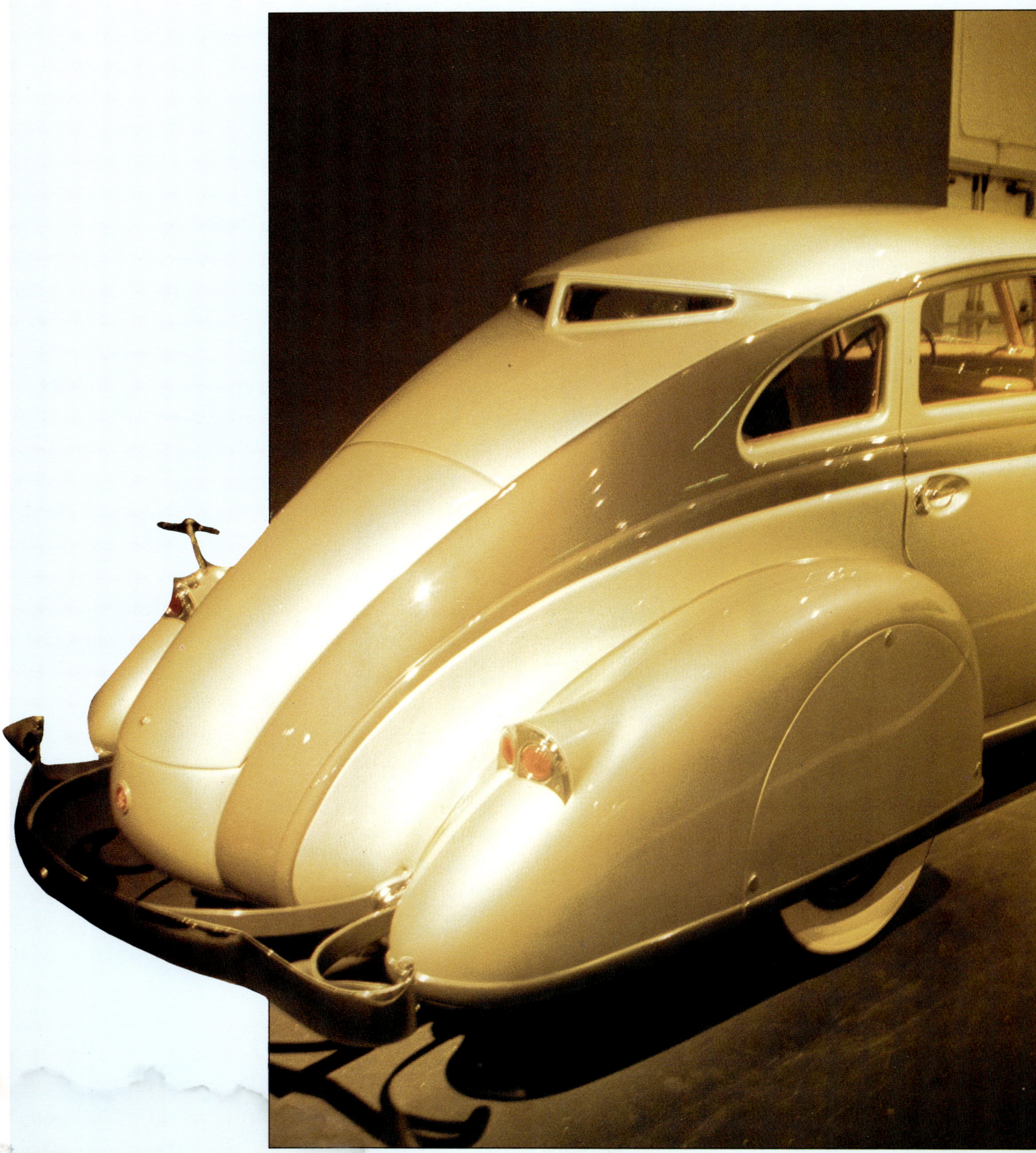

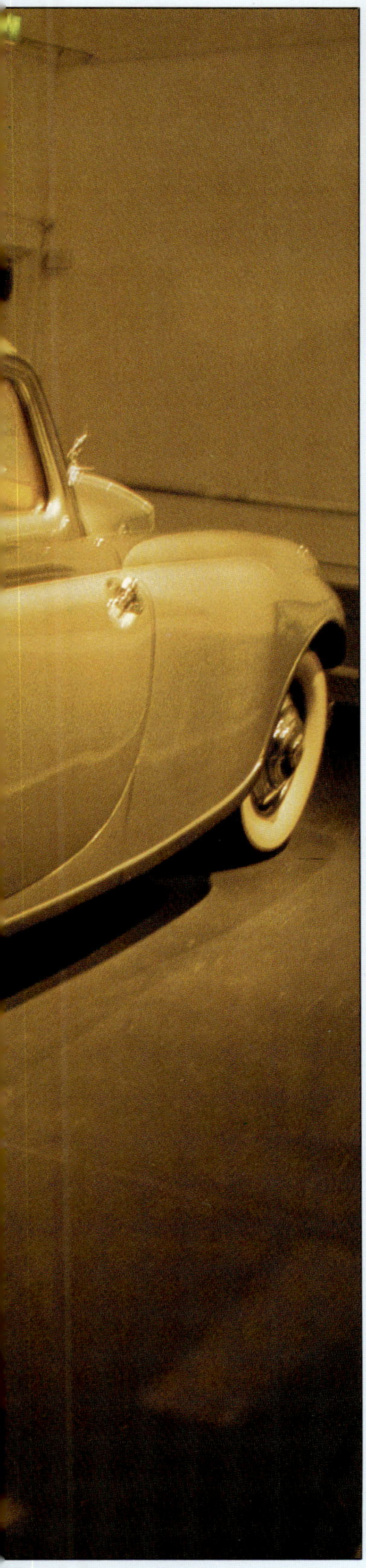

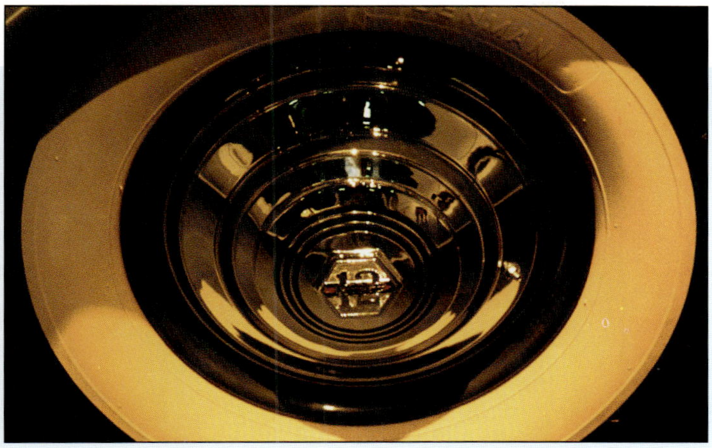

Pierce-Arrow, despite producing this stylish vehicle (left), was one of the many fine American automobile makers that failed to survive the death blow dealt by the Wall Street Crash.

businessman who had interests in the American Peerless Motor company in Detroit, to the USA to visit several American automakers with the idea of selling them some of the Bucciali engineering patents, and hopefully manufacturing rights for their cars also. This last throw attempt to save their company failed doubly, because not only was there no interest in their cars, but several of the Bucciali transmission ideas for military vehicle use were incorporated most successfully into American military vehicles. No royalties were ever paid to the Buccialis. After 1945 Paul-Albert spent all of his money on unsuccessful litigation in European and American courts to claim his financial rewards on these patents. It is sad to have to report that he was equally unsuccessful in the courts as he was as a luxury car maker.

One of the loveliest cars of all time must have been the Cadillac V16, not only a great car, but one that can be said to have represented the very peak of Cadillac quality. Unlike the poor Bucciali, the Cadillac went on to become one of the most successful, and profitable, divisions of the giant General Motors Corporation. The Blackhawk Cadillac V16 that really catches the eye is the one that is simply known as 'The Tiger Car'.

The Maharaja of Indore commissioned Pinin Farina to design a tiger hunting car for him based on the Cadillac V16 chassis. Now this Cadillac model was more suitable for cruising, chauffeur-driven, down 5th Avenue in New York, or Piccadilly in London than being rushed across the hot Indian plains chasing after tigers. Nevertheless a special elevated shooting seat was fitted and six individual gun compartments.

Today the design of a car for this purpose would be more like a stretched Land Rover—very functional and basic, which highlights even more the sheer beauty of the Cadillac 'Tiger Car'. The Cadillac is so elegant that even today it would not be out of place delivering its owner to the grandest of occasions.

The V16 Cadillac really does make sense of the hackneyed phrase, 'They don't make them like they used to'. A Cadillac collector, a man who has a selection of the world's best from the 1940s still runs Cadillacs but has to change the car every six months to avoid mechanical problems! He is of the firm opinion that from the mid-1930s Cadillac quality has steadily declined, and that the V16 models were the greatest cars that the company

During the late 1920s the small Belgian automobile industry produced its finest vehicle, the Minerva, a car built to the highest standards, and valued by many fastidious buyers. Sadly it did not survive the economic depression of the 1930s.

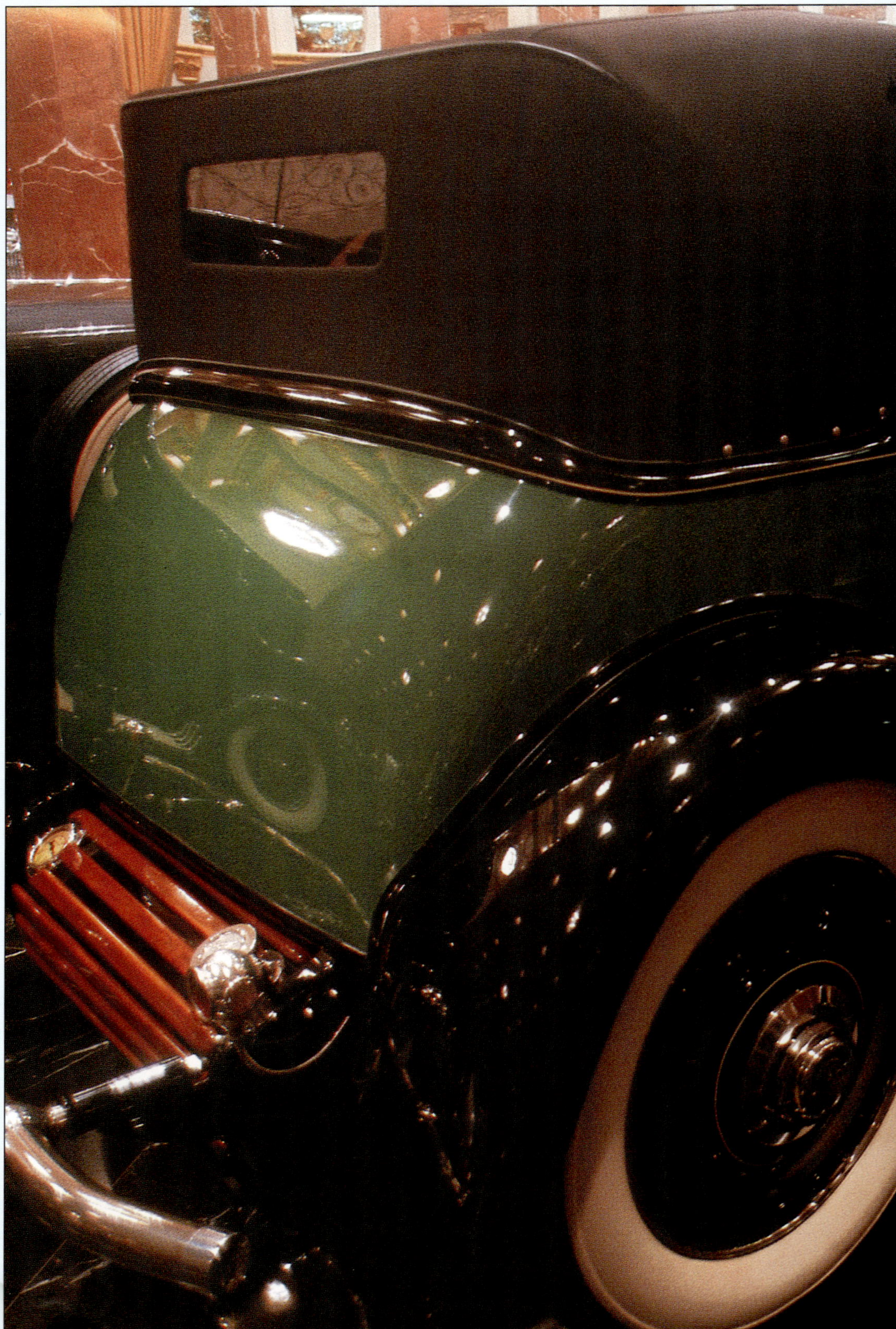

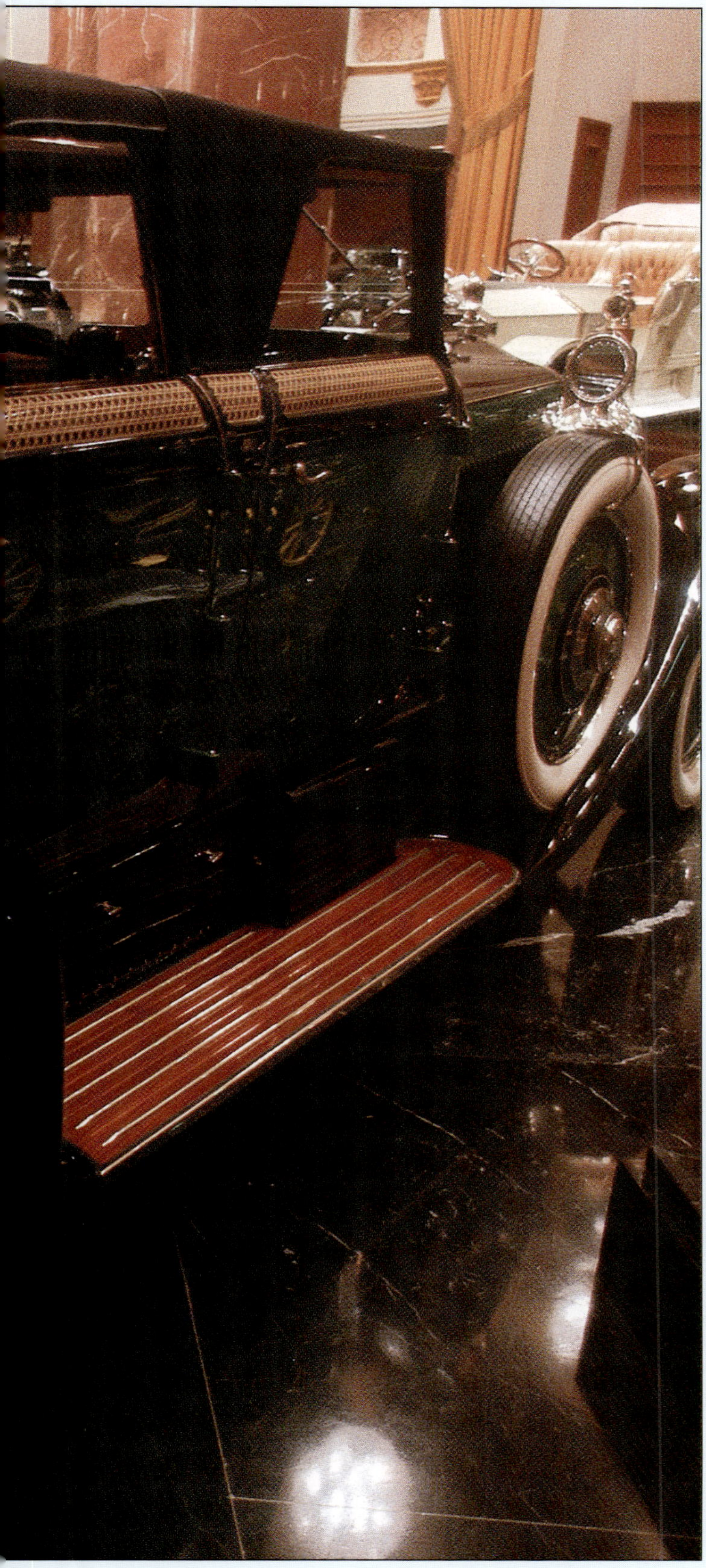

ever produced.

In 1933 the Pierce-Arrow factory, makers of many of the very best American cars of all time, shocked the crowds at the New York Car Show with their Silver Arrow model.

This car, the brainchild of designer Phil Wright, introduced the all-steel roof, radical styling with concealed sidemounts and running boards, and 12-inch thick doors with recessed handles. The car was a sensation, but the Pierce-Arrow concern was in serious financial difficulties, and only five Silver Arrows were ever built, with only three left in existence. Like the Cunningham (James, rather than Briggs) the Pierce-Arrow was built in Buffalo, New York, but unlike the Cunningham, after closing down their car production the company faded away. Cunningham do not make cars anymore, which is a very great pity, as their automobiles were truly fine machines, but their engineering business is alive and well.

Not much is generally known about the Minerva car because, like so many luxury car makers, they were forced out of the business by the depression of the 1930s. Made in Antwerp, Belgium the Minerva was one of the very finest cars made in the world. It was beautifully designed along conventional lines, exquisitely constructed with the strictest of quality control, and purchased by owners with the highest standards and fattest wallets.

The Minerva in the photographs resides in the Nethercutt Collection in Sylmar, California. It was given the gorgeous coachwork by Floyd Derham, the son of the original Derham bodymaker. Floyd had set himself up in competition with his father, but after making only three bodies he went bankrupt. Before going into total decline he did complete the Minerva contract, and the results indicate what a great craftsman was lost to the luxury automobile world.

The Nethercutt Minerva's beauty can be judged by the fact

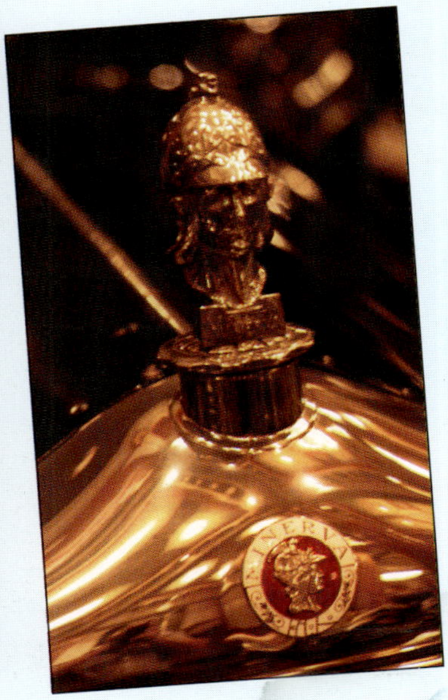

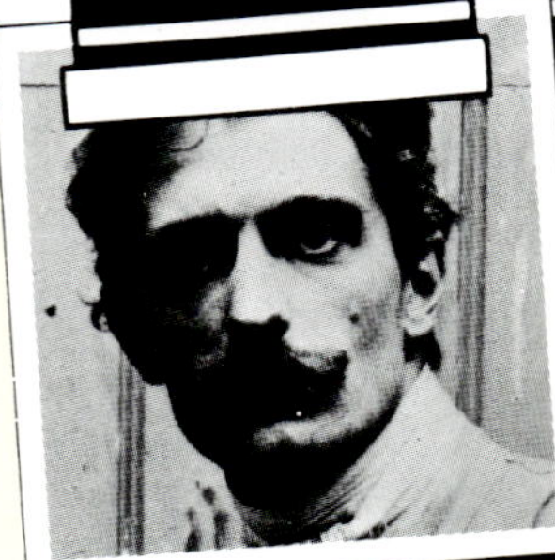

## GABRIEL VOISIN

Gabriel Voisin (1880-1973) lived to be 93 and he would have been the first to agree that living to the hilt, with passion, is the best recipe for a long and interesting existence! His autobiography, *Men, Women and 10,000 Balloons* fully reveals his extrovert nature in work and play.

Voisin was a dynamo of a man: he worked with skill, dedication, judgement and more than a touch of genius. He was an aviation fanatic and built, tried out and flew kites and balloons.

He turned away from aircraft production, after the First World War, towards car production at his Issy-les-Moulineaux factory to take up the slack as aircraft orders fell away.

His cars reflected his individuality — they all used the sleeve-valve type of engine. In 1936 he even presented a 6-litre straight twelve engine, highly unusual! Lightness of weight was, perhaps because of his experience with aircraft, always a major consideration in his cars and he consistently favoured the use of light alloys.

that it scored a perfect 100 points in the 1978 Monterey/Pebble Beach Classic Car Show, and won the Best of Show award.

The 1923 Twin Valve McFarlan Knickerbocker Cabriolet was at one time owned by a great American personality, the film star 'Fatty' Arbuckle.

Made in Connersville, Indiana the model 154 McFarlan was one of the many excellent American automobiles of the period. Its six-cylinder engine produced 129hp. At the time the McFarlan engine was so 'torquey' that it was described as 'big enough for a truck'. Two interesting features on the Arbuckle car should be mentioned; a set of snap fastenings on the outside edge of the roof, (and it was some long time afterwards that it was realized that they served to attach an awning to the side of the car to protect 'Fatty' when he was filming on location). Secondly, the supplementary mudguards fitted in front of the rear guards so as to protect the passenger's clothing from road dirt thrown up on to the car by the wheels on entering or leaving the McFarlan.

'Fatty' Arbuckle is remembered today, if at all, because of his involvement in a rather nasty criminal case. It is now believed that the charge was trumped up against him, but at the time it was

CENTRE: The T. V. McFarlan was selected by the film star 'Fatty' Arbuckle as his location vehicle. It was a quality car, made in small numbers, and is practically forgotten today.

Rudolph Valentino favoured the unusual in his choice of automobiles, hence his purchase of the Voisin Sporting Victoria (far right), a French vehicle made to aircraft standards, and very collectable today.

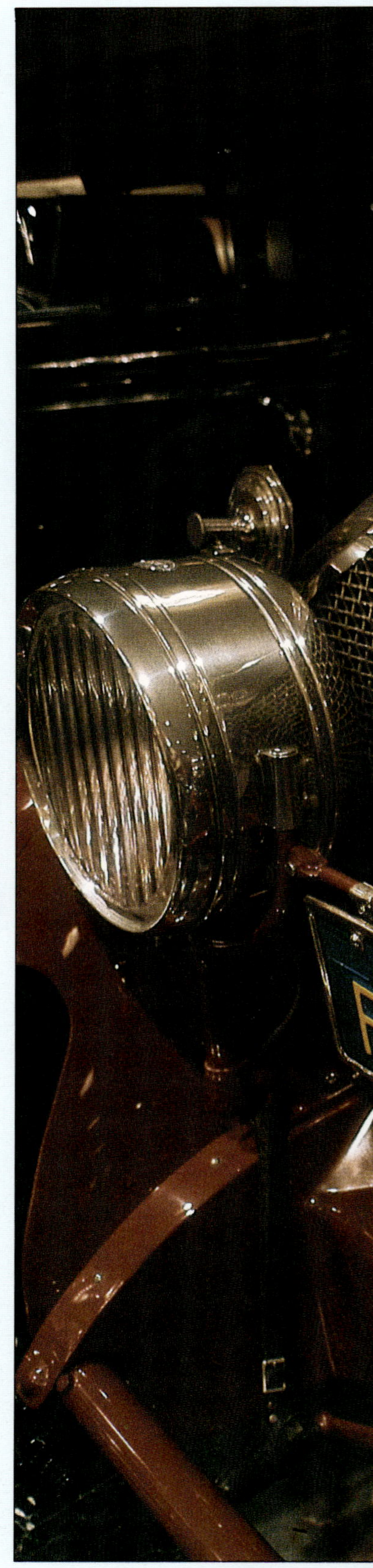

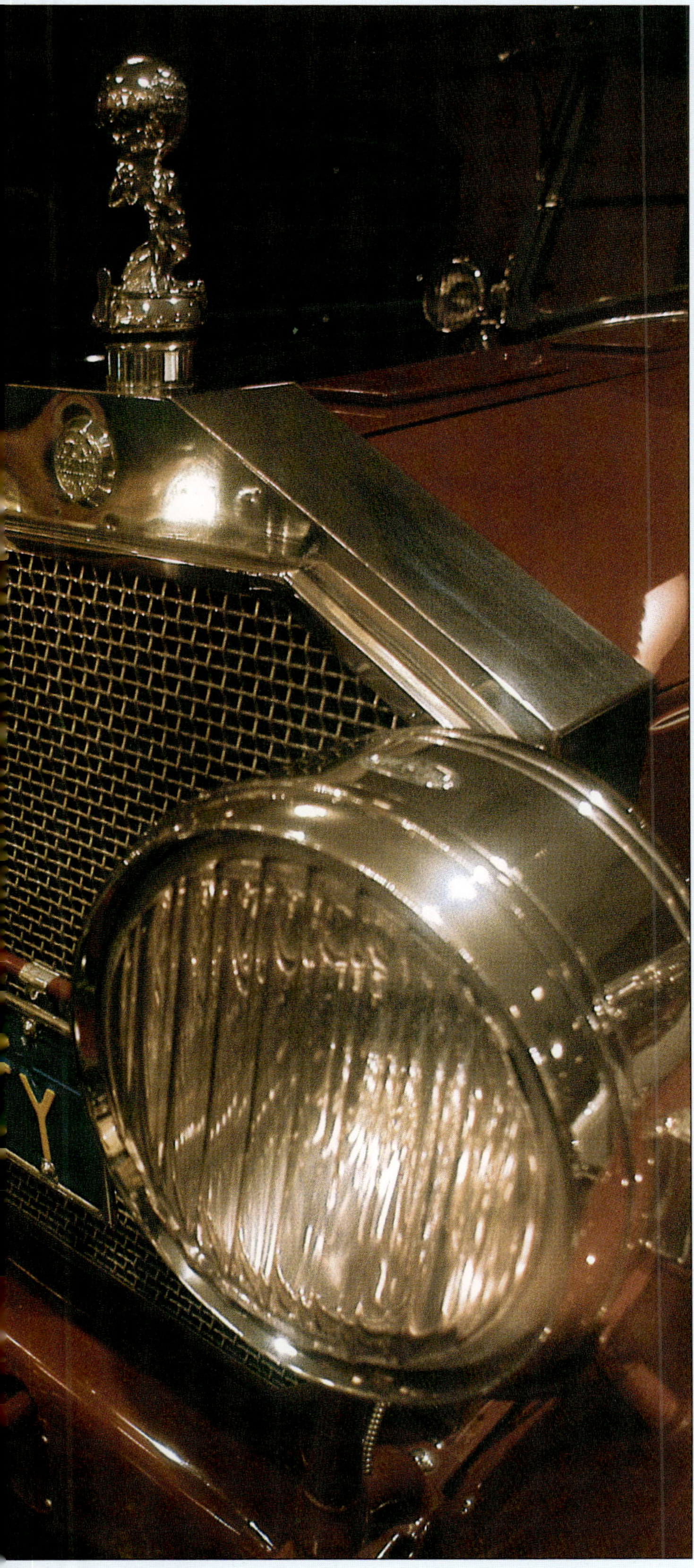


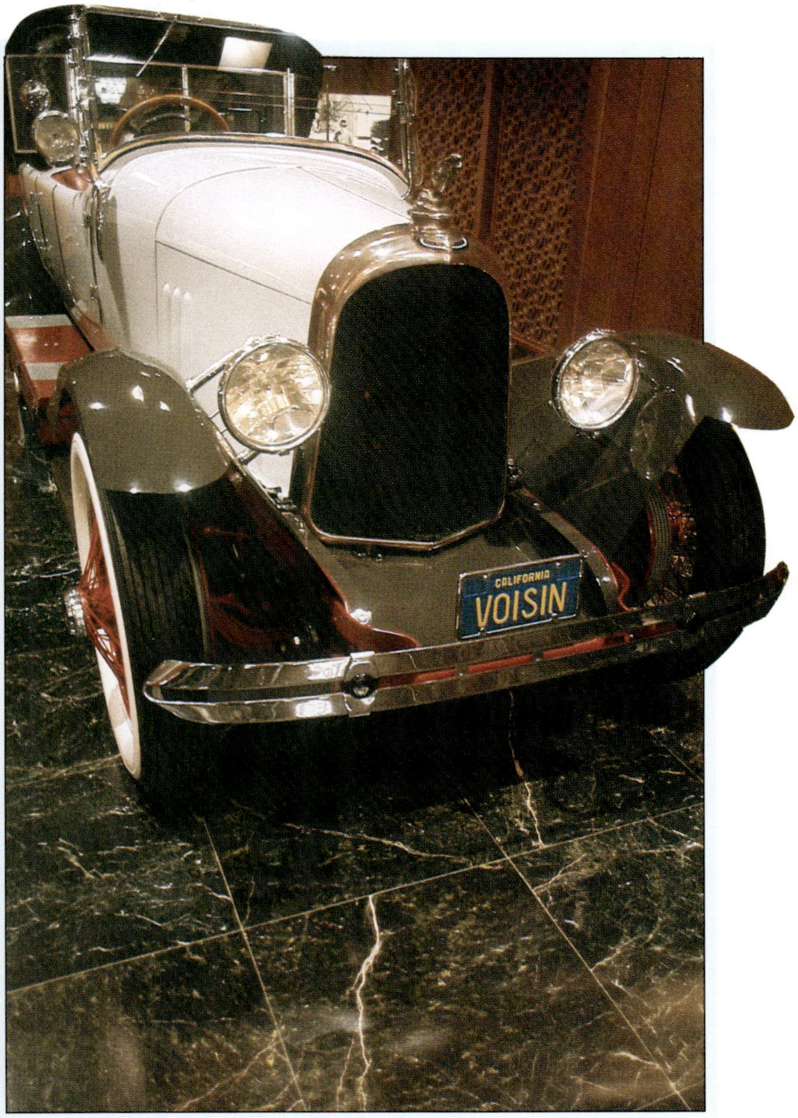


enough to finish his career in the movie business.

The 1923 Avions Voisin Sporting Victoria was first owned by the acknowledged greatest silent film star of all time, Rudolph Valentino. His films, 'The Sheik', and 'The Four Horsemen of the Apocalypse' were two of the biggest films of their time both in terms of numbers who paid to see them, and box office takings. Valentino died a very young man after a simple appendix operation, from blood poisoning. On news of his death fans all over the world went into mourning, and a few supposedly even committed suicide because of their grief.

Valentino's Voisin model C-5 was made in France by one of the most original aero and automobile engineers, Gabriel Voisin. Voisin has claimed, with some justification, that it was he who first flew in a powered aircraft, and not the Wright brothers at Kittyhawk. Voisin argued that the Wright brothers used a catapult-assisted take-off to get themselves into the air, as their puny engine did not have the required power to perform this

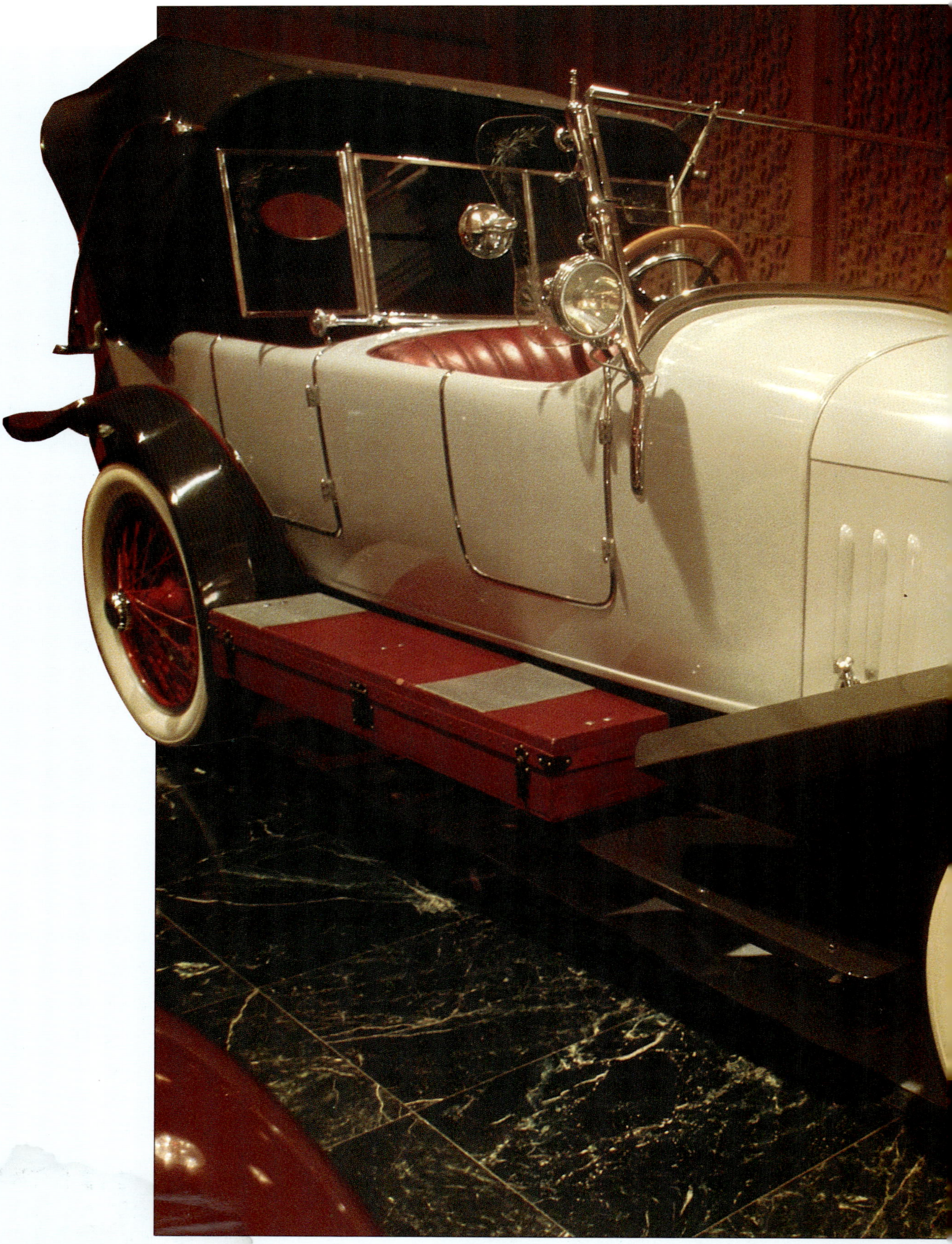

task. Less than a year later, and before the Wrights could find and fit a powerful enough engine, Voisin had flown under powered flight, ie covered the necessary distance etc to meet all the criteria set for defining genuine powered flight, and landed safely. Gabriel Voisin went to his grave convinced that he should be considered as the father of Powered Flight!

The C-5 was one of Voisin's best cars, and the body fitted for Rudolph Valentino a great asset to the rest of the vehicle. Voisin commissioned J. Rothschild and Sons of Paris to build him a suitable carriage for the number one film star, and they did a fine job. The coachwork is both stylish and simple, and reminiscent of the passing horse-drawn age. Like the T. V. McFarlan, the Voisin has supplementary mudguards, but this time for the front wings, so as to afford protection to passengers and bodywork. These can be seen behind the front wheels, and below the mudguards proper. The car is in perfect running order, as are all the Nethercutt Collection cars, needing only gasoline and a battery to be driven away.

The cars in this chapter are special, either by virtue of their makers or because of their owners. All of them are more than simply vehicles, and were so even when new.

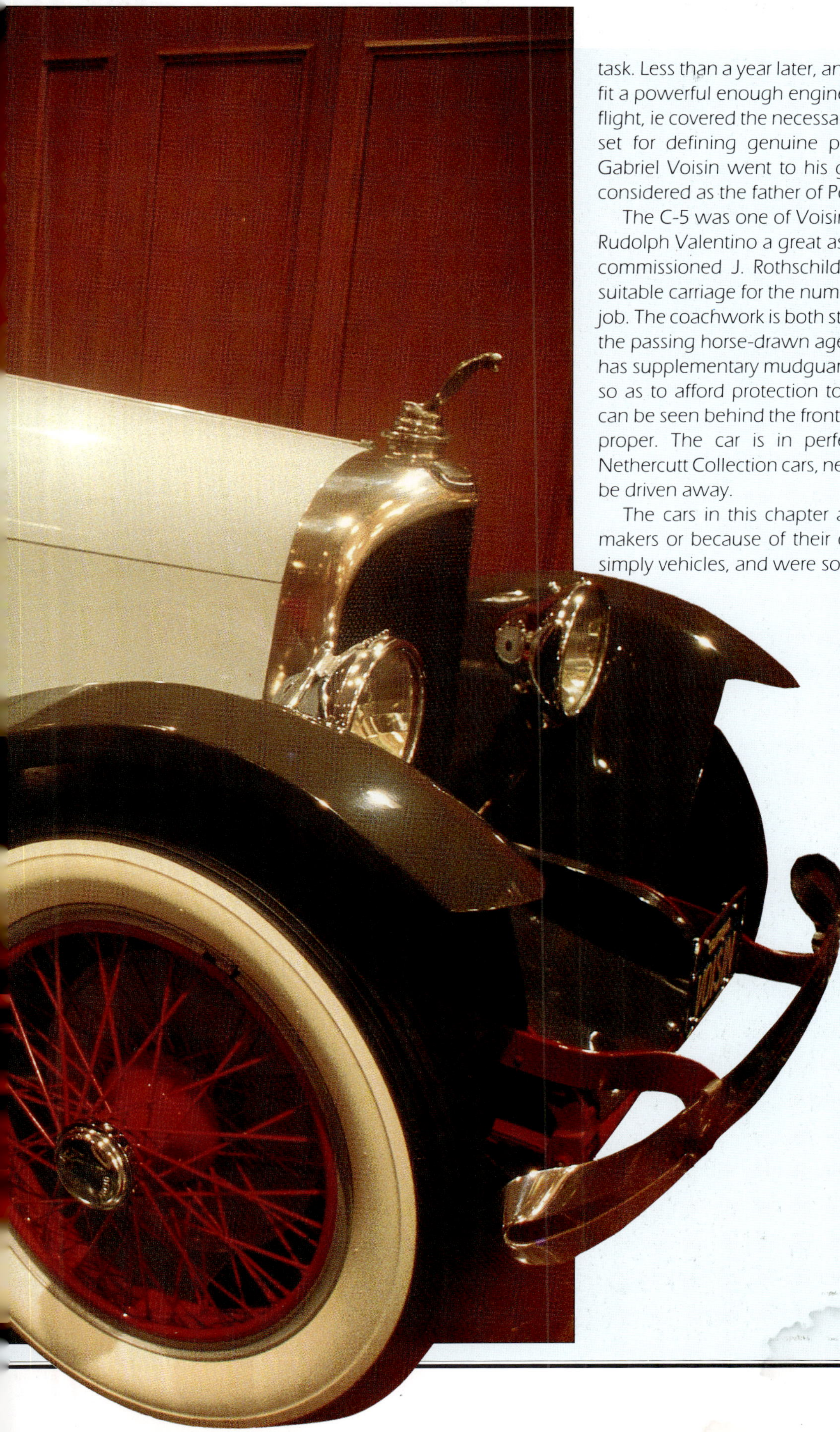

The elegant Voisin that belonged to Rudolph Valentino required very little restoration to bring it up to as-new condition, a tribute to its original builders, and the kind Califo[illegible]an climate.

# CHAPTER EIGHT

# Sportscars

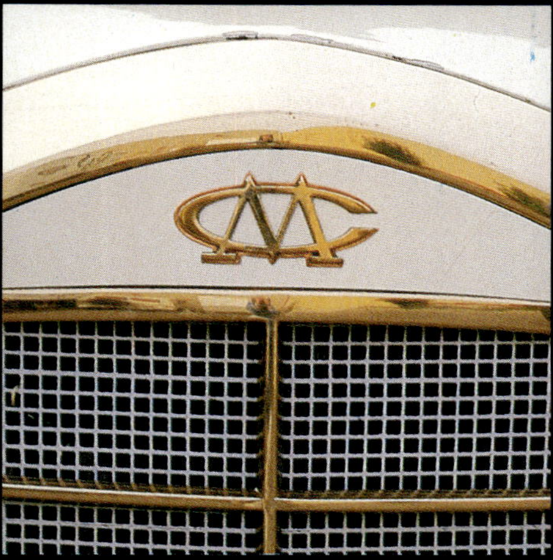

Carroll Shelby's Cobra, with its 427 cubic inch engine, was essentially a racing car slightly modified for road use, with very little concession made to real comfort and convenience. It is avidly sought after by collectors the world over.

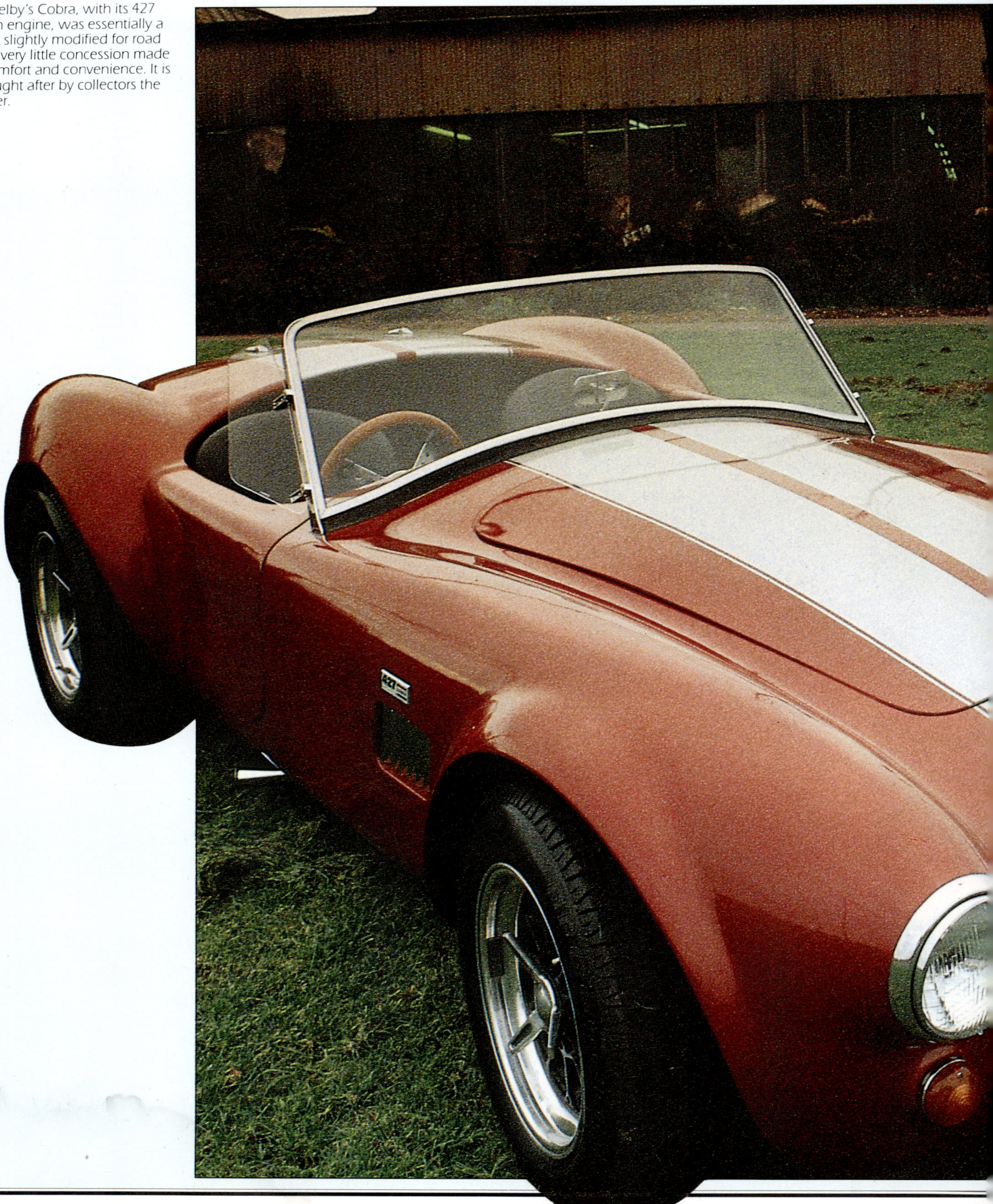

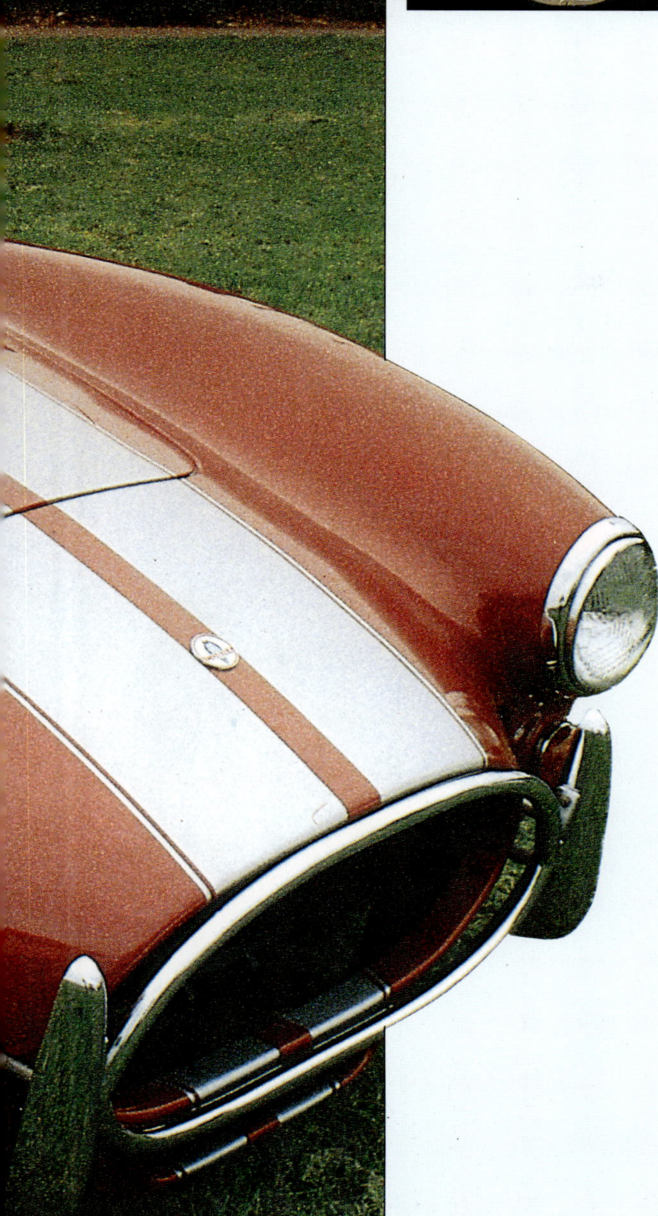

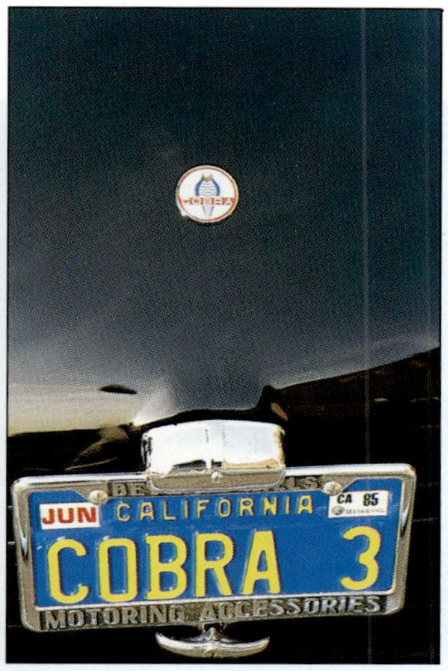


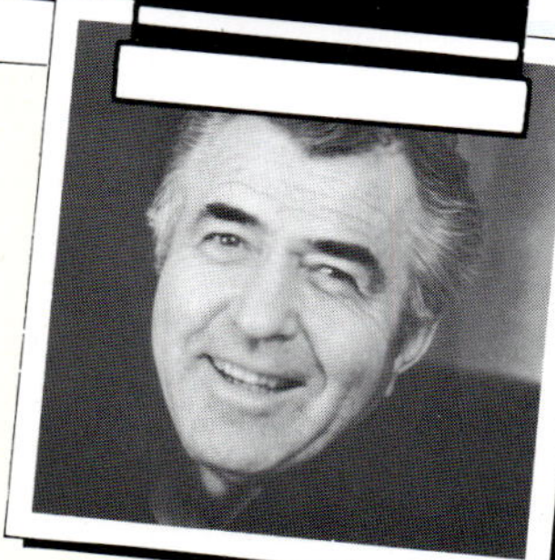

## Carroll Shelby

In 1962 Carroll Hall Shelby retired early from a career as a top line driver of Formula One and Sports/Racing cars. His greatest success, in terms of international fame, had come in 1959 when he had co-driven the winning Aston Martin at Le Mans.

He persuaded the Ford Motor Company, and A.C. Cars in England to combine a Ford engine and an A.C. chassis to produce one of the greatest sportscars of all time, the Cobra.

Today he is still 'fixing'. He is fit, busy — not too busy to keep closely in touch with the Shelby/ American Car Club, and follow motor-racing.

There have been many candidates for the title of the greatest sportscar during the near hundred years of the automobile. Mercedes, Mercer, Alfa Romeo, Bugatti, Bentley, Jaguar, Aston Martin, Shelby Cobra, Stutz, Porsche, Ferrari, Maserati, the list is endless and the choice entirely dependent upon personal taste and national preference. One method many people use to judge the ultimate value for the greatest is to consider the cash value of the car in question on the open market. While not all people will approve of this idea, it does at least have a bearing on the status of the vehicle being considered. A true sportscar in the simplest terms (and again, different people have different views on this subject), should be an open model, very fast, and with good styling. It is not necessary for it to have the best brakes, steering, and roadholding, because many of the accepted great cars in this class did not have these attributes, but they all *were* good looking, fast cars. The Shelby Cobra is a case in point. The Cobra came about following the early retirement, of Carroll Shelby the American racing driver. After his best season, 1959, when he co-drove an Aston Martin to the marque's only Le Mans win, it was discovered that he had a heart condition that made any future driving a hazard, so he hung up his famous striped racing overalls and retired as a driver.

Wanting to stay in the sporting car business he persuaded the Ford Motor Company, and the tiny British sportscar makers A.C., to allow him to put the Ford 260 cubic inch V8 engine into the A.C. Ace chassis, and then made additional chassis modifications so that the new car would handle well and stop. By late 1961 his new sportscar was ready to go into production in the Shelby-American plant in Los Angeles. The story goes that it was in the middle of the night that the name for the car, 'Cobra', came to Carroll, but however it came about, a better name for the Shelby/Ford/A.C. concoction could not be imagined.

75 260-engined cars had been made when Ford introduced the 289 cubic inch engine which Shelby immediately set about using instead of the 260. In this form the Cobra really took off, and 579 of the bigger-engined Cobras were produced in the next three years. In 1965 Shelby substituted the 427 engine in a successful bid to keep the Cobra competitive on the race tracks of the world. Shelby made 348 of these cars in the following two years.

As Carroll Shelby admitted, the Cobra was an old-fashioned sports car, but what a fire-eater it was. Performance was its sole reason for existing, and despite marginal brakes, massive heat transfer into the driving compartment from the engine bay, a distinct lack of torsional strength, and a firm, harsh, ride, the Cobra was king of the roads, and the best value for money of any sportscar in the world. Armed with the 427 engine Shelby won the G.T. world racing championships in 1965 with his Daytona Cobra coupé.

Despite the advantages of the massive horsepower produced by the stock 427 engine, the 289 Cobra is generally better balanced in its handling. There is more than enough power together with quite reasonable fuel economy, and the brakes have an easier time than with the 427!

Today a mint-condition Cobra realizes a vast sum of money on the market, and this fact has encouraged many copyists both in Europe and the USA to attempt to cash in on the popularity of the twenty-year-old sportscar. Only one succeeds in duplicating the original, and that is the highly expensive 'official' Autocraft A.C. Mk. IV, made from the original A.C. patterns, so Shelby's creation still stands supreme. Carroll Shelby's reaction to all the copies being made of his car was, 'I find it strange that anyone should want to copy a car that was already outdated when we developed it. Surely their money would be better spent on producing a modern car?'

This is accepted as an indication of just what a realist he is, and it is not surprising to learn that Carroll Shelby will be helping the Chrysler Corporation develop a series of production-based high performance cars. The early signs are that he has not lost his touch!

A sportscar that failed, but should have made it, is the Triumph

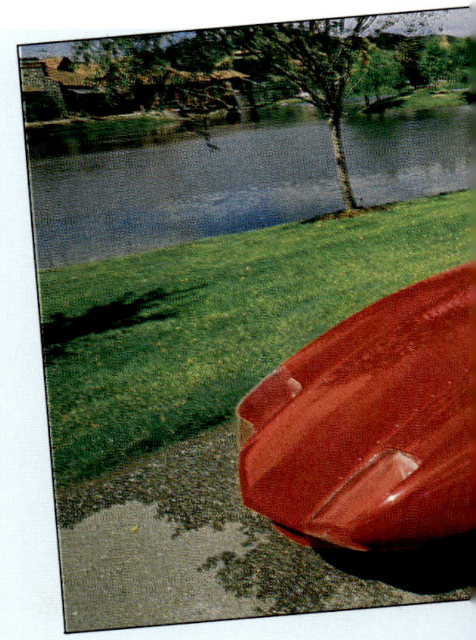

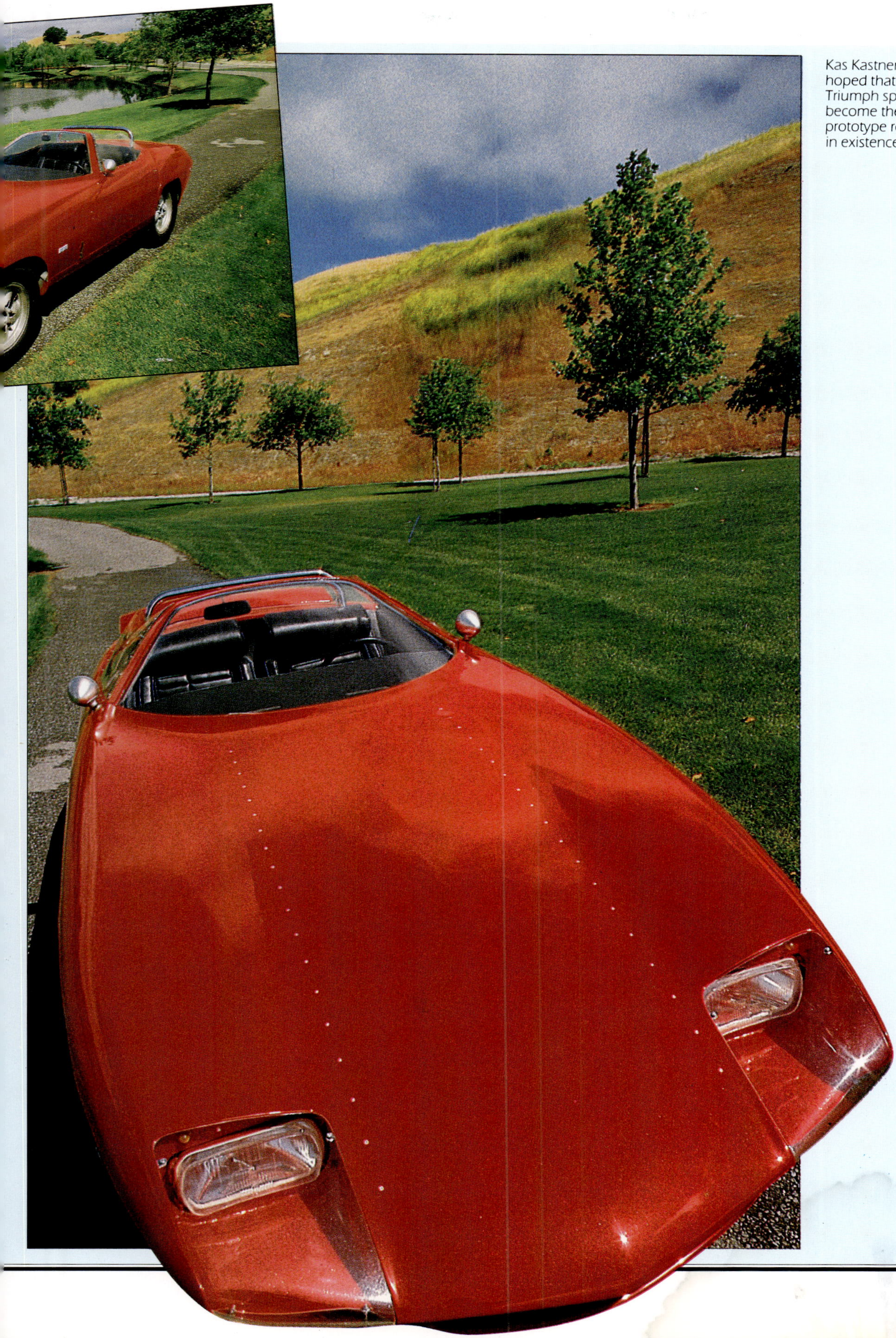

Kas Kastner and Pete Brock had hoped that their interpretation of the Triumph sportscar (the 250-K) would become the new TR-7. But this prototype remains the only example in existence.

The super-charged, six-cylinder engine in the Lyon sportscar is based on a Jaguar unit, but very heavily modified by Russ Lyon to produce reliable high performance.

Entirely hand-made by Russ Lyon and his wife, their car's driving compartment gives a good idea of their artistry and high standards of work.

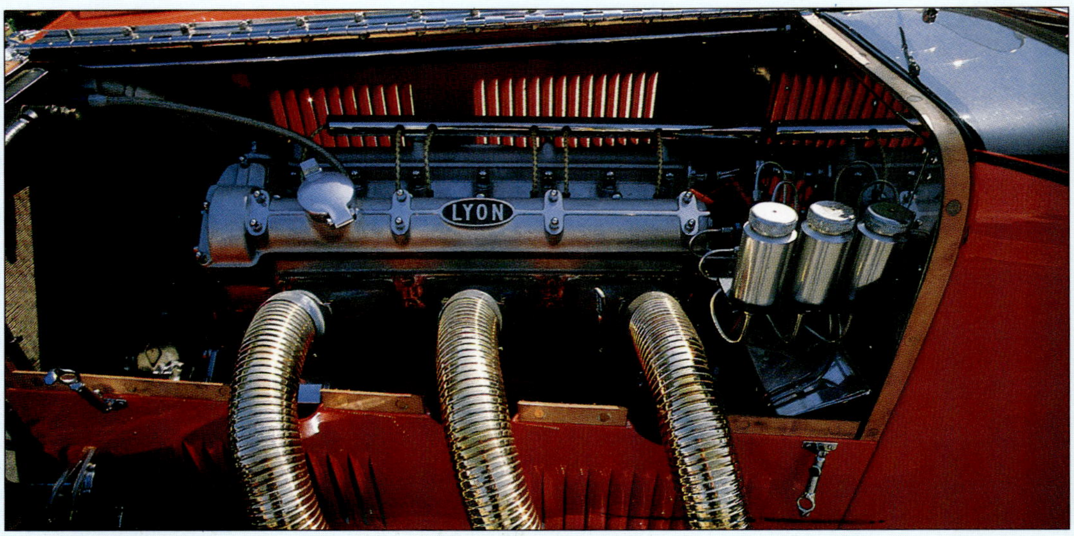


250-K. This car was the result of a collaboration between the Triumph North American racing team manager Kas Kastner, and stylist Pete Brock.

Kastner had made the American Triumph racing team into the most successful and feared, outfit in American racing. He is not only a very fine engineer, organizer and motivator, but also (behind the wheel of a racing car) a frequent US champion. In June 1967 Kas was called to Triumph's Headquarters in Coventry to discuss racing matters for the season. It was his custom always take something new with him which he had under development. On this occasion he was caught napping, and was going to have to arrive in England empty handed. However, for some time he had been examining possibilities for the replacement of the TR-6 model which was selling poorly in the USA. In this connection Kas had discussed design ideas with Brock, who had roughed out some sketches of the car that they felt could replace the TR-6, and boost Triumph sales.

With less than two hours before flight time Kastner called Brock around to his house, and asked him to produce some better layouts of their dream car for him to take to Coventry. Kas just made the flight, and during the short stop-over in New York he showed them to Leon Mandel, then editor of *Car & Driver* magazine. Leon agreed to feature the 250-K, as Kas called the car, on *C & D*s front cover three issues later. This must have been worth a massive amount of publicity, and armed with this additional weapon Kas presented his 250-K to the Triumph top men. He persuaded them to come up with $25,000 of development money to allow the car to be built, but they insisted that it be ready to RACE in the following February's Sebring meeting! What Triumphs were getting for their money was a free magazine front cover and an actual prototype car which would feature in the Sebring races in six months time!! It must have seemed like the bargain of the century to Coventry, because Kas Kastner had never let them down.

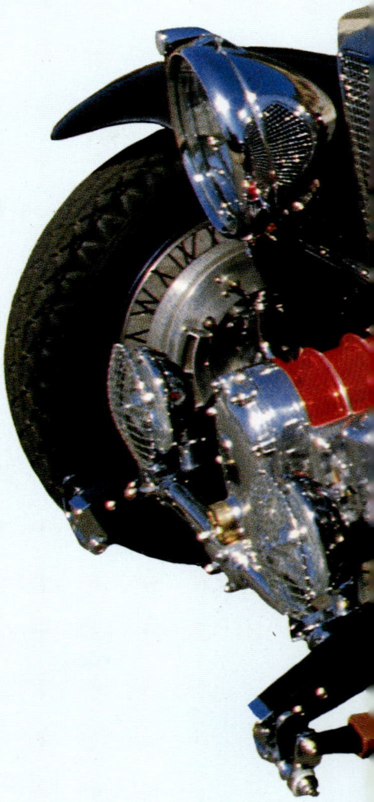

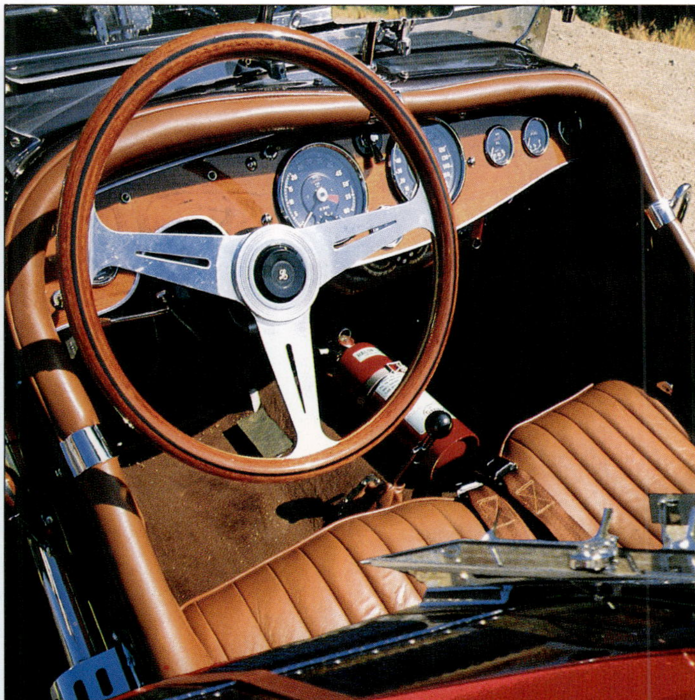

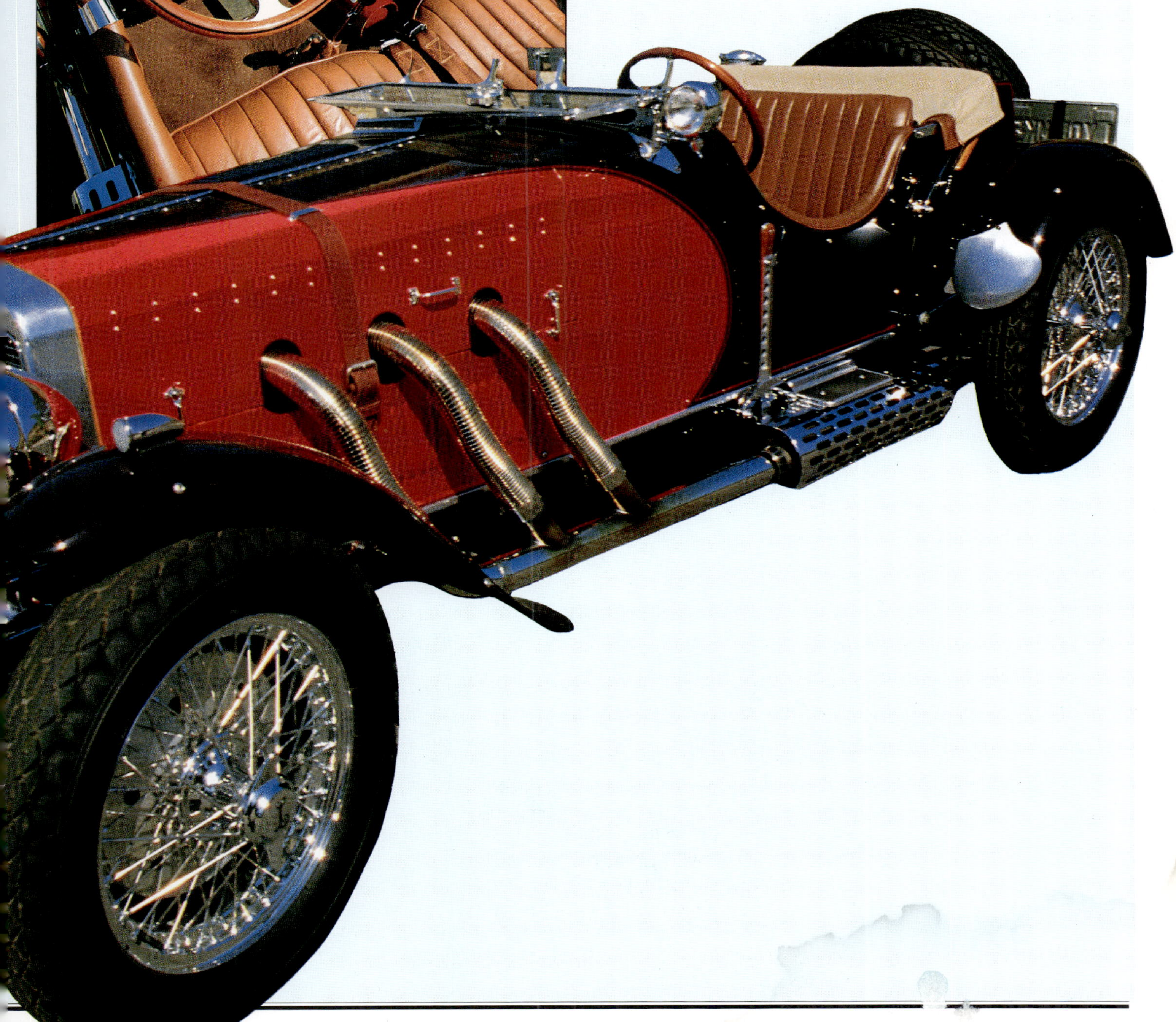

The Lyon sportscar is the fruit of 13 years' hard work by Russ Lyon. A vehicle cast in the mold of a 1930s sportscar, it combines many modern design features with vintage looks, and delivers astonishingly high performance, but at an equally high price.

Kastner built the car and race-prepared it in less than six months, a miracle compared to modern automotive development schedules. Unfortunately, with only five laps of a race track completed to sort the whole machine out, the 250-K went to Sebring, and was retired with a broken wheel, but not before it had been pored over by the world's motoring press, with valuable follow-up coverage. Triumph did not put the car into production in an attempt to rebuild their fading image, in the export markets especially, possibly not liking the idea of making an American-designed sportscar, maybe considering that Coventry should be the source of the new vehicle. So the one and only remaining 250-K sportscar lives in the Blackhawk Collection in California. Everyone who has seen it remarks on its superb looks—on looks alone it would have been a winner against the TR-7.

Another American who nurtured a dream of making a sports car that would set the world back on its heels is Russ Lyon. He has been planning his car for the last 13 years and this year sees that ambition realized in his Lyon sportscar.

With qualifications in mechanical and aeronautical engineering behind him, Russ has produced his first prototype Lyon, and has taken several orders for production models. Each Lyon is hand-built over six months by Russ himself, and costs $135,000—the Lyon is something very special.

A Jaguar-derived six-cylinder, supercharged engine powers the Lyon, giving it a very high performance with a top speed of over 130mph and acceleration from 0-60mph in under 5 seconds—fast in any language. The whole car is most beautifully finished with Russ making the patterns, having castings made from them, machining the castings, fitting and adjusting the components. Even the Roots-type supercharger was designed and made this way by Russ. About the only items he did not make himself are some brake parts, tyres, electrics, basic engine, gearbox and differential, and the chromium plating!

The finished article not only looks fabulous, but it goes just as well. It may look like a sportscar from the 1930s, but it goes, brakes, and handles like a modern machine. With a production rate of only two cars per year Russ looks like being a very busy man for the next 8 or 10 years just meeting the current demand for his creation.

In a similar fashion, Chris Lawrence is making his own sportscar, but basing it closely on the famous Maserati 450S sports/racing car from 1956. In his tiny Norfolk workshop Chris is reproducing this marvellous competition car using Maserati engines and transmissions assembled into his own chassis (which closely follows the original car's design). His bodywork is as the 1956 Maserati, and it is difficult to tell between the Lawrence car and a genuine 450S, the results are so good.

The original Maserati 450S was the car that Stirling Moss, and his navigator, Denis Jenkinson, were to use in the 1956 Mille Miglia. They had won the classic race for Mercedes the year before, setting a new course record for the 1000-mile circuit. The

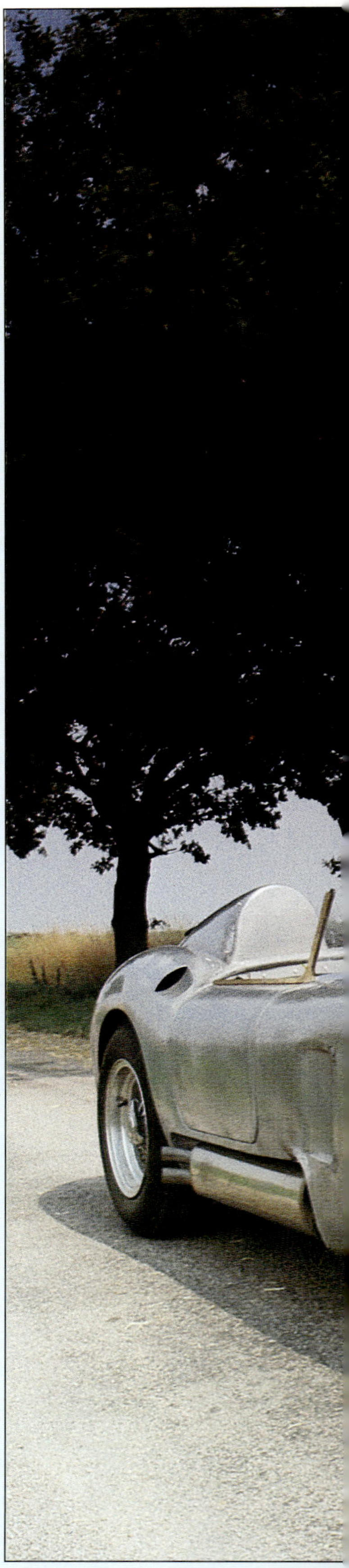

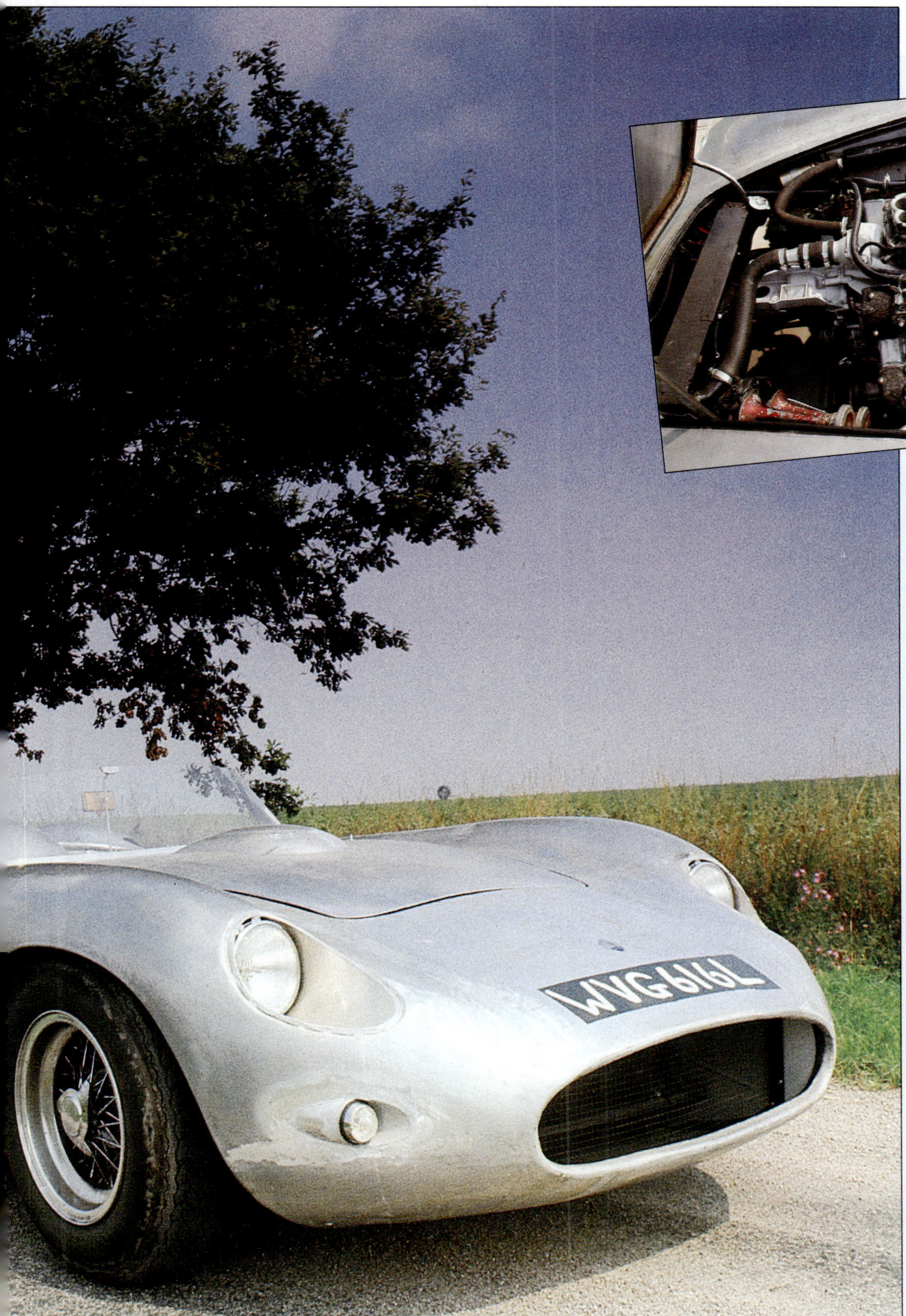

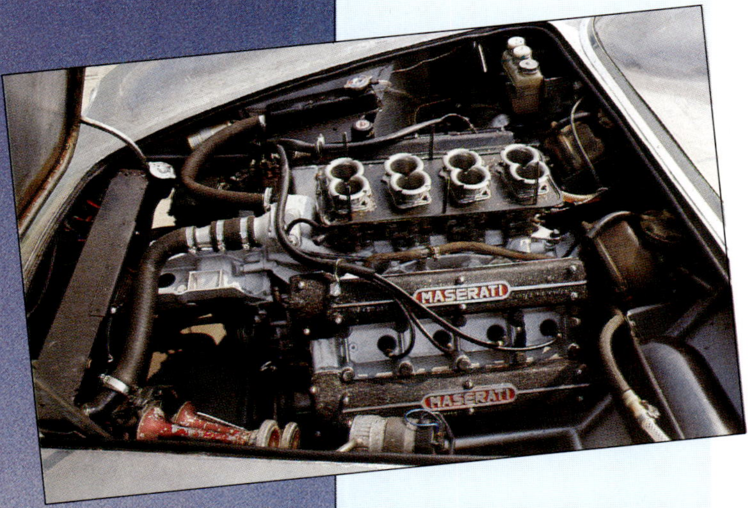


The V-8 engine in the Lawrence Maserati 450S delivers more than enough horsepower to make the car very fast, yet flexible and easy to drive.

The work of one man. It accurately recreates the famous Italian sportscar that promised so much in the late 1950s.

The last Bugatti to leave the Molsheim factory was rebodied by Virgil M. Exner in the early 1950s in a vain attempt to keep the company in business, but it was doomed to failure.

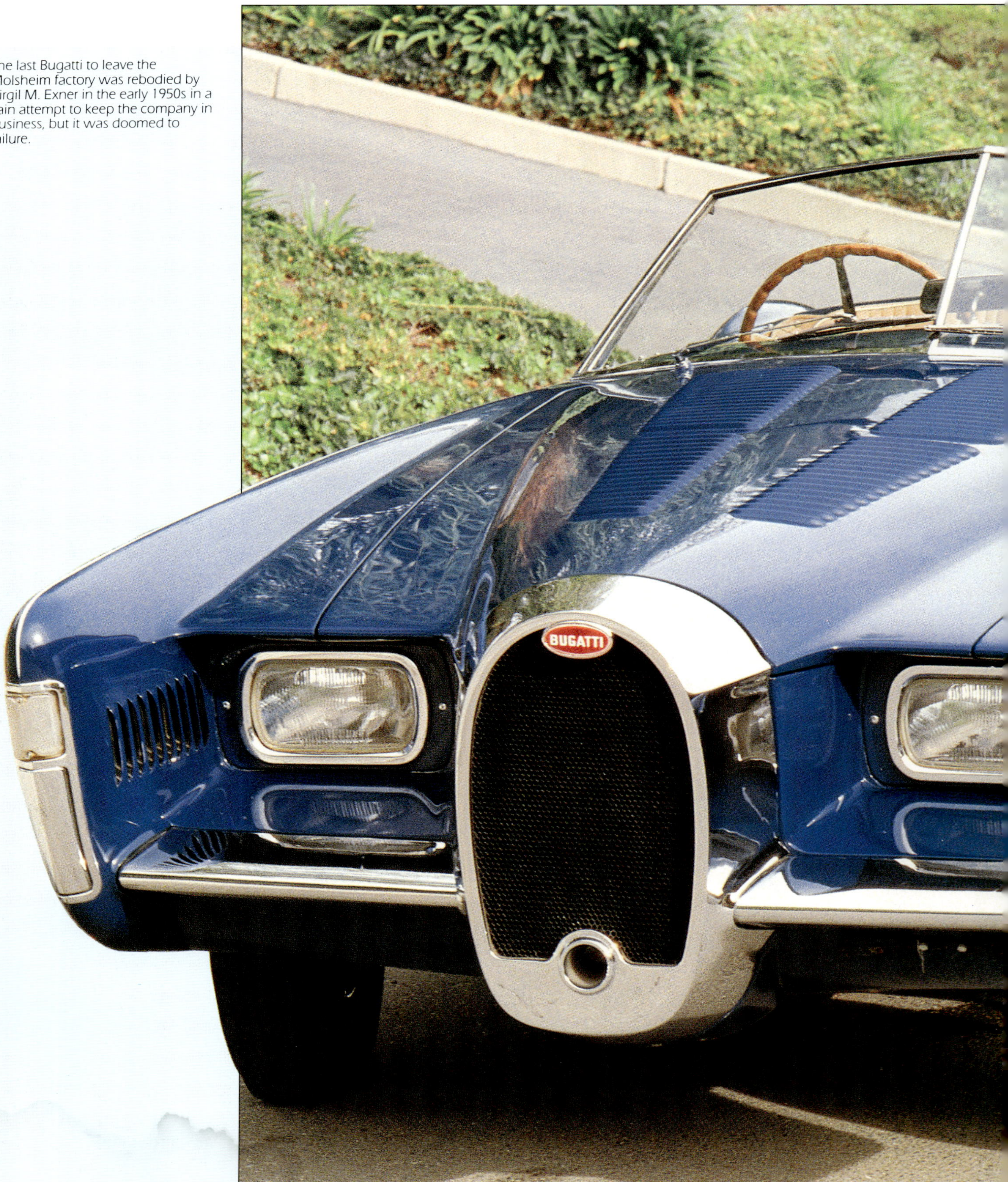

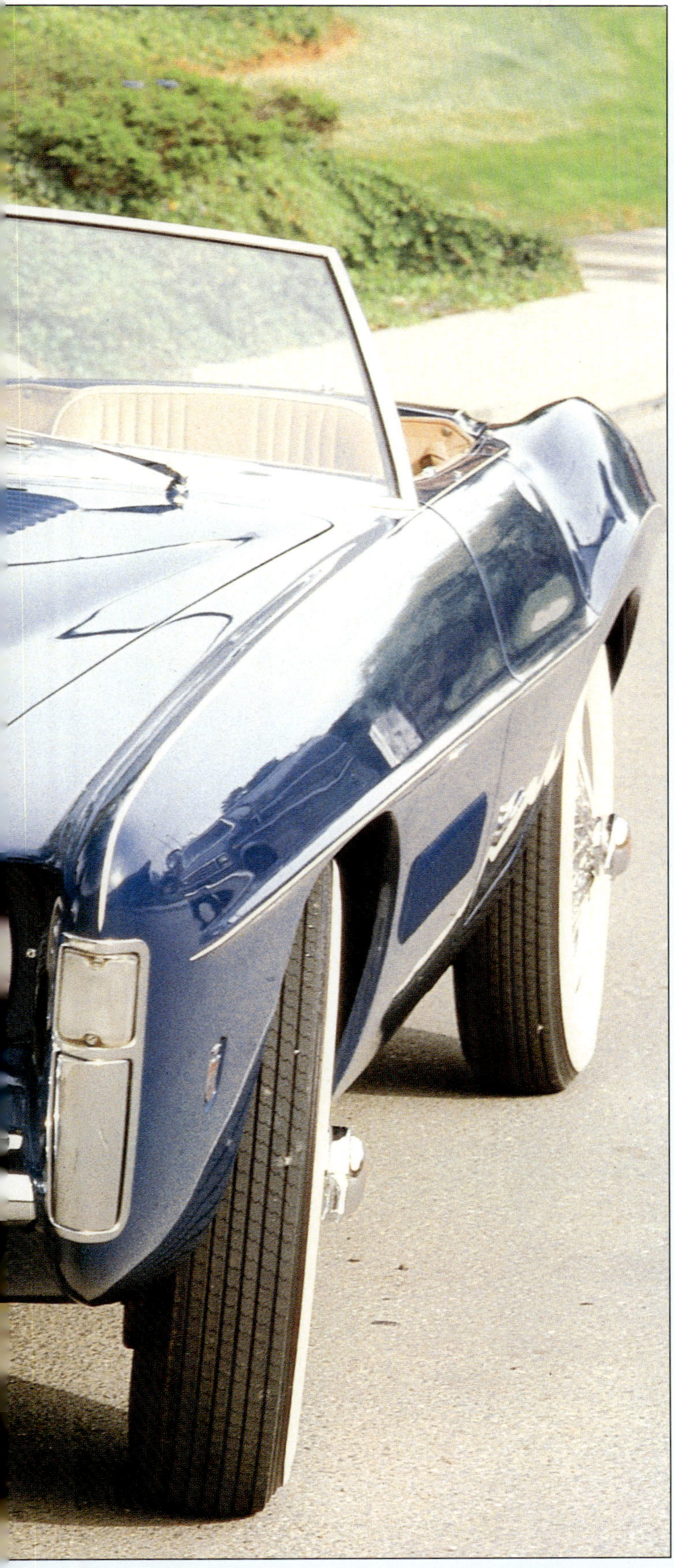

Maserati, with its very high speed potential was to be the machine in which they expected to gain a repeat win. After weeks of testing and practicing race day came and the Moss/Jenkinson car was flagged away from the start in Brescia. Less than ten miles down the road, braking for a medium-speed corner, Moss was horrified to feel the brake pedal snap off under his foot! But a combination of superb driving skill and more than a modicum of luck enabled the car's occupants to climb out unhurt and hastened the 4505's exit from the race.

The Maserati 450S continued to be unfortunate as a race car, although its engine carried on to become the power unit for several production road cars from Modena. A combination of lack of money, and an overstretched racing department meant that the 450S never received the development that it deserved. The final blow came when the World Sports/Racing engine capacity formula was reduced to 3 litres, and the car could no longer qualify to race. Maybe the new Lawrence 450S will give the model a new lease of life.

A car that every enthusiast would fervently wish to see back on the road again has to be the Bugatti. But with the deaths of Ettore (1947), and his son Jean, the company too faded away, not immediately after Ettore's death but three years later. The Bugatti automobile is so tied to the life and style of *le patron* that it really would be difficult to imagine the Molsheim factory without him. When the small Bugatti factory finally closed its doors in early 1951 there were six chassis waiting for customers (and bodies) sitting on the workshop floor. One of them, a type 101-C was purchased by Virgil M. Exner, who had the idea of somehow continuing the production of Bugatti automobiles, but with much more up-to-date styling. He commissioned the Italian designer Bertoni to style a two-seater body, and Ghia to build it.

It was ready for the 1965 Turin Auto Show, and was judged to be a styling success, although today the marriage of the 1930s chassis and road wheels with the 1960s coachwork looks uncomfortable, the skinny wheels appear to lift the car too high off the road giving the whole machine a rather 'strange' look.

On the road, this Bugatti drove like the late 1930s car that it is under the modern skin, with a stiffly-sprung chassis, heavy steering and even heavier brakes. This clashed with the overall styling which promised a more civilized road manner. As a work of automobile art it is excellent, the fit and finish to a very high standard, but as a vehicle it must rate below par for the intentions of those involved in it production. But it is the last complete Bugatti, and as such has a place in automotive history. It is one of the very few cars that should end its days in a collection or museum rather than being driven on the road.

Commissioned to promote the increased use of copper, brass, bronze, and their alloys, the Mercer Cobra rolled out of the bodyworks of Sibona-Basano in Turin in 1964.

Virgil M. Exner accepted the job of producing a unique, one-of-a-kind automobile to travel the world's auto-shows and, hopefully, catch the eye of car makers and persuade them to

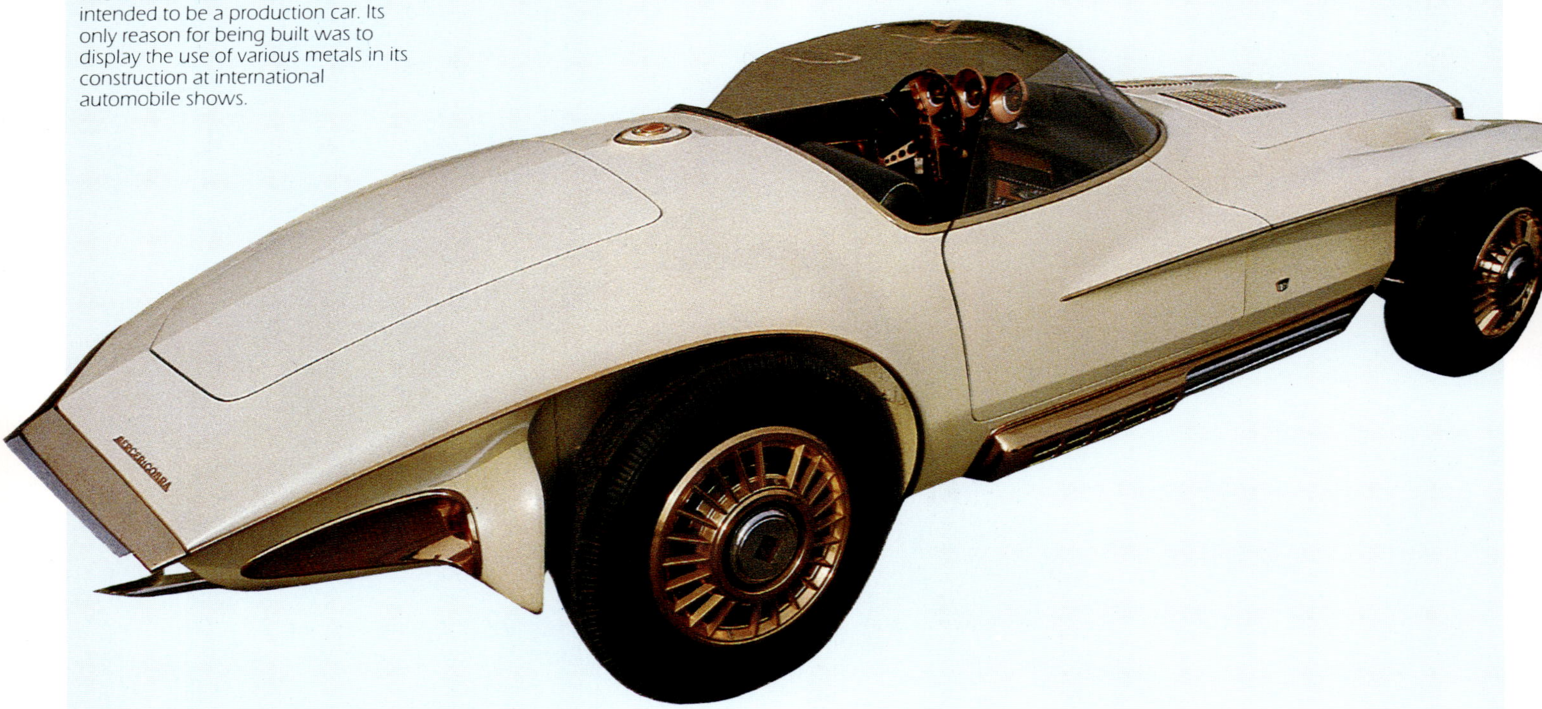

The Mercer Cobra was never intended to be a production car. Its only reason for being built was to display the use of various metals in its construction at international automobile shows.

make more use of these metals.

In association with Sibona-Basano, Exner designed the extraordinary body for the car and took as his inspiration the Mercer Type 35 of 1912. He loved the stark racer-look of that famous model with its liberal use of highly polished brass fittings. He used an A.C. chassis and lengthened it to 182 inches, with a wheelbase of 108 inches. The car has the standard 289 cubic inch V8 engine, but with special Shelby twin carburettor intake manifolds.

The copper items on the car were available in eleven shades, and the brass trim was of cartridge quality. Exner wanted to give the Mercer Cobra a 'warm metal look', as he felt that it would be more eye-catching than cold chromium plating. Of special interest are the disc brakes which feature copper discs, this metal having a ten times greater thermal conductivity than cast iron, the usual material used. The valve covers of the V8 engine, the air-cleaner, oil filler cap and dip stick tube are all in cartridge brass. The steering wheel is made from a chromium/copper alloy, and the exhaust shield is of silicon bronze.

Its pearl-white body colour makes the Mercer Cobra most eye-catching, with its pivoting headlights being another striking feature. On the auto-show circuit the car interested many people, but the use of copper and brass as alternatives to chromium plating has never caught on.

The Mercer Cobra remains a unique one-off motor car, and is a new addition to the Blackhawk Collection.

# Index

# Index